Commentary *on the American Scene*

COMMENTARY

ON THE

AMERICAN

SCENE

Portraits of Jewish Life in America

Edited by **Elliot E. Cohen**

Introduction by **David Riesman**

New York **Alfred A. Knopf**

 **1953**

L. C. catalog card number: 52-6413

THIS IS A BORZOI BOOK,
PUBLISHED BY ALFRED A. KNOPF, INC.

FIRST EDITION

To the **American Jewish Committee**

that exemplary liberal organization on the
American scene whose faith and imaginative
insight into the possibilities of Jewish life
and creativity in the United States prompted
it to provide the wholehearted encouragement, intellectual freedom, and—not least—
the funds, without which neither this book,
nor the larger continuing book from whose
pages this book is taken, would exist.

David Riesman

Introduction

"Idle" curiosity about themselves, like alcoholic excess, is something that American Jews in the past
have not felt able to afford. They feared inquisitiveness
from their enemies; and over their friends they preferred
to exercise a certain power of enchantment, controlling
the image they presented of themselves—whether as suf-
ferers, as Bohemian and uninhibited, or as just like
everyone else. Those nearly official guardians of disinter-
estedness, the social scientists, were also slow in getting
around to studying the Jews. Compared with certain other
immigrant groups around the turn of the century, the
Jews seemed not too disorganized, and perhaps for that
reason were left alone; our best study of immigration,
Thomas and Znaniecki's *The Polish Peasant in Europe
and America*, was concerned with one of the most dramatically disorganized groups. Only much later did
Thomas, a man with an extraordinary gift for curiosity,
get around to studying the *Bindelbriefe*, the advice columns in the Yiddish press (his collection has never been
published), and Louis Wirth write his brief study of the
Ghetto in Europe and America.

Meanwhile, fiction had discovered the Jews as quaintness to be patronized or as victims to be succored—both old traditions, reapplied to the American scene. Fictional treatment of Jews as intensely interesting individuals came much later, and was the work of a few brilliant and gifted writers. In Daniel Fuchs's *Homage to Blenholt*, Budd Schulberg's *What Makes Sammy Run?*, and other works in similar vein, it is often the non-Jews who are victims, while the Jews themselves, strident, violent, hysterically driven and driving, are self-victimized by the very American demons to which they have sold themselves. For the Jews among these authors, neither the Ghetto nor America offered enchantment; each alternative, whether cultural orthodoxy or assimilation—or the tension between them—had its savageries; and these could only be expurgated by art, not by life.

In general the tone of fiction today is more subdued (of course the older genres survive), more aware of shadings and ambiguities. Think, for instance, of Isaac Rosenfeld's *Passage from Home*, or Saul Bellow's *The Victim*, or the elegiac mood of Alfred Kazin's autobiographical homage to Brownsville, *A Walker in the City*. There is no wish in these works to shake one's fist at either America or at the Jews, but rather a resignation to both and a recognition that the existential dramas of daily living are colored rather than created by ethnic and cultural localism. In other words, now that it can be admitted, without rancor or apology, that Jews are different, emphasis can be put on the similarities between their fate and that of other people. It is on that assumption, indeed, that the essays in this volume rest: the assumption that Jews are interesting but not particularly special either in privilege or underprivilege. That is, the Jews are chosen not by history or God but by the writer, because of his familiarity with them or his fondness for them or by his interest in them.

The portrait painter has to place his easel; the essayist, novelist, or social scientist has to locate himself vis-à-vis his subject. Most of the subjects in this book, whether college students, delicatessen owners, or the Jews of San Francisco or "Spruceton" in New England, fall, I suppose, within the broad band of the urban middle class. (There are, to be sure, some garment workers of a bygone day and some chicken farmers who are as up-to-date as Space Cadets, but, as we shall see, there is scarcely a representative of the upper social strata.) Now, the urban middle class has been the butt of aristocratic satire since it first rose into prominence; socialism took over much of the aristocracy's contempt for the bourgeois, so much so that for Karl Marx as for Brooks Adams "the Jew" could be a despised symbol of the banker, the merchant, the soft yet calculating city slicker. When, after 1929, the American middle class, which, much more than Europe's, had escaped such contempt, turned out to be not only Philistine but unsuccessful too, the intellectuals, most of whom were themselves members of the same social group, heaped bitterness upon it. Since the Jewish middle class was hardly less unsuccessful in the Depression and since it had fewer traditions, the Jewish intellectuals made good their liberation from it by either merging Jewishness with the cause of the oppressed-at-large or by reserving their most savage digs for the "petty-bourgeois" closest to them, the very types now celebrated by affection in this volume.

Since those days, two things have happened. Hitler and Stalin have made it plain to many that there are worse vices than the alleged bad taste and softness of the middle class, worse exploitations than those of "the bosses" or landlord or storekeepers of American capitalism. And at the same time, the middle class has itself become more differentiated, more sophisticated, more interesting and various. Indeed the revaluation of "ordinary" Jewish life which these collected pieces represent is part of a more general revaluation of the American middle class by its erstwhile more aggressively alienated sons. The authors of some of these articles have sought, not for a gambit of savagery and fanaticism, of wanting to do away with all that is merely local, but for a gambit of tolerance, wit, and "idle curiosity." Thus, they do not propose to sweep the petty-bourgeois Jew into the "dustbin of history"; in fact, Shlomo Katz's piece is a paean to dust, if it be only old and settled enough.

Yet there are obvious dangers in this shift in perspective—dangers of becoming merely pious, sentimental, and hortatory about Jewish, and, more broadly, about middle-class life. The middle-class American's attitude towards the Jews has often degenerated into the corniness and schmaltziness we are familiar with in many radio and movie "treatments" produced by both Jews and non-Jews. Likewise, the "turn to religion" of many intellectuals often takes, among Jews, the form of an artificial identification with whatever can be labeled as part of an authentic folk culture. We already see the tendency to idealize the life of the Shtetel, the small Jewish village community in Eastern Europe, now that it has vanished, much as we idealize the Indians, the pioneers, and other small folksy groups. (Of the analogous tendency to sentimentalize life in the kibbutz, or in Israel generally, we need not speak here.) Similarly, when our parents and earlier ancestors have become too weak and defenseless further to cripple our emancipation, we can sentimentalize them—"killing" them by the false kindness of applying the maxim: *de mortuis nihil nisi bonum*. Perhaps the Jews are especially prey to the two extremes of a vindictive and aggressive and contemptuous attitude towards tradition and a honeyed and sentimental one, and a loss of all tension between these in any orgy of reconciliation is a particular risk today when the Jews, because they have been victims, and the Americans, because they have been victors, are threatened by complacency.

Thus, what *Commentary* is doing is precarious; a sharp and acrid curiosity is a needful preventive against any tendencies to become false and pious about the Jewish past and present. Not all essays in this volume escape. But fortunately the refugees in Ernest Stock's article are not treated with tears, nor the boyhoods of William Poster and Milton Klonsky with excess nostalgia. Then, too, sentimentality is eschewed in those pieces which recognize that, on the whole, the Jews of America do pretty well—and despite the long faces they may pull when they launch fund drives for "defense." These articles are rich—perhaps, from my ascetic background, I should say overstuffed—with consumables, whether in a city delicatessen or a summer "kochalein." (Indeed, the addiction to food—brilliantly dealt with in Kazin's book—seems to be at once frenetic and sedative, and talk about food among Jews may be a kind of ersatz sexuality, a proof of one's belonging both to a gender and to a cultural group.) Then there are the intangibles: for instance, the library in which Brownsville's intellectual youth nourished itself in preparation for escape; or the "yichus," the aristocratic airs of a self-styled elegant and minatory grandma. And on the side of occupations, the essays also indicate a certain richness: Morris Freedman, in his article on the contemporary Jewish student, even regrets the disappearance of the older penury, radicalism, and vocation for the intellectual life as he watches his students prepare for such formerly *Judenfrei* professions as engineering. Anti-Semitism, where it exists at all in these pages, is only smoke from a distant fire. When the Jews of Park Forest, as described by Herbert Gans, set out to provide a "Jewish" cultural and religious life for their children, they are beset, in this moderately well-heeled and unashamedly amiable Chicago suburb, by the artificiality of forcing on their youngsters a group consciousness which they themselves have no urgent reasons to preserve.

Take, for another example, the problems that beset the "Jewish paintner" of Mr. Gersh's article. They are essentially the same problems which (as my colleague, Everett Hughes, has described them) confront any occupational group: how to keep customers cowed and at a distance; how to prevent one's own routines from being upset by the client's emergency (in this case, a passionate desire for a particular color-effect); how to control one's own pace of work and guard one's own sense of craft even though one operates under the ever-present eye of the client (in this case, abetted by the home-decoration magazines). Such tensions are common to all occupations, though they may be less well-concealed in the humbler ones. Thus, there is nothing in this article which is distinctively Jewish—nothing but the vocabulary (no small matter). But that is just the point: it is intriguing to see what patterns of speech and modes of insolence Jewish painters have contributed to one of history's oldest struggles, the struggle between the seller and the buyer of service. And I am especially glad to see a study made of an occupational group that is neither glamorous nor oppressed nor oppressing, for here curiosity and personal accident guide us to what is interesting or near at hand, without portentousness or the need to make some kind of thesis for which the workers or consumers are mere pawns.

The Jews, then, have moved far enough along in America to be able to afford the same problems—of work, of consumption, of community life—as their neighbors. They do not need to be buoyed up by an apocalytic future, a menacing present, a chauvinist past. They take their Jewishness sufficiently for granted to permit us the luxury of examining in detail the enormously different ways there are of being at the same time both Jewish and American.

I must add, in fairness, that my own way and that of many other Jews I know is not represented here. The well-to-do and highly assimilated German Jews who in Philadelphia have been referred to as the Grand Dukes; the Jews who constitute what in Catholic circles would be termed "the leakage"—those who have severed all or virtually all Jewish ties; the few old-family upper-class Jews who have not lost their identity either in Christianity and change-of-name or in Zionism and other forms of fraternization with the later arrivals—none of these are included in the circles of sympathy and interest in this volume. Largely, the book grows out of the East European and Yiddish cultures which are those of the great majority of American Jews.

There is no harm in this; a book or a series must start somewhere. And for those who, like myself, were brought up with an almost hermetic ignorance of all things Jewish—an ignorance much greater than that of many non-Jews in New York or Chicago—there is a great advantage in this concentration on the middle and particularly the lower-middle strata of Jewish community life. Jewish culture coming from these strata has had such a large part in shaping American urban culture as a whole that Jews and non-Jews alike who have moved in more sheltered circles may find their way, first vicariously and later in person, to cross-class and cross-culture adventures. I might add in passing that such adventures downward in the class system seem more common in contemporary intellectual life than adventures upward: I find it easier to interest my middle-class students in lower-class than in upper-class life—sometimes they deny the very existence of the latter, save in terms of income gradations—and fiction, save for Marquand and one or two other writers, avoids the upper class much as sociology does.

One reason for this, perhaps, is that the writers in this volume have risen above the class and cultural origins they describe and, like the traditional American self-made man, can reminisce, so to speak, downwards; not being ambitious to move higher still—they have become intellectuals and, as such, partly side-stepped the status game—they can accept without bitterness or concealment the ethnic and class base from which they have graduated. One reason for this lack of bitterness is that the parents of today's Jewish intellectuals seem to have been not only willing but eager to see them graduate—which may be one reason why the Jewish college graduate (as *They Went to College* reveals) makes more money than his Protestant, and much more than his Catholic, classmate; family ties have helped the Jewish intellectual rather than held him back. At the same time, these Jews, unlike Scott Fitzgerald, the Irish boy from St. Paul, do not want to crash into an exclusive set—and so they either ignore the existence of such a set or find no fascination in it.

It follows from this that these essays characteristically combine two American themes: democracy and social mobility, both harmonized by not pushing each too far. The mobility may take geographic form—witness the movements into and out of such areas as Brownsville, Brighton, the West Bronx, and the Grand Concourse. It may take religious form—as, for example, in Grace Goldin's historical description of patterns of worship. It may take financial form—as in the Alger stories of Milton Kaplan and in Wallace Markfield's picture of the Seventh Avenue "bosses." All these shifts in taste, assimilation, worship, residence, and understanding are direct and unequivocal. But the very existence of this volume is indirect testimony to the social mobility of Jews as a group. For if its writers and prospective readers were

not themselves reasonably secure in their Americanization, they could hardly profess such an interest in the
humble incunabula of Jewish communal life; rather, they
would have to establish their distance from it. As the
Italian immigrant has to go through a gastronomically
bleached and bland period before he can again publicly
eat garlic and spaghetti, so the Jewish immigrant must
also become Americanized before he can again comfortably take pride and pleasure in his ethnic cuisine,
idiom, and gesture. It is evidence, then, of his having
establishment as an American that he can afford a sprin-
kling of Yiddish in his speech, a Jewish dish at his table.
I speak here, of course, about Jews for whom the non-
Jewish audience, real or imagined, is an important influence—even if only an influence to be righteously rejected. Assimilation works less dramatically but perhaps
even more surely among the Jews who live, in fact and
feeling, in an almost entirely Jewish world; they move
as a group, and by imperceptible steps, away from the
ethnic culture, although with less pronounced cycles of
ambivalent rebellion and return.

To be sure, this metaphorical mobility within
America, in terms of what one can accept of one's lowly
or immigrant past, has been speeded by developments
outside America. The stolidly conservative Spanish and
German Jews, under the impact of recent immigration
and recent history, have lost ground much faster than
conservative Protestants of similar class position—*They
Went to College* shows that only 6% of Jewish college
graduates today classify themselves as Republicans. Thus,
to have a working-class background or perhaps even
working-class manners can be as much a source of pride
among American Jews as among Israelis—both reflect
the worldwide tendencies towards democratization. Furthermore, the fight against Hitler and Nazi anti-Semitism,
the widespread crusade against ethnocentrism and preju-

dice of race as well as class, has had as one of its minor consequences a willingness on the part of many Jews to accept—even to flaunt—a Jewishness they would once have wished to play down. And for the many American Jews for whom European events are still pretty far away, the local chapters of national organizations, and particularly their ferocious fund drives, have served as continuing and only half-welcome reminders that one was a Jew, that—anti-Semitism or no—one was stuck with this Jewishness, and that one might as well attend the rally, enjoy the food and the "Jewish" jokes, and pay the collector.

On the other hand, non-Jews, out of shame, sympathy, or simply an altered focus of attention, have sought to familiarize themselves with Jewish matters. Indeed, the use by non-Jews of Yiddish phrases, their knowing references to the Jewish worlds of New York, their fondness for Jewish foods, are sometime symbolic ways of indicating sympathy, lack of prejudice, and the urban sophistication for which Jews are supposed to stand. In the increasing venturesomeness of American leisure and consumption, Jews play a large share as models and pacesetters, and the Protestant revolt against Protestantism makes frequent use of them: to be emancipated in America means to have Jewish friends, either in fact or fancy.

The economic well-being of the Jews in contemporary America thus appears to have at least two aspects. Coming here as one of the few immigrant groups which already had something of an urban, intellectual culture—and a certain experience in combatting discrimination—the Jews succeeded in rapidly adapting themselves to the business and professional opportunities of an expanding metropolitanism. This adaptation, however, was never internalized. Most Jews never learn a true devotion to their vocations, to substitute for their devotion to family, fame, career, and the main chance. Thus, the Jews were prepared, somewhat in advance of other groups, for the

general shift of cosmopolitan America towards leisure-
minded rather than work-minded attitudes. My guess is
that a study would show that Jews were among the first
to ride commercial airlines for ease as well as for business
reasons, to install air-conditioning, to run hospitals that
didn't smell of ether (sickness may be regarded as a form
of leisure), to take winter vacations, and otherwise to
pioneer on the frontiers of comfort. In "West Bronx:
Food, Shelter, Clothing," Mrs. Glazer describes some of
the pioneer styles, and she grasps (as Jacques Barzun
does more generally in his brilliant *Harper's* article on
"America's Romance with Practicality") the substructure
of idealism beneath this seeming devotion to the things
of matter that matter.

But of course there are many Jews of whom all this
is not true—Jews who have had no part in the progression
by which the casserole and the icebox have replaced the
melting pot as America's contribution to ethnic harmony.
For some of the Jews reported on in this volume are
Puritanical; those who obey the Law, and those who, in
Brownsville's library, prepare to leave it behind, live
lives which may be intense but which are hardly gay or
colorful. Where it is not simply a stereotype, the American image of the Jews has been set in the mold of a few—
of a minority within the minority. Both Jew and non-
Jew may find in this volume a greater range of "Jewish"
existence than they had known of.

And this leads me to recur to the view that such a
volume should be thought of as a first instalment in a long
series of portraits. There are recorded here some vanishing, if not vanished types and scenes: the old-clothes man,
the genteel lace-curtain grandma of "My Grandmother
Had Yichus," the early *shul* in Tulsa, the new Eden in
San Francisco. Doubtless, the amateur and gifted anthro-
pologists represented here wanted to describe these persons and places before acculturation should alter them

beyond recognition. But Jewish life in America is changing so rapidly that new kinds of persons and new kinds of places are always being thrown up—Morris Freedman's article on the new-model Jewish college student is one such attempt to capture the future as well as recapture the past. And in turn our other ethnic groups in America need to be looked at with the kind of attention illustrated here. Matthew Arnold's conclusion, in 1883, that America was simply "not interesting" was not true then; today, it would be a fantastic statement about so various, so enterprising, so spirited a culture. Good reporting about that culture is itself part of that variety, that enterprise, that spirit.

Elliot E. Cohen

Foreword

      Most of the COMMENTARY *pieces* that make up this book were published in the department of the magazine called "From the American Scene." They are written by Jews about Jews. Inescapably, one might think, they would be anxious, defensive, aggrieved, purposeful. Paradoxically, they are not. They aim neither to prove anything, to solve anything, nor to make a "contribution" to the times or the ages. They are written for enjoyment, and *with* enjoyment, we guess—and need no introduction. *So*—they have two, by the editor himself and a guest professor—and of sociology, no less.

      Perhaps it is that one feels that *Commentary*, even after all of seven years of existence, still needs a word or two of explanation. The official statement that it is a magazine devoted to "Jewish affairs and world issues" for some reason doesn't suffice. People ask questions, plenty of them. We like best of all the definition which one of our subscribers overheard his eldest giving: "Well, *Commentary* is like the *Atlantic Monthly* or *Harpers*, you know, serious, but more serious . . . but more funny too—say, that's funny!"

Well, perhaps *Commentary* is a bit odd, as befits a Jewish magazine. One oddity is that so "specialist" a magazine gives so much of its pages to "general" affairs; another, that by now so large a proportion of its non-Jewish readers read it, as they say, "religiously" and find it "represents them," reflects what they feel and think. And of all its oddities, many readers profess to find most odd the department "From the American Scene"—so "popular" a department in so "serious" a magazine.

As a matter of fact, this department has from its inception been, in the editor's view, nearest of all to the heart of the magazine's purpose. It was our thought to use many methods to help bring American Jews and their concerns into their own and the public view with fuller knowledge and insight than generally obtains—historical reconstruction, intellectual analysis, reportage, religious reflection, sociological and other scientific study, fiction. But from the 17th century we remembered one way of writing about human life that has fallen into disuse, though it was once immensely fruitful and indeed may be said to be the mother method of journalism. We refer to those informal sketches from daily life called "characters." Less specific than the individual incident or personality, less general than the scientific or philosophical essay, these sketches of representative figures and scenes built up a typology of the familiar life of their times.

In "From the American Scene" it was our hope to provide a similar picture gallery of Jews and their familiar ways of life "on the American scene." What could be simpler than to look about and write of what you saw and remembered of the landscape nearest to you? Of course nothing is more difficult to do than just this, especially in these times, and especially with Jews. It is the very last mode in which it is fashionable to write today —and who writes about Jews except problematically, creating new problems where, heaven knows, enough exist already? Who writes of human beings simply as human beings, taking the stance of neither the scientist, nor the objective reporter, nor the detached social or psychological novelist, but *con amore*, identifying oneself with the common life and being open to it and about it—and about oneself?

But it can be done, as this book shows. Whatever the novelists and the deep thinkers and the apocalyptic politicals dredge up—alas, all too accurately!—about this desperate world, and whatever they discover about the Jews, that most desperate of peoples, it is still possible for Jews in America to look at their lives with a new ease— an ease that comes from the realization that here they, like a hundred other kinds of people, are at home, and can at last permit themselves to sit around once in a while in their house slippers, and even let the neighbors see them through the windows *en famille* with their hair in curl-papers and their suspenders dropped.

In the introduction he has written for this volume, David Riesman speaks with great penetration of what these pieces show of the Jewish group in the American setting—their origins, their socio-economic status, etc. I should like, myself, to mention briefly an aspect which he does not much touch upon, possibly because he is looking chiefly elsewhere, as, indeed, the writers of these pieces were, too. I refer to that extra dimension given to Jewish personality and life by the fact that each Jew moves, consciously or not, in the context of a long and special history and a religious-ethical tradition that lays upon him, whether as a burden or a badge of pride, the sense of being "chosen," and so creates in him the tendency, even the obligation, to carry himself "with a difference." It is this that plays a persistent counterpoint— humorous, pathetic, tragic, farcical—to whatever Jews do or are.

Under the caftan in the ghetto we were princes of

the most royal of all lineages—as Sholom Aleichem's Tevye the Dairyman said, "the envy and admiration of the world"—and vestiges of this magnificent pride remain somewhere in each of us. The Jewish "paintner" behaves as he does—and how he behaves!—because, in addition to all the good reasons Mr. Riesman cites, what kind of life is it anyway for a grown Jew to be daubing cinnamon-bun tan on some silly woman's dinette?

More than once in a while in these sketches there shows through, often undefined but still real, the enduring hold of Jewish historic memory. And perhaps as *Commentary* goes on into the years following, we shall see it exhibited more often and explicitly—and more often, too, without the nostalgic sense of loss, but as something cherished that is felt likely to continue.

Still another last word. Why are these "Jewish" pieces so "American"?—this has been asked with speculative wonder by a hundred readers, Jewish and non-Jewish. Why am I reminded of my Congregationalist grandfather, my mother's eccentric cousin who runs a filling station in Tennessee, my very Italian mother? Well, maybe the old saying will help us: the Jews are like everybody else—only more so. This need never have been such a paradox—for haven't we found, the common belief to the contrary, that to be most individual is to be most representative? Is not the commonest element shared by all common men the fact of difference? So it is, we venture to say, that most of the paradoxes about "the Jew" apply to all people, and especially to "the American," who is always something else besides American, whose very Americanness perhaps consists in being something else—Jew, Catholic, Italian, Negro, Irishman, Pole, white native Protestant, Westchesterite, Puerto Rican, Mexican—"and proud of it."

It is all of this, and much else, that makes the sum of these states and its peoples add up to the richest country in the world to live in (and to write about)—and in every sense that the word "rich" has meaning.

And it is only the beginning. For over this land, too, whether by the accidents or the predestinations of history, there hovers that extra dimension, a sense however dim of some high promise that keeps this "most materialist nation on the globe," as more than one has called us, the most conscience-ridden of all.

Jews, we said earlier, traditionally feel that they live under a covenant. What if—suddenly it occurs to us— it is the fate of American Jews to live under a double covenant, our ancient one and that which we feel crystallizing in the American firmament? Awful thought! But need a double covenant be a double burden—may it not prove a double blessing, not only for the lot of us, but for lots of others?

Special acknowledgment is made to my colleagues on *Commentary*—Nathan Glazer, Clement Greenberg, Robert Warshow, Frances Green, Sherry Abel (and to Irving Kristol and Richard M. Clurman, who now labor in other vineyards); to Elaine Dreyfus, who worked on the proofs; and, above all, to the writers, who put up with unconscionable demands on their time and nerves with patience and fortitude. Our gratitude to the Publication Committee of *Commentary*, whose confidence in this and other of our projects has never flagged or faltered, and, among them, for special mention, Alan M. Stroock, our chairman, and Ralph E. Samuel, his predecessor and founding chairman. Our most respectful, appreciative salute to Joseph M. Proskauer and Jacob M. Blaustein, presidents of the American Jewish Committee during this magazine's not always untroubled life, and to John Slawson, executive vice-president, who include among the freedoms they stand for, and fight for, freedom of expression for writers—and editors; and who have, despite harassments, never given ground. A particular bow, lastly, to William Cole of Alfred A. Knopf, Inc., who was this book's *shadchan* (marriage broker) in the first instance.

New York, November 1, 1952

Contents

Contents

Commentary *on the American Scene*

I

Shlomo Katz

Heritage

The small narrow room overhanging the stairway used to be a bedroom. Its single small window is only about four feet from the blank wall of the adjoining house and the air within it may not have been completely changed since the house was built. But many years ago, before the family had dispersed throughout the country, it had to serve. An immigrant family of six—there was no help for it; every square inch had to be used. When the parents finally remained alone, this small room gradually took on the functions of an attic, storeroom, and—whenever one of the scattered flock came back for a visit—guest bedroom. Every time I briefly visit my parents in St. Paul almost the same scene is enacted in that room on the day before my departure.

The first few days of the visit—or rather the hour or two each day that I spend with my parents—are full of questions, attempts at conversation, and food. The questions are nearly all impersonal. The "old genera-

tion" learned a long time ago not to ask personal questions. The "younger generation" is always right in whatever it does. Aren't they educated? Haven't they seen
the world? Even when they are wrong they are right
and an old person must neither question their inscrutable ways nor inquire too closely into their doings.
After the few brief, permissible inquiries about health,
the talk runs somewhat as follows: "What do they
say in New York? Will there be a war?" Or: "Such a
calamity! Floods in the country. No wonder prices are
going up."

I try to classify in my mind what "they say in New
York" in order to provide some answer, and I find it
difficult. Who speaks for New York? The editorial in
the *Times* or in the *News?* My landlord who insists that
there will be no war and that "those Bolsheviks in Albany and Washington" should be forced at once to do
away with rent controls, or my neighbor at the *Stammtisch* in the Waldorf Cafeteria who has it figured out
to the minute and the inch when and where the next
businesslike (not for purposes of diverting rivers in Siberia) atom bomb will be dropped?

I try to get at the source of my parents' information
about the floods. The Ohio, it is true, had been on a
rampage, but that was weeks earlier. When I ask where
they heard about the flood, a faint resentment comes
into my mother's voice. "Don't you think we know what
the papers say?" It turns out that a member of the one
congregation of now scarcely more than ten that still
holds daily services in a synagogue on the West Side
was a subscriber to the Jewish *Morning Journal*. He
read it regularly but not always consecutively and repeated the news to his colleagues in the house of
prayer. His report about the flooding of the Ohio thus
reached its limited audience weeks after the event. I

hasten to reassure them about the flood. The conversation lamely proceeds from one subject to another. The gap of years is in the way, and the still greater gap of estrangement.

Then there is the food, with the meal a pathetic version of the prodigal son and the fatted calf. No sooner do I enter than the entreaties begin: "Eat something." I assure them I am far from starved. They don't believe me. After a trip? Such a trip too! As with most old people, their memory vaults over the immediate present and the recent past to the far time when any trip meant a journey of at least a day for which one had to prepare adequately—with, among other things, a basket of food conveniently tucked away in the straw in the wagon.

The proffers of food have many overtones. They are an outstretched hand of reconciliation between generations, an attempt to do something in common, for the table is really an altar and when three sit at a table and there is good will among them the divine spirit hovers over them. The insistence on food is also a covert attempt to reassert authority. The "child"—whatever its age—must be looked after.

I give in and "eat something." But they are not satisfied, for I do not eat enough. If they had their way I would eat constantly and ask for more. It is a problem in group psychology, I think. I am reminded of the distasteful and indelicate superabundance of Jewish restaurants, the staggering mounds of food in delicatessen stores in Jewish neighborhoods, the endearing diminutives applied to a *gut shtikele* ("fine piece of") something or other. I can't help thinking that a similar diminutive of endearment used to be applied to a child's mental capacities; then it was said that he had a *"gut kepel"* ("good head"). Wasn't there originally something very tender and self-contradictory in the exaggerated concern for the eating habits of the children? It was necessary that the children should be sufficiently buttressed against the hostile world. And yet at the same time it was proper that they be not too well developed physically, for weakness was also a symptom of spirituality: the *"shvach"* ("weak") child was also the delicate, sensitive, and scholarly one. And, after all, spirituality and scholarliness came first: to give up these would have meant bowing to the values of the enemy world—a final and fatal surrender. So, while the "weak" and other-worldly child was plied with food at every turn, he was never asked to learn to fight and no effort was made to encourage even his more safely aggressive urges. Indeed, what profiteth it a man if he win the world and lose himself?

"You've lost weight; you are so thin," Mother says. I have not lost weight; but I don't argue. While chiding me it is her intention to compliment me also. Having lost weight means I have gained in the finer qualities of the spirit.

Some time during the day preceding my departure I am asked obliquely: "Would you care to go through the things in the small room?" Then, by way of explanation: "There may be some things that can be thrown away."

I consent. I would go through "the things" even if I were not asked to do so.

"The things" fill three cardboard boxes and are the accumulations of a lifetime. Each year some of the acquisitions whose sentimental value was not great were discarded—school report cards, textbooks, old notebooks and similar documents, as well as articles of wear and household use. Some were thrown away with no more than a slight pang of nostalgia; others caused a

considerable emotional wrench. A natural process of selection had its way and the things that survived the
wastebasket were no longer likely to be discarded. But
the re-examination of the permanent collection took
place regularly. The invitation to go through "the
things" was in the nature of an annual communion with
the "usable past."

The term "usable" is hardly correct, but the objects
in those cardboard boxes do represent a segment of the
past. One can only marvel at the inner logic of the process of selection which preserved such a strange conglom-
erate of articles and documents. At times the logic
becomes apparent. Of what value, indeed, are high school
and college textbooks or report cards of twenty-five
years ago when compared with an ancient birth certificate signed by an "official rabbi," now that the particular
rabbi in question, the entire institution of "official
rabbis," and even the town where he once officiated,
are no longer in existence?

No surprises await me. I know exactly what is in
those boxes and where each item lies. But there is always a certain newness about the experience, perhaps
because the things have grown older by one year, and
have therefore become more venerable and of clearer
historical validity.

I know that the prize, the bundle of documents
tied in a large kerchief, is at the bottom of the box in
the corner. But the ritual must be gone through in
proper order. Also there is always a faint possibility of
discovering something new in the accumulation of objects, something not new as an object but with a new
meaning.

I begin with the box of clothes. Mother provides a
running commentary; I know it by heart yet I do not
find it boring. On top and half filling the box is Father's

winter overcoat, the one made of black cloth and lined with fox skins. "These days," Mother says, "everything is junk. Nothing lasts. Just look at this coat, it's still good." I know what she means. Her parents had ordered the coat as a wedding present for Father. That was more than fifty years ago. Once, about twenty-five years later, it received a new cloth outside as a gift from new in-laws. It still does duty in the frosts of St. Paul. The fox skins, it is true, are getting quite bald, but when Father puts it on and turns up its huge collar, even Minnesota's winters are powerless against it.

When I made the coat's acquaintance it was already about thirty years old. During the winters in the Ukraine, when it was too cold for the smaller children to play outside and Father was at home, we used to stand the coat up like a tent and play hide and seek around it. At night, when the built-in oven failed to give enough heat, it became an extra quilt.

The chief movable wealth of the family consisted of three items: a large number of books, the silver, and the coat—the *tulup* as it was called. During the pogroms and pogrom-scares that abounded immediately after World War I, the last two items were always hidden away at the first disquieting rumors. The books were too bulky to move and, furthermore, *pogromchiks* were not interested in books. Then the Bolsheviks came to town. Life was safe again, for the moment. They were welcomed. But they had their ideas of sharing the wealth, and individual soldiers felt it would be accounted a good deed to deprive a bourgeois of a heavy fur coat, even one in the fourth decade of its life. They were also establishing a public library in town, and any household with more than a handful of books was made to contribute its literary possessions for the public welfare. The searchers naturally helped themselves to

8

whatever else caught their eye. As the search committee began its work at the end of the street the silver was quickly hidden away and Father put on his coat and went for a walk in the orchards that bordered the town. The committee came to the house. Their literacy was not of the highest order and they were dubious about the revolutionary quality of some of the books. One of them struggled with the name Nietzsche. He transposed the clumsy consonants and read it as "Nishchi"—"the poor," in Russian. "Friedrich the Poor" struck him as particularly appropriate class-conscious stuff for the new library. The books were loaded on a wagon. The search committee was given tea and smiles; they might take books and other belongings, but when they were around there were no pogroms. As soon as they left I was sent to call Father. The coat was safe.

Nearly everything else was abandoned on the trip to America, but not the coat. Over the long journey it served as coat, blanket, mattress, pillow. Then spots began to appear in the fur. But it held up.

"Yes," Mother says as I put the coat aside, "they used to make good clothes once, but not any more." She begins telling a story to illustrate her point. I do not listen. The first box is still half full.

Several other articles of winter apparel nearly account for the rest of the space in the box. Reaching the bottom, I lift out a circular piece of bright yellow damask, frayed at the edges and covered with stains. "A human being is such a fool," she says, "clinging like this to rags. Better throw this away. Why should it lie around?"

This time I object. This is a cape that was part of her wedding dress. How it came to be brought to America I don't know, but since it has been preserved all these years, why throw it out now?

Once before, when I was similarly engaged in going through "the things," she had talked about it: "It is the cape from my wedding dress. When Father was taken into the army and I was left alone with a child on my hands, I cut it up to make a dress for G. But the cape was left. It was a style like that when I was married."

"Everybody else managed to stay out and not serve Fonia, only he had to be taken," she said, and her bitterness at my father's failure to evade service in the Czar's army was as fresh as if it had happened the day before.

As a matter of fact it wasn't true that he was the only one taken. Many Jews in town were drafted. But some took extreme measures, even to the extent of crippling themselves, to evade serving in the Russian army. He refused to take such drastic measures.

It occurs to me that my father's army service took place in the 90's of the past century. Every history book now has at least a hundred pages after that period. But my mother's resentment has not abated a whit, and the sight of the ancient bit of bright yellow cloth revives it. Many times I suspected that Father had had a secret liking for military service despite the severe handicaps that a Jew had to labor under in the czarist army. To him it had been an opportunity to assert himself as a Jew. She only remembered that he had not been as quick as some others in avoiding military service.

When we were children he used to talk about his four years of service, and there was a note of pride in his voice. His victories had been small. It had been a battle of simple, enduring faith against a wicked oppressor. There was the time when a particularly vicious and anti-Semitic lieutenant tried to make life more than normally miserable for his Jewish charges. He especially tried to trick them into breaking regulations when they were on guard duty, for then the punishment would be severe and Jewish soldiers as a group could be blamed for laziness and inefficiency. "One night when I was on sentry duty," Father told us, "this lieutenant wrapped himself in a wolf skin he had. He thought that he could sneak up unnoticed and grab my rifle from me. It was a very serious offense to lose one's rifle. But I detected him as he crawled up in the dark and I let him have it with the butt. He hollered out who he was but until he managed to disentangle himself from his wolf skin I gave him a good beating. When he finally stood up I came to attention and saluted. There was nothing he could do to me and he was afraid the other officers might laugh at him, so he didn't even report me. After that he left us Jewish soldiers alone."

Other triumphs were of a more sublimated nature: getting up half an hour before reveille each morning to pray in shawl and phylacteries, despite the angry murmuring of the Russian soldiers at being disturbed; performing all the arduous and tiring duties without eating pork and other meat rations; walking many miles to the nearest town on an occasional weekend off for the privilege of praying in a synagogue and eating kosher meals in a Jewish home. Then there was the time when he was sent on some mission that required considerable presence of mind. Two other soldiers had been sent before him and had failed. He succeeded and the major gave him a five-ruble gold piece. A Jewish soldier could not be given rank, so money had to take its place. But why bother about rank—his self-esteem as a Jewish soldier had been given a boost. Let the *goyim* keep their rank.

These were victories of which he spoke for many years after. But Mother could not share in them. She only remembered that she had been left alone.

"So I cut up the wedding dress to make a dress for G. And then every year I used to make it over and shorten it and fix it up for the other girls as they became big enough to wear it. Six times I made it over. But the cape remained. I don't know what made me take it when we went to America. But we were in such a hurry. Some things that should have been taken were forgotten and other things, useless rags, were brought along."

We were in such a hurry. Relatives, neighbors, friends came to say goodbye and hurried us along. There were rumors of an impending pogrom that spring of 1921. A day delayed and all might be lost. But I myself was in no hurry. I would have liked to enjoy a few days longer the glory of my impending Americanism and boast before my ten-year-old friends how I no longer had to bother with Russian declensions. Who needed Russian in America? But still they kept coming and telling us to hurry. They came to buy household belongings and hurried us. They came to bestow tearful kisses of parting and urged haste. They brought small gifts for the trip and pushed us on. The gifts consisted mostly of food. One well-meaning soul brought a string of garlic. "They are good against seasickness," she said. She herself had never been to sea. The garlic was wrapped pell-mell into a bundle together with a lot of other odds and ends, and somewhere among the hastily packed belongings the cape was included. The soldiers who helped to smuggle us across the frontier searched everyone thoroughly at the border. Garlic was an item of food, so they took it. They had no use for the bright yellow cape from a 19th-century dress.

The first box is empty and I carefully replace the

things, leaving the big coat on top. It can do service again next winter.

"Rest a while," Mother urges before I begin on the second box. "There is no hurry. Maybe you'll have a bite to eat," she tries tentatively. "Such a long trip ahead of you."

But I tackle the second box, somewhat smaller than the first. Once it was filled with discarded school books as one member of the family after another added his accumulation of unsold or unexchanged texts. But most of these had been disposed of. Now in the upper part of the box is the metal base of a small table lamp, a spare electric iron so long unused that it is doubtful whether its coil is still in working order, a folding yardstick, and similar gadgets once bought and used and now retired. I suggest throwing them away now, but my mother says, "They may come in handy some day."

Beneath these are several Mahzors (prayer books for the holidays), a set of the Bible with commentaries, other religious volumes. Father's eyesight has been failing and he can no longer use them. Moreover he knows every word of them by heart. The Bible set is bound in parchment and in good shape. The prayer books on the other hand are dog-eared and falling apart. "Let me buy you some new ones," I suggest. She won't hear of it. "Besides," she says, "where will you get them here in town?"

These books are among the first things my father bought when he got to America. The volumes still bear the purple oval imprint "Lebanon," the emporium on Fairfield Avenue which specialized in wholesale *matzah* distribution, religious books and other items pertaining to worship, Yiddish newspapers, and also a line of delicatessen and groceries. Lebanon was not only a book and delicatessen store; it was also a social center for new immigrants on the West Side. Now Lebanon is no more. The owner is dead, and his emporium in new hands is a prosaic grocery store. "There is someone in the city who sells prayer books, but he lives far away. But why should you bother? These are good enough. Last Rosh Hashanah I almost lost the Mahzor. The second day of Rosh Hashanah was on a Saturday so I asked a little boy to carry it home for me. On the way he met some other children and did not bring it to the house. But some days later his mother returned it to me. Things don't get lost and these are good enough."

Things don't get lost, she said, and I was reminded of the curious formula which as pupils of the *cheder* in the Ukraine we were taught to write in our best calligraphy inside the cover of any new book: "This book belongs. . . . To whom does it belong? . . . It belongs to whomever it belongs to. . . . Nevertheless, to whom does it belong? . . . It belongs to . . ." followed by the name of the proud possessor. No one knew who authored this evasive version of *ex libris*.

Father comes in as I begin on the third and last box. His *tallis* (prayer shawl) and *tefillin* (phylacteries) are on top for easy access every morning. "Do you still have your *tefillin?*" he asks. I nod assent. "Do you use them?" I maintain a discreet silence. Mother intervenes, fearful that the younger generation might feel offended: "Stop bothering him with your questions. All of a sudden he's inquisitive." She addresses no one in particular. "He knows what he has to do without your reminding him." The younger generation always knows best. How much heartbreak through the years must have gone into the shaping of this state of resigned approval. Father stands rebuked but unyielding. "But you do have them yet?" he asks again. I shake my head in confirmation. I see that he doubts my word but prefers to ask no more.

Beneath the prayer shawl is a thick layer of photographs and receipts of all sorts—receipts for rent, from the electric company, from doctors and hospitals. I know better than to suggest that some or all of these be thrown away. Once I did make such a suggestion and it was vetoed without any ado. The reasons were not explicitly stated but the firmness on the subject could have been formulated somewhat as follows: Assuming that no one is likely ever to ask for these receipts it is nevertheless possible that one may be called upon to prove that the rent for the month of February of six years ago was paid. One may, at any time, be asked to give an account of oneself on earth as well as in heaven. The proof of innocence and of duty performed must be at hand always. With the photographs it is a different matter. I feel impelled to look at each one of them. They are nearly all of relatives in Europe. The "American" photographs are on the walls. During the first years in this country there was a fairly intensive interchange of letters with those who remained behind. As the years passed it slackened until the trickle of communication dried up almost entirely. Now the poorly developed pictures yellowing with age are the only remaining contact with that remote world.

The faces on the pictures already say very little. Only at rare intervals does one of the faded images evoke any appreciable emotional response. But though the likenesses themselves have ceased to be moving because time has blurred their features, the people they represent still have a claim on the emotions. This one is still alive but long not heard from, another died, these three perished at the hands of the Nazis, two others are lost without trace. Thus it goes through the

entire collection. Strange faces of lost people, faded images reposing in a cardboard box in the corner of the
small room.

Only one thing remains in the box—the bundle of
documents tied in the large kerchief. I lift it out and
gingerly untie the square knot. It is always something of
a thrill to go through these papers. It gives me a vague
feeling of anticipation, like that of an archeologist examining a new find of ancient tablets.

The pile of papers spills over sideways on the table.
At the bottom is a huge sheet folded in four. It is the
passport on which the family entered the country. It is
cracked apart at the creases and one side is covered with
stamps and transit visas.

It was 1921 and we were already safely in Bessa-
rabia. Together with hundreds of other refugees we
stayed in the women's section of a synagogue which had
been made available for the exiles from Russia. The
pews had been taken out and hundreds of cots placed
one next to the other. Families, children, single men
and women slept next to each other with but an occasional blanket as partition.

In the middle of the hall several wood-burning
stoves had been put up and were used for cooking. Before dawn we would be awakened by the plaintive
chanting of the Psalms in the main section of the synagogue below. Babies cried, women stirred about the
stoves preparing breakfast and quarreling over their
turns at the fire. Later in the day the men went about
the city looking for work and consulting the "delegates."

The "delegates" were mysterious creatures sent by
relatives of the refugees to facilitate their coming to
America. They transmitted money allotments from the
United States, helped in obtaining visas, arranged for
transportation. We had a fancy "delegate." He stayed

in the best hotel in Kishinev, a building that made an indelible impression on me with its four stories and elevator shaft but no elevator. He wore horn-rimmed glasses and always received his clients in shirt sleeves and wearing suspenders. Up to that time we had never seen horn-rimmed glasses. Where we came from, intellectuals—such as teachers and pharmacists—wore pince-nez on a thin black silken cord and never went about in their shirt sleeves. But Americans were different. It was even said that he was a graduate of an American university. One can't be a stickler for form with the great of this world.

After months of promises and encouragement he suddenly informed us that we could not get a visa to the United States because the Soviet government still had not been recognized and we had no passports, but he promised, not very convincingly, to fix matters up. More months passed. At length Father was sent to Bucharest and was there provided with the huge sheet of paper, made out by some officials of the czarist regime. The American consul promised to honor it. We got our visas. The "delegate" was all-powerful, despite his shirt sleeves and suspenders.

Years later I came across the "delegate" in New York. He sat behind a desk in a small bank. The location of his desk indicated that he was far from being a power in the institution. He wore the same kind of horn-rimmed glasses. But he was not in shirt sleeves. For a moment I doubted that it was really he. I went up closer. I recognized the face, and there was the name plate before him to dispel all doubt. *Sic transit*. . . .

The passport is always interesting if only because the family photograph is pinned to it—the first in which I ever figured. Taking it was quite an occasion and also one that lasted an unbearably long time. After duly slow-freezing us into the desired posture the photographer communed with himself behind his black cloth for what seemed like an hour. I nearly bit through my tongue trying not to laugh. The result was that on the picture my mouth is pursed into a tube. The others did better and when the end product was shown around among other refugees it met with complete approval. "A good picture, *nu*, worried Jewish faces," they said. "May you have luck in America." Everything was as it should be. The child was "*shvach*," the adults had truly Jewish worry on their face. It would be a genuine passport, though signed by a displaced czarist official without authority.

Next to the passport repose the affidavits sent by the American relatives undertaking responsibility for our not becoming public charges. In triplicate, notarized, and with a blue heavy paper backing, they look as impressive today as they did thirty years ago. With the affidavits had come a letter from the relatives explaining their significance. The message was written on a letterhead showing a skyscraper in the upper left-hand corner. We looked at it with awe. Could that building really be theirs?

Disillusionment was not long in coming. They did not own this or any other building. But there was a grain of truth in the picture. There was such a building in St. Paul. Months later I faced it and recognized it. The President was stopping in St. Paul for a day and was lodged in the "presidential suite" of the best hotel in the city. I went to gaze from afar at the building thus made historic. It was our old friend of the letterhead. There was no bitterness among our family on the subject. For a little while it had aroused such wild dreams. If our relatives did not own the huge hotel, one of them must have had lunch in it at least once—though he may have merely gone into the lobby to write the letter and taken a piece of the stationery.

Documents and more documents, ancient pieces of paper, stamped and countersigned, refusing petitions, granting approval, giving instructions, classifying by name, number, age, sex, employment, destination, origin. All of them are answers to questions once asked. Now the questions have long been forgotten but the answers still lie wrapped in the big kerchief at the bottom of the cardboard box. Next to the affidavits are Father's naturalization papers taken out many years ago. He is a patriarchal-looking man with a long white beard. "You are not an anarchist?" he was asked, and even the questioner must have smiled at the absurdity of the question. Yet questions must be asked and answers must be given. Bakunin, too, had a beard, and so did Marx.

Some old letters in their torn envelopes lie next to the naturalization papers. The most recent is more than twenty years old. They have been saved because of the return addresses. Father had quoted the Talmud: "Mountains don't meet, people do. Let us keep the addresses, just in case. . . ." One is from a man who came on the same ship. He went to California and in his letter he complained of his lot and asked whether he might not do better in St. Paul. A second is from some distant relatives who had taken up their abode in New York and urged that we too move there. "Millions of people make a living in New York, why should you settle in *oisraisenish?*"—that is, in a place torn out of the context of human habitation.

Still another letter is from a fellow refugee from our native town. During the many weeks that his family and ours squatted in the women's section of the synagogue there were numerous and heated discussions about where to go. He had chosen Palestine. "I know it's poor and small and there are Arabs," he used to argue, "but enough. I want to go to a Jewish country." (I was inclined to agree with him in a general way, but personally I wanted to go to America: the trip was longer.) He did go and for a few years a thin trickle of communication was maintained. He was satisfied with his choice, but in his last letter he added nostalgically: "There is one thing I envy you—that you have snow in the winter. I am happy and I never regretted the choice I made even though life is hard here, but every now and then I get homesick for good, deep snow in the winter." I wonder if he ever got over his homesickness. Letters from acquaintances in Israel inform me that one of his grandsons born in that country is now a high-ranking officer in the Israeli army. I conveyed this news to Father. He said nothing. But I wondered whether he did not wish to ask, "Why didn't you become a high-ranking officer in the American army?" I may have been wrong; though his eyes were fixed on my arm, he may only have been thinking of the *tefillin*, not of the corporal's stripes.

"That's nothing," Mother says as I pick up the next piece of faded paper. I quickly replace it. It is the *ketubah*, her marriage contract, and even at this late age she acts self-conscious about it. If old people could, I think she would blush. I once tried to read it. The ink is faded almost to illegibility, the script is fanciful and hard to decipher, the Aramaic is virtually a sealed book to me.

There is also a bunch of diplomas, one from grammar school, three from high school, and a number of certificates from various evening courses. Among these there is also one small certificate from the Hebrew school which lasted for one brief summer in our town in the Ukraine. It is handwritten and only the single word "diploma" on top is printed.

The Bolsheviks had come and new winds began to blow. A trained Hebrew teacher appeared from some big city and, utilizing such local talent as was available, he established a Hebrew school with a regular curriculum and well-organized classes for the children between nine and twelve. The school was a success and we loved it. But autumn came, the Bolshevik authorities frowned on the idea of a Hebrew school, and there were rumors of pogroms. The families of many of the pupils fled or thought of flight abroad. The teachers, too, prepared to emigrate. Our class, the oldest, was disbanded and we were given these diplomas—the first diplomas we had ever had. There were no facilities for printing these documents, but in order to lend them a greater degree of authority and thus enhance their value in our eyes, a few letters of Hebrew type were obtained somewhere and the word *teuda*—diploma—was printed on top. With our ingrained attitude of reverence for the printed word, especially print in the "holy tongue," that one word was enough to give the small piece of paper a magic quality.

When the class was disbanded, the departing teacher organized those of us who were to remain behind into a Hebrew-speaking group. We met regularly all through that winter. Our Hebrew was a bit halting, it is true, but we made up for it in enthusiasm. For one thing, we had an organization of our own at a time when the very word "organization" was a charm. Then, too, we had to fight for our existence. The meetings were held in private homes and on the day we gathered it was our duty to scrounge around for fuel—sticks, branches, straw, reeds, anything that would burn—to warm the house in which we met. Very soon we ac-

quired still another incentive—the disapproval of the
Bolshevik authorities. We were in a revolutionary
mood. There was revolution all around us. What could
be more revolutionary than to say yea when the authorities, real, genuine city authorities, said nay?

The brother of one of our members was a power in
the local "revcom"—the revolutionary committee. This
brother appeared at one of our meetings and told us,
kindly but firmly, to dissolve our organization. There
were more important things for boys to do in a
Bolshevik-ruled town than speak Hebrew once a week,
he said. We refused and decided that henceforth we
would speak Hebrew whenever we met each other. The
next time the commissar's kid brother came to the meeting there were outcries of: "Spy! He is a spy! Kick him
out!" Then and there some sort of trial was held and it
was decided to exclude him from membership because
he told our "secrets" to his brother the commissar. The
boy denied tattling. He was expelled just the same. Out
of spite he said he'd tell his brother "all about us"
and that from now on he would be a Bolshevik. We
were ordered bluntly to dissolve our children's group.
In reply we staged a protest before the office of the local "revcom." Somebody dashed out with a broom and
chased us away. We scattered, our loyalty to Hebrew
greater than ever as a result of this persecution. Alas, it
did not last long.

The leader of our group, the one who was first to
shout "Spy!" and to lead the demonstration against the
"revcom," was a boy whose father, a man named
Velvel, had been murdered in a pogrom the previous
year. The son always took the lead in our Hebrew
group; it was as if he had vowed to his martyred father
to remain true to his people, its past, its culture. But
several years after we came to America we received a

letter from someone in our town, with this postscript attached:

"Do you remember N., the son of Velvel who was killed in the pogrom? He is now a fanatical Communist and he has already reported to the Cheka a number of secret Zionists in town and they were exiled to Siberia. He is now a big shot in the local administration and when one speaks to N. Vladimirovitch it's best to be careful." N. Vladimirovitch—from Velvel to Vladimir. Vladimir means "rule the world": the martyred father had attained a strange posthumous triumph.

"Enough, enough," says Mother. "Do me a favor and have a bite of something. Tomorrow you have to go on a long trip."

I am almost finished going through "the things." Only a few old birth certificates remain. They had been thought lost for a long time. Then they were accidentally rediscovered after many years and I found out that I had been using the wrong date for my birthday. At home we had naturally used the Jewish calendar for such occasions as birthdays and death anniversaries. When first asked in America what my birthday was, I guessed at it as closely as I could. The rediscovered birth certificate showed that I was more than a week off. I was not quite the same person as the boy who pursed his lips so hard in order not to laugh when posing for the passport photograph.

II   *Harry Gersh*

The Jewish Paintner

A delicatessen store man is different from a candy store man or a merchant, but not much. A little of the spice of the pastrami, a little of the fat he didn't trim off the corned beef enters his soul. But basically he is a small businessman with all the same faults and virtues.

A furrier is different from a dress operator or a hat blocker. But essentially he's a needle worker, argue though he will about it—and he will.

But a paintner—he's really different. Who could confuse a paintner with a plumber, a carpenter, a brick-layer? They all work on buildings, but who works like a paintner?

A sociological definition of a paintner would include the following: he is Jewish; he makes his living (some living, he would counter) with brush and paint pot; and his attitude to his customers is like that of a Spanish grandee to a peasant, a king cobra to a worm. Think of the butcher during the war or a candy store man with a case of Chesterfields and a box of Hersheys during the same years, multiply by ten thousand, and it still isn't the same. At best these gentry were nouveaux-arrogants, and it didn't last long. The paintner's attitude has a patina.

Let's get one thing clear from the start. A paintner is more than a painter with a Jewish accent. There are a hundred thousand painters—poor, middling, or expert practitioners of the brush and pot—not a bit different from a million other building tradesmen. A paintner, now, is something else again. He is a painter with a difference. He is a mechanic, a *balmalocheh*, an expert craftsman—but still that's not the whole story. Other trades have older histories, but none has the paintner's special traditions. No other craftsman has his personal psychology molded, tempered, permeated by his craft. A paintner remains a paintner, awake, asleep, or at the movies. The world is colored by his paintnering.

He didn't deliberately adopt his biased view of the world. He didn't sit down in convention and argue it out and pass a resolution to that effect. Part must be written down, I suppose, to economic and social determinism—the rest is sheer trauma.

It might be interesting to investigate the etymology of *balmalocheh* as it refers to the paintner. Some suggest it derives not from "master of the tribe" or craft, as is commonly thought, but rather from Baal Moloch, the master of the abomination.

The paintners' trouble began forty or fifty years ago, much antedating the recent movement to encourage Jews to enter the handicraft trades. To be sure, even then they were masters; not only of the brush and palette, but of the cut direct, the snub superior.

A newly arrived Jewish immigrant, circa 1900, had little choice of new occupations. If he couldn't afford a store, or even a peddler's pack, he became a garment worker. But for a few, the fast talkers, the adventurous, the strong of back, there was painting. Any of the other building trades might have done as well, but painting had two great advantages—the boss supplied the tools and skill came after the job.

A carpenter needed a plane, a hammer, a saw, a chisel, and ease at handling these intricate machines. A plumber needed other tools and the ability to light a blowtorch. A bricklayer needed years of training and waterproof feet. But a paintner—anybody could *shmeer* and look good in a dark hallway.

The boss paintner knew all this—he may have started the same way himself—and he took advantage of his knowledge by paying the greenies half or quarter scale. After all—was the customer an expert on painting? And in that same dark hall who cared? So it wasn't painted so perfect.

So an old-timer (he came over last year) took a greenie (he came over last week) and made a paintner of him. First he established relationship. He was a relative or a friend or a friend of a relative. Then he took the new one to a paint store for outfitting and training.

Since a paintner needed only one tool in his kit, the buying of that tool became highly important, almost a ritual. However, after a good deal of arguing, weighing, and measuring, the greenie was fitted to a putty knife. Then came a pair of white overalls. Union rules specify white overalls, changed each week. But the second pair would come after he had earned some money at his new trade. If the trainer were finicky he might order the new one to buy a duster. But that was ostentation.

The sale of the putty knife and overalls entitled the trainee to a tour of the store for an eye acquaintance with the rest of his trade. He was shown paint brushes and kalsomine brushes and ceiling brushes. Also enamel, flat, oil, turps, and varnish. Then he was ready to swing a brush.

The next day the newcomer was taken before a boss paintner. "He's a good mechanic from the old country yet," the old-timer stated, "but he doesn't know American materials so good. So he'll work for a little less for a while." And another paintner was born.

With the birth of this new craftsman there was the attendant psychic trauma. The new paintner knew he wasn't a mechanic, knew that another trade took better tools and greater skill. He knew it and the other paintners knew it and the boss knew it—and he knew that they knew it. But the customer didn't know it. The customer didn't know anything. And a tradition was born—the customer doesn't know anything. And who has respect for a person who doesn't know anything?

Feeding this disdain was another factor—proximity. Most building craftsmen—for example, plumbers—see their ultimate consumers only in an emergency. Others, such as bricklayers and lathers, never see the householder. But the paintner comes around year after year, always working under the customer's eye. He is cursed with having the amateur over his shoulder, with housewives' indecisions, with spots on the furniture and floors. And he curses right back.

Products of a literate culture, the new Jewish paintners immediately set out to make the language of the trade more esoteric. Some superficial students in the field have ascribed the trade patois to unfamiliarity with English. A more realistic study would indicate that they were only trying to do for painting what others before them had done for law, medicine, and the dance. In the interest of impressiveness they were clothing what is essentially a simple art in verbiage outside the ken of ordinary people.

The new language had so powerful a hold on the trade that I, a very literary high school student in my youth, never knew the simple original English words for the paintner's tools I worked with—I carried a "straisel" around during several summer vacations without embarrassment, but blushed when we bought a new one and the bill was marked "1 Straight Edge." And I painted many windows with a good "seshtel" before I heard ordinary folk call it a sash tool. But, being a good union man, I must keep some of the other words secrets of the trade.

The paintner has other troubles. He is forced by the eccentric fancies of women folk to live in a world of strident off-key hues. He is beset by lemon yellows, babyblues, and pustulent chartreuse, when all he wants is a decent, honest eggshell off-white. This spectrum conflict further colors his approach to people. Exhausted by the many whirling, clashing colors thrown at him, he sees the world in dull grey, the world and half its people. With women he usually sees red.

The boss paintner, more interested in money than in artistry, has also wounded the craftsmen. Anxious for the job, the boss offers a little carpentry and plastering with the painting. The paintner is stuck. He must fix plaster and refit the window sash before applying his colors.

It is this list of psychic and physical wrongs that has made the paintner what he is today. His uneasy sense of his own lack of craftsmanship, the lady of the house eternally over his shoulder, a growing color-phobia, and the pressure to dabble in other skills in which he has even less artisanship than at painting—all these make

him feel persecuted. And what do the persecuted do?
They find a scapegoat to persecute.

The genius of persecuting someone involves setting
the right tone at the first meeting. In order to create at
once the correct rapport between himself and the householder, the paintner has developed the classic opening
gambit:

"And what kind of *miseh-meshineh* [evil-looking]
color do you want now?"

At one stroke the paintner has established the fact
that the customer has no color sense, that she is looking
only to make trouble for a poor workingman, and that
it would be far better if she left the whole matter in
his hands without further hints or interference—especially if she values peace of mind more than some silly
partiality to some non-existent color.

Sometimes, out of a feeling of delicacy usually foreign to the paintner (or because the boss is present),
the classic opening is more devious or hidden. I remember being witness to the following scene, a silent witness
because the customer was a family friend and the
paintner was a fellow craftsman who worked for us.

Mrs. Lewin was having the whole house painted.
It was a long-thought-out and long-planned affair. She
and her husband had spent hours creating the color
scheme, rearranging the furniture to suit, deciding
when they would have enough money. She had read
one full year's back issues of *House Beautiful* and
American Home. She knew what she wanted.

Enter Schmiel to survey the job. He arrived early,
carrying a parcel of overalls, a bucket with his scrapers,
putty knives, and spackle. When Mrs. Lewin answered
the door he announced:

"The paintner is here."

This is the correct third-person approach.

Once the door was opened wide, he entered, and without further invitation or ado he walked right through to the kitchen. There he deposited his bundles, and seated himself in a chair. Again without waiting for an invitation. Why not?

"Am I a salesman? I'm a mechanic, I came to do a job, so I should be bashful?" he would have explained.

Mrs. Lewin was forced to tag after the man who was going to execute her fond plans. Having little experience with paintners she had not even assumed the traditional no-use-trying-to-do-me-in expression attempted by more sophisticated householders in addressing paintners.

Excitedly she invited Schmiel to follow her about the house, so he could see what colors she wanted in what rooms. They went upstairs and she began her "spiel."

"In this bedroom," she began, "we want a light yellow. Almost like early sunlight."

Schmiel didn't bother to look at her. He didn't even bother to shake his head sadly. He just stood in the exact center of the room and looked about at the four walls. Mrs. Lewin went on talking about the almost sunlight yellow. Schmiel just looked. When he had looked enough, he walked into the next room without saying a word. Mrs. Lewin followed.

"And this is my daughter's room," she continued. "We thought it would look just right for her in a pale pink. An ivory with a pink tinge. Do you think you can make that color?"

This time Schmiel did look at her. The look was almost expressionless but it conveyed the sense of a busy man whose patience was beginning to fray a little. He said nothing.

The next room was the bathroom. Mrs. Lewin had ideas there. It was going to be gay and bright. Not just antiseptically utilitarian like most bathrooms, not violent like the new Hollywood bathrooms, but laughingly gay. Schmiel shuddered just so slightly. Now downstairs. The living room was going to be papered, said Mrs. Lewin. The *balmalocheh* stalked out into the dining room. This room was to be a soft grey. Not a blue-grey, nor a brown-grey, just a soft even-toned grey.

"And now the kitchen," Mrs. Lewin ended, "I want this room in ivory." Schmiel nodded. But she continued, "So I can put some gay decals on it and make it look Pennsylvania Dutch." That did it. The paintner sat down heavily.

First, he tried the artistic approach. Mrs. Lewin looked susceptible. "It won't look good so many colors. Such a mish-mash. How could anyone stand it? Every time you go into another room your eyes will blink. Better leave it to me. A nice ivory all over. Hah?"

Mrs. Lewin wasn't having any. He had misjudged her. She started in again listing colors and rooms. Interrupting, the paintner made his second move:

"It's going to cost you a lot of money. Every time a new color is ten dollars extra. Five rooms all different is fifty dollars more. Hah?"

Of course, here he was daringly off-base. The price had been set, and it wasn't any of his business, anyway. But he tried. Mrs. Lewin was firm. Third move.

"It's so old-fashioned, all these colors. Last week I worked by very rich people in Westchester. With high-priced decorators yet. And by them was all eggshell." He looked hopefully upward. It didn't work.

Schmiel had now used the three standard anti-color gambits. Basically Schmiel was not dull- or mono-color-minded. He enjoyed Christmas ties. But color was a nuisance and anyway not within a layman's province.

Unfortunately, Schmiel had no opening for standard argument number four. This one is reserved for a customer who asks for something new. A paintner's definition of new is within the last twenty years. This argument goes like this: "There isn't any such thing." And if confronted with printed proof, the next move is: "It's just in the advertisements, it's not on the market yet."

To Schmiel's and the trade's sorrow, Mrs. Lewin won the argument and got her way. But before the four days were over there must have been many an hour during which she wondered whether it was worth it, whether anything was worth it. Schmiel had many resources.

Another of the paintner's gripes—inevitably let out on the customer—is that he cannot leave his tools in the shop. That *shvere-arbeiter* the plumber, called upon only in emergencies, has developed a method for making customers pay for their temerity. He leaves his tools in the shop. He does carry a bag of tools, but the one necessary for this particular job is in the shop. The paintner is caught by fate. The boss delivers the paint, ladders, and brushes. These materials are ample for the work. And that means seven hours of work for seven hours on the job. It's not right.

To counter this wrong, the paintner has developed several time-wasting techniques. For example, the "you got a rag?" angle. Technically there is no reason in the world why the householder should supply rags to the paintner. He is supposed to leave her premises broom-clean and without spots. But the lady of the house knows that it doesn't pay to take chances. When the paintner says, "You got a rag I should wipe up the spots?" she starts tearing sheets, shirts, and dresses. Usually they are sheets, shirts, and dresses she is still not sure she can spare. Meanwhile the paintner examines the pictures on the wall with a jaundiced eye. Every day he needs more rags.

Another technique involves coffee. Let the slightest aroma of coffee rise through the house and the paintner appears in the kitchen for a drink of water or a question about some room. There he will hover about, sniffing. Each sniff will seem to exhaust the air from the room. The rest is always automatic.

If the lady of the house is not a between-meals coffee drinker the paintner will broach the subject delicately. "Hummah," he'll say, "I thought I smelled coffee." Usually she gets the idea.

For recalcitrant housewives, there are several "get-even" techniques. One is a subtle method of making fun of the customer, known in the trade as *macht choizik*.

I once sat entranced while the same Schmiel exercised his techniques on a lady who had insisted on a peach ceiling. He would put a drop of color into the paint pot, mix it, dip his brush, and climb laboriously up the ladder to take one swipe at the ceiling. Then he would climb down, go to his lunchbox, take out a peach, climb back up with the fruit and compare the ceiling color with the real thing. After some hours of this the woman fled her house for the movies.

A historic crisis in householder-paintner relations was precipitated in New York by the New School for Social Research, some years ago. The architecture and interior painting of the New School building on 12th Street were advanced. Classrooms were painted with walls and even sections of walls in different colors. Theoretically this method of painting was calculated to even the light throughout the room, eliminate glare, rest the eyes, and focus attention on the lecturer. Maybe it was fine for the New School. But a lot of apartment dwellers got ideas.

The paintner, as a creature of tradition, resists change. But this idea of two walls of different colors was more than change—it was revolution. So the paintners rallied for the counterattack; they used all the old methods and some new ones. And today they have routed the enemy. At any rate, two-color rooms aren't as popular as they once were.

During this battle the paintner made telling use of a new ally, a part of his equipment that heretofore he had looked upon as an inanimate enemy—the dustcloth. The dustcloth is the canvas affair to cover the furniture and floors to prevent spotting.

Now a dustcloth looks inanimate, but it has an animate malignancy. Householders do not believe this but I have seen it with my own eyes. These great squares of cotton can develop feet and crawl. A new, whole dustcloth can instantaneously open its fibers and let a paint spot through onto the piano it is supposed to be protecting—and close up and look whole again. The paintner carefully covers floors and furniture with dustcloths. He paints, and then he lifts the cloth, and there under the cloth he finds spots, dried hard. One more thorn in the paintner's side. But in the New School imbroglio it was the secret weapon in the paintners' arsenal. I recall the case of the West End Avenue lady who had some lovely new Swedish modern white birch furniture, and for the walls of her living room she wanted nothing less than moss green and Algerian beige. . . .

Most paintners have wives (and live in apartments that badly need painting), but no tribe of men dislike women more. For that, by and large, women must bear the blame. Why do female householders assume that men working about the house are half-blind—or rather blind to half they see? A woman who normally would redden with shame if she knew that her slip was showing will walk about the house half undressed, oblivious to the paintner.

Gas meter readers, either because they work for a major utility or because of special training, can walk into an apartment in the early morning with their eyes fixed on a point near the ceiling. They can read the meter and walk out of the house without even having seen the woman of the place clumping about in her nightgown. Paintners cannot do this. It bothers them. A strict morality goes along with the rest of their conservatism.

To make matters worse for them there are the "matchers," the women whose sense of color is so literal that they can only visualize what they have right at hand. This one comes up to the paintner and, grabbing the front of her shocking-pink peignoir, shoves it in his face.

"Here," she says, "make me this color in the bedroom." It is frightening. ("Lady," ends one of the many rueful paintners' jokes on this theme, "I am an old man.")

From this paintner trouble comes another and—from the householder's point of view—worse trouble. The artist, averting his eyes from the deshabille, makes mistakes. For example, he paints over things. It is sad but true that, if not closely watched, the *balmalocheh* will paint over the door hardware, any wall lighting fixtures, and an occasional piece of furniture too heavy to move. But it's not his fault.

To counteract this and other forces working to undermine their craftsmanship and probity, paintners often work in pairs. Working as a team, the two mechanics carry on a running conversation, usually about their customer. It is *de rigueur* that the householder be always spoken of in the formal third person, even though he may be standing right beside them. When the customer addresses them, one paintner always paraphrases what the householder said to the other paintner, using the third person, of course.

Two paintners are working on the window sashes of a living room. The man of the house is sitting in an armchair, reading a book. Suddenly a large splash of ivory enamel appears on a pair of grey kid gloves carelessly left by the customer on a window side table.

"Shlemiel," said paintner No. 1, "look what you've done to the man's gloves."

"So it happened an accident," No. 2 answers, "a little turp and it'll come out. Don't get excited."

He climbs down from the ladder and attacks the spot with a paint-dirty rag and some turpentine. The owner of the gloves sits mesmerized. The conversation continues.

"A nice pair gloves, soft like butter. But not a paintner's color. Gloves like this you don't find on a paintner. It must be a fine man, an artist, maybe a writer, to wear such gloves in the middle of the week."

Paintner No. 1 by now has stopped working and is watching the proceedings with great care from his high perch.

"Be a little careful, you *yold* you," he says, "a five-six-dollar pair gloves you'll ruin for the man yet."

Eventually the spotted glove is put aside to dry. To be sure, it doesn't look perfectly clean, but No. 2 explains to his partner that only a snob and an aristocrat could be dissatisfied.

"And this glove he doesn't use anyway. He has to take out a cigarette, or maybe a nickel for the subway.

How can he wear a glove on the right hand? In the pocket it can have a little spot," he adds.

That's the way it goes. You think you have troubles? Ask any paintner, he'll really tell you.

III *Grace Goldin*

I Remember Tulsa

We had quite a Simchas Torah in Iowa City last year. The celebration of our "rejoicing over the Law" took place at night, of course—everybody had to be at work the following morning. We are a congregation of grocery owners—how better celebrate Succoth than among stacks of Iowa apples and squashes?—but running a grocery all day doesn't dampen Jewish fervor at night after the store closes. Quite the contrary—though the spirit is not what it used to be. The mothers worry about the children staying up too late, with school tomorrow. Once upon a time, when the men of this Yiddish-speaking generation were younger, they did the *kazatsky* on Simchas Torah. Now they import a hora from the university crowd. But how they can drink and sing!

There must have been a lot of sleepy children in school next day, because the big doings went on until ten forty-five and later. At nine-thirty the occasion ceased to be an aim in itself for the youngsters and became a test of endurance, which they found even more delightful. At ten-thirty little Shirley, three years old, rendered "Ani Maamin" in an off-key soprano from the *shulchan* (lectern).

All in all, it was the kind of Simchas Torah my friends in New York go from shul to shul trying to find.

We out here in Iowa are not offered much choice of shuls. Either God deserts us utterly and drops us shul-less in the middle of the prairie (as happens often enough) or for some merit of our ancestors we are granted a man like Mr. M. I cannot decide whether he would like to see his name in print or not. Well, perhaps he would. Mr. Samuel Markovitz, then, is our *chazan*. He is big-time stuff—professional. He was once offered a good round sum to sing to the Jews of Rock Island over Rosh Hashonah and Yom Kippur. He came home after the holidays so desolately homesick that we have been gladdened by his presence in Iowa City every Rosh Hashonah since.

Mr. Markovitz runs a coal and oil company, but that is not his real business. You see him as he really is, doing the work God gave him to do, at Kol Nidre services and at Neilah (concluding service on Yom Kippur). He has the temperament of a big-town chazan—and the voice; but what impresses you most is his fervor as he stands before the open Ark. There his great talent emerges—a talent for throwing himself into God. He is no more sincere, perhaps, than the religious poet who, pouring out his heart to the ineffable, still keeps his eye on untidy prepositions and ragged meters. Mr. Markovitz is aware of the effect every cadence has upon you. Yet as he *davens* in his white chazan's hat, his back to everybody but the Lord, he is at the same time rapt above the Pole.

This Simchas Torah he was at the very top of his form. He has trained the whole congregation as his chorus. There are only about three Jewish families in Iowa City anyway—everybody has married into one of them, and all the children are first and second cousins. We had a family party with trimmings—apples and candles for the children—the candles lit the first time around: afterwards we blow them out. Mothers, I'm sure, must have been quite as terrified of burning down the Altneuschul in Prague.

This year's crop from the university gathered round Mr. Markovitz. Leo, from the Law School, looked as pale and pious when he laughed and beat his hands —who would expect to find this in Iowa City?—as he had looked all day on Yom Kippur standing continually propped against the slightly peeling wall. Our shul itself is a bit disheveled; one shoulder strap of the white curtain over the Ark hangs broken, and the women have almost talked the back benches smooth. I am a little afraid, though, of the new shul that our townspeople are planning to build. I am afraid they will stand in awe of it, and then the younger generation might take over. And that would mean that decorum might win out, and the pepper and salt of Iowa City Judaism be lost forever—as I fear it will be anyway with the passing of its founders.

Ours is only a corner of Judaism—not a very clean corner either—but a genuine corner. No one can doubt that who has seen Mr. Markovitz before the Ark, or heard his singing from among the whisky bottles on Simchas Torah. . . .

That evening I kept thinking of another small Midwestern town we lived in for a number of years, and of the Temple there, that lives for me in a single symbol

—its Torah. Yes, though they believed in ultra-Reform (and had heard nothing of the change of heart since the Pittsburgh Platform) that congregation did possess one Torah, a little object approximately the size of the scrolls of prophetic books—*neviim*—we used to carry about on Simchas Torah when we were children. They kept the Torah clothed in a white satin robe held together with a girdle, an actual girdle, that fastened down the middle with a number of hooks and eyes. Every year the same two men of the congregation, chosen for integrity, marched at a signal to the front of the Temple, where their Torah stood housed in a pointed, shoulder-high Ark. The signal was: "Who shall ascend to the mountain of the Lord, and who shall stand in His holy place?" A proud, silent, solemn moment for the two men—a sort of accolade: "What shall be done unto the men whom we delight to honor?" A once-a-year *aliyah*, in a ritual that had long since discontinued the practice of calling six men to the Law every week at services.

The first year we lived there—after which we made an awful row about it—we worshiped on Yom Kippur in a borrowed church with a great cross, a black cross on a red velvet field hanging just where the *bimah*— platform—should have been. The bimah in that cold and marble vault stood to the left, slightly elevated, carved and also marble, with Gothic writing around its rim: "In the beginning was the Word and the Word was God." I stared at that sentence all through Yizkor one year until I cried as bitterly as the mourners.

It was a revelation to visit the Jewish corner of the cemetery of that town. The ancestors' names one discovered on the tombstones of all the well-known Episcopalian families! Some of their children still gave to the United Jewish Appeal "in memory of Father." Others no longer chose to acknowledge even that tenuous link.

The year we arrived my husband made an attempt —probably the first in the congregation's history— to read the portion of the week out of their little Torah. He unhooked its covering and tried to roll it over to the proper section, but the Torah, so rudely forced, immediately tore in two. My husband hastily gathered the two scrolls together, bound them with their girdle from bottom hook to top, and so far as we know that Torah has never since been disturbed.

That was the congregation whose high point every year was Yizkor, the memorial service, on Yom Kippur afternoon. We adjourned for lunch on Yom Kippur promptly at noon and the members would come over to us solicitously: "Aren't you eating *anything?* Do you feel all right?" And Mrs. T. would come over, her head on one side, shaking sorrowfully: "You're looking so well, *poor* thing!" Not knowing what to do with ourselves until three o'clock, we paid our annual Yom Kippur calls at lunchtime. Our friends learned, when we came, to hide the welcome-box of candy. At three we reconvened to read enlightening spiritual selections from the Hymnal. We read for an hour, taking turns: then Yizkor.

Autumn light fell through the stained-glass windows; leaves crossed the open spaces of blue sky, leaves like chips of spinning yellow glass. And from the pulpit the names of the dead were read—just names, but they produced a powerful cumulative effect. Then the congregation came nearest to religion, though I hesitate to call it Judaism.

All this brings me by strange and devious ways to

my grandfather's shul, which for the first eight years of my life *was* Judaism to me.

My grandfather was an ordinary New York Jew, neither very rich nor very poor—or, if he was extraordinary, it was along the same lines as a number of other New York Jews. His wife's father was a rabbi. His own father, after struggling for years to bring twelve children and a business to a point where he could well abandon them, disappeared one morning leaving a note for the older children on the breakfast table: "I sailed for Palestine. Send Mama and the babies after me if you want."

My grandfather was a man of considerable Jewish and secular learning, self-taught. He also enjoyed writing verse. I do not know whether he would ever have left his family for Palestine: things turned out quite differently for him. The second of his four daughters married an oil man from Tulsa, Oklahoma (and points East European), and she moved out west with him.

It takes only one oil well to make or break a man. The *nagid*—rich man—of the present Tulsa community used to be our grocery-man. He bought one day, instead of a stock of canned goods, a corner of a corner of an oil field. That was all he needed.

By exactly the same kind of purchase my grandfather, who had gone bankrupt in New York, moved to Tulsa and built himself one of the fanciest homes in town. Then he paid off his creditors—with compound interest fully covering the duration of the loans. I met one of those creditors twenty-five years later. He looked me over with profound attention and complimented me as only he could: "An apple never falls far from the tree," he said.

When the new house was built, it contained a shul.

43

Naturally, if he makes that much money, what does a Jew do? The town shul was too far away to walk, but that was only an excuse. This was a God-given opportunity for my grandfather to rule his own shul: an autocrat, defining policies, outlining the order of prayer, compelling decorum, making those improvements in the service every man on every board of directors yearns to bring about—all-powerful—and singlehanded.

The shul took up one whole wing of the house. Nothing but a porch was above it, and when it was explained to me that nobody should stand above a shul and be able to look down upon it, I never went out on that porch but with fear and trembling. The room was beautifully proportioned, like the rest of the house—no one felt cramped for space because one wing of the house was given over exclusively to religious use. One entered at the back of the shul, from the garden, through a double glass door. On each side of the room were three long windows; on the men's side they looked out on the driveway, which was their hard luck: we women had the flower beds and shrubbery. The bimah extended across the front third of the room, raised by three marble steps that also went clear across; and on those steps stood potted plants all year round. I realize now that someone must have watered them— but at that time, for me, they grew right out of the marble. On the High Holidays we had white flowers, and for weddings a greenhouse came indoors.

Shul was separated from house by a double door at the back of the bimah, to one side. It was such a door, I thought, as locks up only a shul or a safe. With the house side of the door open, the shul part not yet, one stood between two worlds. Nowhere else does a door open into a door.

Sometimes we would enter the shul by the garden

door, and sometimes we would come from the house and walk across the bimah. When that happened I invariably felt the faint giddiness of stage fright, no matter how few were the faces looking up at us.

The ceiling of my grandfather's shul was decorated with a repeating design. I don't know what architects call it—it was a kind of double square letter "c" going on from one "c" to the next until, following them overhead around the room, one fell into a sort of trance. I heard my first Hebrew—long before I could read—to the rhythm of architectural patterns, and one phenomenon became related to the other.

But the chief delight of our shul was its silver—Bezalel School work. The Torahs carried bells, one heard them tinkling. And since for the first seven years of my life I was nearsighted without knowing it, breastplates and crowns seemed but a great brightness to me, briefly visible when they came round to be kissed, but otherwise moving back and forth above like silver clouds.

Then what a revelation on Simchas Torah when, for once in a year, we were allowed on the bimah and could watch the Torahs being dressed! Open, they were nothing—one could see ink-writing in the Siddur, or in school. But to watch their fat sides tied together with white ribbon, their red velvet dresses slipped on, fringed in gold, and with lions—from my seat I could never see the lions. And then over the lions clanged their silver breastplates! I could see now that they were not mere blank silver, those breastplates. They too had little crowns, with green beads bouncing from the tips. And they had two tiny doors that opened and locked on a little all-silver Torah; they had a slot where you could change the name of the holiday, each name engraved in Hebrew on a silver calling card. And with my finger,

I rang the bells—I could almost see the bells clearly, standing on tiptoe: I thought the crown like that of any Russian czar (and I was quite right). The other Torahs had double crowns that you might take up—on Simchas Torah—and shake like silver gourds.

There was a pointer, too, with filigree handle and a tiny pointing hand, like a back-scratcher but ever so much more beautiful.

I remember my grandfather's shul as it changed its appearance and its atmosphere for many different occasions. I remember the weddings, with baskets of flowers on either side of the Persian throw rugs, looped together with wide white ribbons and bows; and the cumbersome gold-painted wood *chupah* loaded with boughs; the feel of rose petals, fresh rose petals in the shallow baskets we used for wedding after wedding, and my amazement—half regret—at watching whole roses hastily torn apart to fill a flower-girl's basket. Then, when I had graduated to train-bearing, I remember rows and rows of white satin buttons: every bride's dress in those days was fastened with innumerable satin buttons from the neck down to the small of the back.

I remember Shabbas because then the shul was slightly boring in a polite and beautiful way, like pleasant company stopping over too long. On Shabbas I had a chance to see how different leaves grew in the shrubbery and to observe the shapes of the Hebrew letters in the Siddur. I would count the number of times God's name appeared on each page—he was always easy to find. But I never realized until long afterwards that sometimes he hid there in disguise—in four letters rather than two. I only knew him in his two-letter form. And I would torment my mother for a paraphrase of longer English words until she whispered, indulgent and surprised, "Don't you know what *that* means?" Of course I knew, but one had to do *something*.

I remember the High Holy Days only because of white drapes on ark and shulchan, and the heavy, yellowed wool prayer shawls the men wore, with black bands falling in angles and squares like the Hebrew letters. There were so many beards on the men's side. There was my grandfather's, white, curly, parted in the middle and bunched to either side (like Max Nordau's, I thought later); and there was Uncle Sam's beard—a little black pointed one.

Uncle Sam was in my eyes the embodiment of holiness. He stayed up all night on Yom Kippur. He wore slippers—I suppose some of the other men did, too, but I looked to make sure of Uncle Sam's. He preached to us—but never having made up his mind whether to talk of holy subjects in Hebrew or English, he compromised—or vacillated—between the two. It was not until much later that I found out that a sermon can convey—indeed is often expected to elucidate—thought. A sermon in the days of Uncle Sam was an indulgence, tolerated after the Torah reading solely out of politeness. It rose to a high pitch of incomprehensibility and nobody ever took it seriously.

Nevertheless, I took Uncle Sam seriously. He always seemed to fast harder than anybody else on Yom Kippur. He always got the first glass of water afterwards. One night I dreamed about Uncle Sam—the only dream I recall from my childhood. I dreamed that he and my grandmother stood at the entrance to Heaven. It was an anteroom, rather like the dressing room under the great stairway in my grandfather's house. At one end, where the coats were generally put, hung a curtain, a rolled-up curtain like the one in the auditorium at school. Behind it lay the conviction of Heaven. My grandmother approached. The curtain did not budge; its painted trees stood stiff and tall. Then Uncle Sam drew near and immediately the roots of the trees curled inward, the whole curtain rolled up, and my uncle went his way to Heaven. I awoke with the most painful sense of disloyalty to my grandmother. What was Uncle Sam to me, that I should put his soul above hers?

Uncle Sam died twenty years after my grandfather. He died in Palestine—just. His boat docked there one day and he died the next—of starvation, having lived on orange juice all the way across because he did not consider the food on the boat to be kosher. I suppose that in the end he did bear out my dream of him.

There were not many men in my grandfather's shul as rigorous as Uncle Sam. As a rule, such persons attended the downtown synagogue, which they held in a grip of iron. My grandfather steered his shul with satin reins, but he had his way. With the help of the Bezalel School and the oil wells, he made Orthodoxy fashionable in Tulsa. He imported a cantor—Pinchos Jassinowsky, newly arrived in this country. My grandfather found him singing in a church choir. When they asked the boy later what he had sung, he replied that it had quite a pretty tune, and quoted the words phonetically: "Jesus-loaf-er-off-my-soul."

The family brought a service with them from the Jewish Theological Seminary in New York, which had been just across the street from them. Whenever there was a prayer that had no tune in that service, Jassinowsky wrote music for it. He set the whole Friday night service to new music. He furnished variants which gave me some excitement on Shabbas—what tune for "Ain Kelohenu"? What length for "Adon Olam"? From another relative, a cantor in Kansas City, we took a third set of songs. Our musical versatility was amazing, and that is just what my grandfather wanted it to be.

He sought a new type of Judaism, which I may say I have never met since the days of his shul and do not consider myself likely to meet ever again. Perhaps Moses Montefiore sponsored something like this in his private chapel, but I doubt it; Montefiore was at once too literal and too Orthodox. My grandfather was willing to stretch a point for effect, quite without loss of sincerity —somewhat in the manner of Mr. Markovitz. There was too much decorum in his shul for it to be Orthodox, too much familiarity with tradition for it to be Reform. We were Conservative—but with a difference. I have always thought of our brand of religion as aesthetic Judaism, since in the final analysis the test of a practice or belief was not: is it true, is it logical, is it commanded, is it traditional?—but, taking all these matters for granted, is it beautiful?

When he made enough money to do exactly what he wanted, my grandfather did exactly what any good Jew would want to do. He published privately his own commentary on Ecclesiastes and saw his name in print— names, rather: our family runs to threes in names. My grandfather's were Lionel Elihu Zorah. Uncle Sam was Vivien Samuel David. And I remember how my husband stared when he inquired into my name for the *ketubah* and was told, "Chanah Chesna Feigel daughter of Alfred Enoch Zundel of the family Aaronson"!

L. E. Z. Aaronson saw his four married daughters and his son build themselves homes and settle in Tulsa within five blocks of him. The congregation was filled with his tribe—on Shabbas we had twenty or twenty-five to services (all singing); on holidays, sixty. Shabbas afternoons he gathered his children round and read them *Perek*, the Sayings of the Fathers. This went on for nearly ten years, and, human nature aside, there was no reason why it should not have continued forever.

But it ended—the Shabbas afternoons, the oil wells, the shul, my grandfather's life. It ended in a family fight and lawsuit that made the front pages of the newspapers. Had that happened fifty years ago instead of twenty-five I might give details. However, the final blow-up only proved what Emerson wrote: "We were not made to breathe oxygen, or to talk poetry, or to be always wise." By the same token, it is just as well we possess other brands of Judaism than the aesthetic in this country. Like every other beautiful thing, my grandfather's aesthetic Judaism lived its moment, and passed. Wistful reminiscence is all I can summon up to protest its passing. I suppose that sort of ritual could be lastingly effective only in very small quantities, mixed with a large amount of something at once more earthy and more fallible.

Once, when I was six, I stood out in my grandmother's front garden while the grownups were in shul, and watched the cars ride by. And I thought to myself with certainty, "There go the cars. In not one of those cars is a Jew. A Jew wouldn't ride on Shabbas." There in the street passed the rest of the world, and here in the garden stood I, amid Jews and roses. Something of that frame of mind persists, and makes it still seem odd that Jews are ever poor, are ever ugly (our family was persistently good-looking), are ever persecuted, hounded, insulted, are ever vulgar or raucous.

What reminded me of my grandfather's shul this last Simchas Torah is that, of all the holidays celebrated there, I remember Simchas Torah most clearly. A child would. I remember the singing—my first Hasidic melodies. I do not remember drinking: perhaps my grandfather would not allow it, perhaps I didn't notice it. We were not given candles to march with at all: we had flags for the girls, *neviim* for the boys. How we marched! It took exactly three choruses to take us round that bimah. I always managed so I would step precisely on the third repeated pattern of the Persian throw rugs. I hopped on one border with the right foot—on the other border with the left foot. Everyone was there, all the family, all the friends; no one was at business, no one was at school, no Jew anywhere in the world was any place but at shul, with the Torah.

Judaism has never lived up to the promise of my Simchas Torahs—or rather, I would say, Jews have not done so. Whenever they approximate it, as in Iowa City this past year, the most that is renewed of old days is a piercing nostalgia for what might have been, for what I thought then would surely be. And I am sorry my daughter Robin will never get the chance to celebrate Simchas Torah in my grandfather's shul.

But Robin had a good time this Simchas Torah just the same. I saw that. Maybe she enjoyed herself just as much here in Iowa as I did in Tulsa. Maybe she makes the same thing out of what she gets.

IV *William Poster*

'Twas a Dark Night in Brownsville

In the 1920's, when I was very young, every New York Jew could feel certain about one thing: he was superior to anybody living in Brownsville. There was a kind of bilingual folk ballad about this Brooklyn Kasrilevke that we Brownsvillians learned to anticipate from a certain gleam in people's eyes. It began, " *'Siz geven a finstere nacht in Brunzvil*"—" 'Twas a dark night in Brownsville"—and it was always accompanied by uproarious laughter. Whenever a Brownsville boy ventured outside his home district, some variant of the following dialogue was inevitable:

"Where ya from?"

"Brooklyn."

"Uhhuh. What section?"

"What section?"

"Yeah. 'At's what I said. What section?"

"Uhhuh."

"So?"

"So what?"

"So what section of Brooklyn d'ya come from?"

"Ahhh, whaddya boddering me for? It ain' exackly a section. Besides, yuh wooden know nuttin' even if I tole yuh."

"I wooden, huh? So tell me an' see already. What section?"

"Well, it's kinda near East New York."

"Ahhh, stop stallin', willya! What street?"

And as you let the answer trickle slowly forth, you would involuntarily brace yourself. "Ahah!" the inevitable eruption would begin, "dat's in Brownsville. You live in Brownsville! Brunzvil, hah, hah, hah, hah, Brahnzvil. Noo? Hahz everything in Brahnzvil? Hahz Peetkin Avenue? Huh? Hahz Belmont Avenue? Hah? Dey still trown duh gobbidge outta duh windows? I heah dey're buildin' sooers der now. It's gettin' classy. Yeah! Hah, hah, hah, ho, ho, ho. *'Siz geven a finstere nacht in Brahnzvil.*"

The formula never varied, and I never saw anyone from Brownsville clever enough to lie his way out of the predicament. A kind of shamefaced loyalty or sense of identity, coupled with a peasant-like inability to pick up social affectations, forced the admission every time. As we grew up, we became accustomed, if never really adjusted, to the fact that we were living in a social zoo: so firmly entrenched was the world's opinion that the Brownsvillian had no choice but to accept it as a mystic, final truth.

Indeed, we found ourselves frequently employing it against each other, boasting about a married sister in East Flatbush, proclaiming how far from the center of Brownsville we lived (I myself, however, lived at its very hub), using every possible means to inch our way out of the mire. And when one of our school teachers in an explosion of rage informed us that Brownsville was one huge cesspool of illiteracy and hoodlumism, and that she had narrowly escaped being demolished by a flying bag of garbage that very morning, we all hastened to agree with her.

When we were about to be graduated from Brownsville's Groton, PS 66, rumors were as plentiful as nuts on Passover. No use trying to get into the choicer high schools—we were told and told each other—because the name of "Sixty-Six" was anathema to every principal in Brooklyn. We were all on a special Board of Education blacklist. Maybe the best thing to do was just to get our "workin' papers" and comply with the law by enduring the brief purgatory of "continuation school," after which society might leave us in the sodden untutored peace we felt was our natural condition. After all, didn't our parents assure us, as we came streaking up from a punchball game covered with grime and sweat, gobbled our food, and rushed off to one of a hundred feverish nocturnal activities, that we were all bums, gangsters, truck drivers, "expressmen," *grobyankes* (coarse louts), *boolvans* (brainless bullies), *paskudnyaks* (sheer vilenesses), accidents of nature who would doubtless end up murdering their own parents?

But publicly sensitive as we were to the opinions of our teachers, relatives, and outsiders, to ourselves our habits and morals seemed not only pardonable but perfectly natural and even praiseworthy. Once back in the inner world of Brownsville boyhood, we were content with being what everyone else reviled, and ardently desired to be even rougher, tougher, dirtier, more ill-mannered, more foul-mouthed, more vicious, more uncompromisingly opposed to every kind of law, order, and authority. True, boys in all the lower-class New York neighborhoods took pride in their toughness; but in Brownsville, somehow, we worked at it full time.

Built up nearly overnight on rundown farmland, Brownsville, in the 20's, had come to occupy an area of about two square miles set apart by such natural boundaries as the IRT El on Livonia Avenue, the BMT El on Junius Street, the junction of Pitkin Avenue's macadam with the greensward of Eastern Parkway at Howard Avenue, and the Liberty Avenue trolley. It was, I believe, the largest solidly Jewish community in the city. Other reputedly Jewish sections may have contained more Jews than Brownsville's two hundred thousand, but they were likely to be strongly Jewish for only a block or two and then give way to a mixed ethnic pattern. Brownsville was a Jewish island. I would guess that the population was about ninety-five per cent Jewish and four per cent Italian, with a handful of Negroes and a few Polish janitors making up the remainder.

Up to the age of twelve or so, a Brownsville child scarcely saw any members of other groups except for teachers and policemen, and never really felt that the Jews were anything but an overpowering majority of the human race. I don't think my contemporaries and I believed that the figures who loomed largest in our imagination—say, George Washington, Nathan Hale, Tom Mix, Babe Ruth, and Jack Dempsey—were actually Jewish, but we never clearly thought of them as anything else.

In a period when most of New York's Jews were striving desperately to become Americanized, perhaps Brownsville's solid Jewishness alone was enough to account for the section's lowly status. But there were other factors. For one thing, circumstances seem to have attracted a specific type of Jew out to Brownsville: I have the impression that the great majority came from the regions of Russia around Minsk, with relatively few of Polish, Rumanian, or any other origin. By and large, they were an energetic, hustling, robust lot, but rarely possessed of any but the simplest material ambitions. The desire for respectability or elegance must have been weak in them to begin with, and Brownsville scarcely supplied the soil on which it could thrive. Essentially, the district was the New York center of the *proste yid*, the "plain Jew," remarkably level-headed, and rarely noteworthy for imagination or lofty aspirations. Most of the older men had their occupations in the neighborhood; they were storekeepers, real estate men, peddlers of fruits and vegetables, the auxiliaries of these businesses, and those professionals indispenable to the community.

The most prosperous merchant of Pitkin Avenue and the poorest potato peddler were likely to live in the same house or adjacent ones, and to buy most of their food, clothing, and furniture at the same stores—if only out of lack of desire or time to do otherwise. Brownsvillians, in general, were either so busy or so unimaginative that "conspicuous waste" or snobbery of any kind was minimal: when one of them finally did get the idea and had the leisure and the cash, he migrated to another section. But as long as he stayed in Brownsville, he remained subject to its prevailing egalitarianism of tone and manners. Likewise, the children all went to the same schools, and played together in packs in which the children of the fairly affluent (like myself) were indistinguishable from those of pushcart venders and junkmen (like most of my playmates).

In appearance, too, Brownsville was egalitarian, with no very distinguished residence within its confines, and the streets pretty much littered and grimy everywhere, though there was considerable space inside and about the buildings, and it did not at all resemble the congested, malodorous slum districts of Manhattan. The dwellings were of every variety and looked as though they had been dropped chaotically from the sky, while the business establishments gave a curious appearance of systematic arrangement: seven blocks of furniture stores on Rockaway Avenue, so that a walk down that street was like a girl's domestic daydream of plushy sofas and gleaming mahogany bedroom suites; five teeming, pungent blocks of pushcarts, groceries, and "appetizing" stores on Belmont Avenue; men's and women's clothing and similar emporia on the ten busy blocks of Pitkin Avenue. A huge six-block square of junkshops, tinsmithies, stables, garages, and miscellaneous small enterprises surrounded these main arteries. How it all rang and clattered and hammered and buzzed and smelled! There wasn't a quiet square yard in the whole district.

For all its reputation, Brownsville in the 20's was scarcely a poverty-stricken neighborhood. The merchants of Pitkin Avenue had prospered in the postwar boom, often accumulating enough surplus capital to open second or third stores or to dabble in real estate (a Brownsville passion). Belmont Avenue flourished on a largely deserved reputation for cheapness and quality that drew customers from a wide area. And while selling vegetables from a pushcart may not have looked very elegant, it was often amazingly lucrative: one peddler was reputed to have three cellars and a fleet of four trucks devoted solely to stocking his cart—which was, indeed, always surrounded by a large group of chaffering *veiblach*.

Junk, rag, and paper dealers, who had gone into business with nothing but a horse and wagon, their bare hands, and inexhaustible patience, expanded their lots, acquired trucks, and even ventured into manufacturing. Stables gave way to garages—alas for the children who in the early 20's could still watch the black-smiths at their forges and stuff old pocketbooks with horse manure for the unwary! The owner of the local barber shop replaced his flyblown mirrors, hired an extra helper, and to the consternation of the conservatives installed a *zaftig* blond manicurist. The tailor, who could be seen in his undershirt sweating over the pressing machine, hired a regular delivery boy instead of luring us from our games with the promise of big tips. The gabbling flock of carpenters, painters, plumbers, and masons that used to swarm on the corner of Stone and Pitkin Avenues dwindled noticeably on weekdays.

Unemployment, the great blight on the prosperity of the 20's, could not have been too great in Brownsville because nearly everybody was in business for himself. Good food could be had cheap and rent was low. Many families lived in two- or three-story houses that were sturdily constructed, relatively spacious, and comfortably, if primitively, heated by wood or coal stoves and gas radiators. Free of the high costs of social conformism and ostentation, Brownsville didn't fare badly.

I once read, in a local newspaper, a series of statistics purporting to show that Brownsville had the lowest mortality rate of any community of similar population in the country. The claim seems plausible. Though ridden by its sense of inferiority, Brownsville was at bottom free of many of the inhibitions, tensions, and pretensions that are among the most lethal factors of modern life. Heedless of medicine, dentistry, manners, child psychology, balanced diets, and social distinctions, Brownsville roared, worked, played, ate, and slept. The major problems of human relations were settled by a yell, a laugh, a shrug, or a slap. There were, surely, heartaches and headaches of every variety, but I think that the people of Brownsville knew in their bones how little one actually needs to cushion oneself against the shocks of life.

In an odd way and for a brief period, Brownsville fulfilled the age-old Jewish need for a sanctuary, an escape from the consciousness (if not the fact) of being a minority in exile. To a child, at any rate, Brownsville was a kind of grimy Eretz Yisrael without Arabs. Living in a world all Jewish, where no alien group imposed its standards, the child was secure in his own nature. What social shame he did feel was simply for his own lack of shame when, outside the boundaries of Brownsville, he ran up against those for whom a nervous consciousness of the opinions of the world had become a badge of superiority.

True, his first vision of the real state of affairs was apt to produce something like a traumatic shock. Indeed, to reach maturity with anything like a normal relation to society was difficult for Brownsville's second generation. All that remained functional to their parents out of the wreck of the European heritage were some simple physical and prudential precepts and a few copybook maxims. Maturity alone constituted the power of the parent over the child, for the reciprocal relation by which parents derive strength from conventions and conventions derive strength from parents was shattered by the break from Europe, by social change and the facts of life. Too often the children were the guides in matters of American language and custom, and the parent could never be certain that even the most outrageous adolescent behavior did not issue from some mysterious American norm that his child understood better than he. The amazing thing, then, was not that Brownsville produced some criminals, freaks, and barbarians, but that so many did manage somehow to obey the laws, attend school and go on to become proper or even distinguished citizens.

When he first awoke to purposeful consciousness, at about the age of five, a Brownsville boy found himself an integral part of what he called his "gang," a group of boys with a whole network of rules, aims, and standards. The gang consisted of twenty to thirty males of approximately the same age. They had names not only like Irv, Joey, Dave, but also Yookie, Dodie, Cockeye Sidney, Cripple Natie, Gimpty, Roobs, Bensie, Baby, Abie Kabibble, Koko, Meetsgah, Knockout, Avrum, Blowie, Moish, Gyp, Heshie, Yushkie, Brownie, Blackie, Whitey, Punk, Zigzag. There were no tomboys in the gang. Until puberty, a Brownsville boy studiously ignored the existence of girls his own age except when they turned up playing jacks on a handball court, in which case the jacks were summarily kicked into the gutter, followed, if necessary, by their owners. Older girls were eyed with fanatic hostility: we bombarded them with ash-filled snowballs, chalked up their coats on Halloween, shouted abuse at them, and elicited screeches by nipping their ankles with our nails while making cat-noises or dropping dead mice in their paths.

Inclusion in the gang was absolute, and human relations outside it were cut to a minimum. Even its territory was staked out with minute precision. When two Brownsville kids who were strangers had some contact, the first question was, "What's your block?" and the answer established identity. A gang might not inhabit a full block but only a specific sector of it. Thus "my block" was Osborne Street between Pitkin and Glenmore Avenues, and the region my gang regarded as its domain took up one-third of this area, starting from Pitkin Avenue. Our territory ended where a small group of Italian families and their offspring took over. The section of the block nearest to Glenmore Avenue belonged to a second Jewish group. Small as the area was, the three juvenile clans were as tightly contained as primitive tribes.

Competition was intense between the two Jewish gangs; the punchball games between the two, with every cent we could muster bet on them, were the gala events of the block. There was, I believe, a real difference between the two gangs, a difference perhaps imperceptible to the outsider but crucially important to the boys themselves. The Glenmore Avenue boys were a little taller, cleaner, and more refined, and they could make us feel awkward and stupid by their sneers and by the greater precision, control, and clarity of their language and action. We were cruder, noisier, more energetic. The punchball games expressed this difference, and it would be hard to say who had the edge.

But such was the disorder of juvenile Brownsville that nobody ever really won anything at all. Whenever a game or contest tended to a conclusion, the party in danger of defeat simply smashed up the system of conventions and rules that made the game possible; it was a deliberate technique of planned anarchy. Whether at checkers, marbles, arguments, fights, punchball games, you simply refused to acknowledge a defeat and developed every possible stratagem to obliterate even the marks of victory. In order to win at marbles, for example, you not only had to have superior skill, but often the ability to beat up your opponent, out-argue him, enlist the sympathies of onlookers, and hang on to your booty and the sensation of victory against every conceivable psychological attack, including the ultimate "OK, dogface, you win, pick up duh marbles 'n go home to your mudder."

Suppose you won all the marbles and pennies of one of your opponents in a game that included four players. He would promptly insist on a loan, with the support of the other two if they happened to be losing. If the game ever dwindled down to two players you could maintain your right to quit, but the loser made sure you never did. After the first loan, one altercation succeeded another and you were lucky if you finally got away with one-tenth of your legitimate winnings— with sneers and catcalls following you for being a quitter (the loser never quit). And at home you were met with a bawling-out interspersed with slaps for being plastered with mud and three hours late for dinner. How could you explain that you couldn't quit if you were losing and you couldn't quit if you were winning?

Punchball games got under way only after a half-hour of skullduggery connected with choosing for first turn at bat, and frequently a game never reached the second half of the first inning, the side at bat either preventing a third out from being called by trampling on the first baseman, or else refusing to admit it when it was called. If the game survived these obstacles, then the losing side would stall till darkness enabled them to enter a claim of no decision, or would break the game up in a brawl in which the stakeholder (if anyone could be persuaded to fill that perilous post) nearly got torn in two.

Between the Pitkin Avenue gang and the Italian clan in the middle of the block, relations were slight, consisting of brief, jittery moments of sociability, and bursts of warfare in which, despite a considerable inferiority of numbers, the Italians maintained equality. We were physically stronger, I think, and won our share of individual fights, but their group fighting tactics were much more advanced than ours: they stuck together like a unit of the Maffia, swooped down on us suddenly while we were dispersed in twos or threes, feinted frighteningly at our testicles, batted us over the head with stockings full of ashes, and sometimes even succeeded in taking our pants down. By the time we could get organized to counter-attack, they would have disappeared into their lairs. Once we went to a lumberyard and armed ourselves with thin twelve-foot lances with which we kept them off the streets for days, but they soon procured lead pipes of equal length and wreaked havoc among us. There were also occasional flurries of ash, garbage, tin-can, stone, and bottle throwing.

The Italian group included the inevitable displaced Jew, and in my gang there were two Italian brothers called Frankie and Brownie, as well as a Polish boy called Petey. The Jewish boy among the Italians was known as Yushkie. He was an unusually tall, thin boy, rather bitter, grim, and distrait in appearance. His bitterness probably came from the fierce baiting he was subjected to for being foreign-born—a "mockery." We regarded him as a renegade, and, since he used Italian fighting tactics, felt towards him a mingled respect, hatred, and horrified repulsion. We never spoke to him or included him in our games, and he was likely to be the special target in any clash between the two gangs.

Frankie and Brownie associated with us simply by preference. Their parents were somewhat more Americanized than the other first-generation Italians on the block, who scarcely spoke English at all, and Frankie and Brownie were perhaps a trifle more refined than the other Osborne Street Italians, who were a very rough lot indeed.

While we were very "race-conscious," once some-one was inside the gang we completely forgot about differences except when the inevitable problem of chalking up boxball boundaries on the Sabbath came up. Many religious precepts were flouted with next to no concern, but writing in public on the Sabbath was an infraction we all avoided because it had become amalgamated with our more fundamental preoccupation with prestige. The taboo was so powerful that even Frankie, Brownie, and Petey, as well as the most irreligious Jewish boys, would refuse to violate it because of the lowering of status that would ensue. We usually bullied Cockeye Sidney, the lowest-ranking member of the gang, into doing it, and then excluded him from the game he had made possible. If necessary, with a few kicks in the seat of his pants.

Despite his inward anarchy, the life of a Brownsville boy was as regulated, definite in its objectives, and ritualized as that of a member of a primitive tribe. Whenever he could wrench himself free from such chores as eating, sleeping, school, and homework, all of which he had to be coerced into by force or the threat of force, he got together with the gang, from which he could never be excluded unless its psychological or physical hazards were more than he could endure. And as long as he had sufficient strength to participate, he was relieved of some of the worst terrors of childhood. All kinds of attitudes were fixed and ordered for him: the limits of his territory, his position within the gang, his relations with strangers and with boys of different ages.

Age groups were marked out by a mobile but definite system. No matter what a boy's age, there was always a group of boys younger than himself which he called "duh liddle guys" and an older group which he called "duh big guys." And he himself to his juniors was a "big guy" and to his seniors a "liddle guy." A cluster of rights, prerogatives, and attitudes was attached to this relation which had so powerful a grip that even when one saw a "big guy" some ten or fifteen years later, some of the old feelings were automatically revived.

Among the "big guys" were to be found all one's "big brudders" and among the "liddle guys" were to be found the "kid brudders." It was an absolute obligation of "big brudders" to protect "kid brudders" and redress any physical injury to them, even if it was inflicted in fair fight with a peer. At some desperate point in a fight between two boys of equal age, the one who was losing would threaten his opponent with the might of the older males of his family. This tactic was orthodox and did not lessen the status of the individual using it, beyond the natural drop in status resulting from his defeat. A skillfully used "big brudder" was an advantage paid for by receiving numerous raps on the head, while a "kid brudder" was on the whole a liability, useful for errands and menial tasks and as a source of admiration, but altogether too likely to subject his protector to the gratuitous perils of fights with all the "big guys" whom he happened to antagonize.

If the hazards of gang life were great, there were many compensations. To its members the gang gave a wide variety of skills, a set of functioning attitudes, and a highly specialized language. If you talked in the right tough style you wouldn't get thrown off a handball court or have your checkers stolen; in fact you could push other boys aside or steal their checkers. A fashionable idiom, used audaciously, served, as it does in many a society with different values, to conceal weaknesses. Humor and wit were also great values, enhancing one's position directly by attraction or indirectly when used to degrade someone else. Words were also intoxicants.

At the age of three or four, boys held hands and pivoted rapidly until they got dizzy, shouting: "Sailor boy, sailor boy, go so slow, sailor boy, sailor boy, go so fast. . . ." Soon afterwards they learned serious and humorous threat language: "I'll mobbilize yuh," "I'll kick yuh teet' down yuh t'roat," "I'll spit down yuh appetite 'n' charge yuh for a seltzer." They learned how to get the proper snarl into phrases like "gidduhhellah-taheah" and "go tell yuh mudder yuh fadder wants yuh." They picked up a score of different chants for choosing who was to be "it," and a number of jingles and songs, usually obscene.

The earliest game I recall playing was also verbal. It was called "Milkman." The "milkman" went to each player and took an order for bottles of milk which he delivered in the form of slaps on the hand. He then came to collect for the milk and the "customer" refused to pay in the most insulting fashion possible. The "milkman" asked for an explanation. The "customer" informed him that he had found some horrifying object in the milk such as a rat's tail or a lump of horse manure. The "milkman" then asked a series of questions to all of which he got the same answer:

"Waddya eat every morning?"
"A rat's tail."
"Wot's your fadder?"
"A rat's tail."
"Wot time is it?"
"A rat's tail."
"Waddya use for brains?"
"A rat's tail."

The "milkman" gesticulated wildly and made weird faces while he asked the questions. If the "customer" broke into laughter or gave any other answer but the original one, he paid a forfeit by doing something difficult or painful, such as "goin' troo duh mill"—crawling rapidly on hands and knees between the straddled legs of all the other players, who paddled his behind as hard as they could (there was always one wise guy who held the crawler between his knees until he got up and started a fight).

Before we were twelve, my friends and I had learned not only what we were required to do in school and an enormous number of physical games and feats, but also a considerable amount about all the local businesses and the society in which we lived. We had learned a score of fairly complicated card games including poker, casino, rummy, pinochle, hearts, blackjack, fantan, banker and broker, and an Italian game called "brisk." We shot dice, placing our bets according to a close approximation of the true probabilities—an intellectual feat beyond the scope of many well-educated adults. Between the ages of nine and twelve, we also read, I would judge, no less than fifteen hundred novels —Merriwells, Nick Carters, Ted Strongs, Tom Swifts, and Baseball Joes—as well as innumerable issues of *Sport Stories, Detective Stories,* and *Amazing Stories.*

There was not a fence, hole, wall, lot, or cellar in the block that we did not use for some childhood purpose, and as we moved towards adolescence our knowledge spread to take in the entire section and then beyond it to Coney Island, Ebbets Field, and the big Brooklyn parks and movies. We also organized half-uniformed athletic teams that participated erratically in interborough competition—though nearly all sports and social organizations were short-lived, breaking up in bitter conflicts over questions of power, privilege, and obligation.

In fact, the battle for status was the chief determinant of our lives. Status came from skill in fighting and in such key games as punchball and basketball, but also from a certain indefinable quality of personality, the gift of making others accept and conform to one's style of behavior. Even fighting was not so simple an affair as it seemed on the surface, and success in fighting was not altogether a matter of sheer physical skill. The question of who could fight whom was constantly on our minds, and hardly a day went by without someone trying to put some newly conceived opinion of himself to the test. The boys at the very top were more or less unchallenged. Those at the very bottom were likewise immune so long as they accepted the humiliations and insults which were their daily lot. But for a boy lodged precariously in the middle ranks, life was a tornado of fists and faces, the faces he was out to damage on his way up or the fists that were hammering him down to the nightmarish, infra-human realm populated by Cockeye Sidney and his similars.

We hunted and fished, too, though making the true metropolitan conversion by which all the quarry tracked down by human beings throughout the ages is reduced to the glittering tokens of civilization.

Mallard and teal the fowler downs in fall.
But season is always open for green game.
All weapons used; hand or enchanting hair,
Instructed dice or dynamite or flame.
To pipe of organ some in chapel tread,
Others in alley with a pipe of lead.
(John Frederick Nims, "Dollar Bill")

The cellars of many buildings in Brownsville went out some distance under the sidewalk and were covered by grates. Peering through the grate you could spy, some twenty feet down, a tangled mass of papers and heterogeneous objects among which, at all times, there might be a coin. A boy who was of a speculative turn of mind would steal a long, thin stick from the lumber yard and then lie flat on the sidewalk, gimlet-eyed, probing the mass of junk. If, after probing perhaps for hours while pedestrians cursed him, shopkeepers threatened him, and other kids sneered and goosed him, a coin emerged, he would go into action. After careful consideration of the ratio of investment to return, he would attach a wad of chewing gum to the end of the stick, and then a tense struggle began. It took an absolutely sure hand, a keen eye, and perfect technique to attach the coin without losing the bait in a mass of papers. Insecurely attached and as willful as any fish, the coin usually wriggled off before it was reeled in. When an elevation was successful, it still had to be gaffed through the narrow bars and defended against possible onslaughts. But any sum from a nickel to a half-dollar went a long way, buying handfuls of sticky candy, soda, flavored ices, chances on a punchboard, or a trip to the movies.

We hunted also in the empty lots, for bits of brass or lead we could sell to the junkyards, frequently stripping decorated panes of glass of their lead linings or scraping the precious metal from milk cans and boiling it down to lumps. We needed money for a hundred different commodities and were always on the alert for every penny, clipping dimes from grocery bills, chiseling from older members of the family, betting, thieving on a small scale from fruit markets and local shops and trading with what we stole. We worked, too—running errands for tailors and printers, stacking boxes for the Pitkin Avenue merchants, shoving fruit cases around on Belmont Avenue, or unloading bananas.

It was in the area of work that the difference between the poor and the affluent began to be felt. The poor boy was usually required to do some work at a very early age, and by the time he was twelve, he worked in the family store or helped around the pushcart and got regularly paid for it, usually by the hour. Thus he quickly established adult economic relations with his parents. The "bourgeois" kids, on the other hand, were held down to the smallest allowances possible, because their parents figured that the less money they had the less trouble they would get into. Thus it was the children from more affluent homes who, in the world of boyhood, were "poor"—and they bitterly envied the poorer children their usable wealth and grownup airs.

Indeed, "workin'" and the maturity and independence it implied held in our eyes an immense glamor. Gathered around a stoop for our nightly philosophical and educational sessions, we spoke passionately of our desires to become plumbers, bricklayers, carpenters, or businessmen. A few romantics wanted to be star athletes and a couple of little cynics wanted to be bookies or gangsters, but I don't think I ever heard anyone express a longing to be any kind of professional or even to go to college. The traditional Jewish passion for higher education as well as many another "Jewish trait" simply fell apart under the violent impact of street life. Out of the hundred or so boys I knew best in Brownsville, I don't think more than ten got to college, despite fairly good opportunities. And many sons of fairly affluent parents never got past grade school, the lure of punchball, movies, and "workin'" proving stronger than parental authority or desire.

Unloading bananas was the biggest working thrill of all, because we were selected primarily for strength and actually worked with grown men. It also had a sensuous appeal that nothing else quite matched. The banana wagon would come clattering slowly down Osborne Street, and when it got about two blocks from its destination the drivers would begin to bawl in loud, hoarse, sing-song tones: "A load! A looooaaaaaad!" Punchball, handball, and boxball games would melt in its path. The chant was echoed and re-echoed with every variety of musical and verbal adornment by scores of kids, and by the time the wagon reached the cellars, a midget army was running after it and clinging to its sides. The drivers would climb majestically down from their perch to inspect the crowd of anxious small-fry desperately displaying their muscles and standing on their toes. I was rejected frequently, until one day by weaseling through the pack, stretching myself till I nearly split, and croaking loudly in the weird imitation bass I used in order to keep from being assigned to the soprano section of the music class (a fate worse than death), I got myself hired.

It was not an unmixed pleasure. The huge green stalks weighed nearly as much as I did and it was touch and go from the moment one was handed to me till I got it (or it got me) down the steps and onto its hook on the ceiling. I suspected the older men of laughing at me and was frequently warned to beware of "tearan*too*las," huge poisonous spiders with a sting that made you turn purple all over and die in agony. You had to work fast and the ache in your muscles became more and more painful and your hands got cut to ribbons by the strings. The ordeal lasted about four hours and I got through it out of sheer pride and fear of ridicule. The pay was about two dollars, which along with the tremendous rise in my self-esteem, was just enough to compensate for a broken back.

The Brownsville juvenile was, to be sure, only a special variant of the genus *boy*, produced out of a variety of conditions: American democracy; the confused, rambunctious energy of Brooklyn; the isolation of a part of the Jewish heritage—its physical, practical component divorced from its spiritual perspective—partially cracking in the long, convulsive effort to maintain the natural continuity between generations despite the actual vastness of the gulf that yawned between the European-born parents and their children.

The relation between generations is basically always the same—the old connections have to be maintained, and at the same time they must give and expand to accommodate growth. But what strains the machinery was subjected to! What wrenching occurred as out from under the tremendous corpus of the centuries-old Jewish development lying motionless as a whale cast up on the strand of the great continent, crept the children, breathing a bewildering mixture of the heavy, humanity-laden air of the Old World and the thin atmosphere of the New! Nature itself seemed to have lost track of its norms, and groaned, baffled by the problem history had set for it. Relations between children and parents reached an extreme of imbalance, not only among the Jews but in all of an America that was going, at different rates, through a prolonged crisis of transplantation in which scarcely anyone has had more than an inkling of what is to be preserved or destroyed, what will grow and what decay. There were cleavages between the generations that were too abrupt, too mental, with an insufficient quantum of the fertile human plasma carried over; and there were continuities that were too fertile, too rich and stagnant to permit the necessary "adjustments."

Everywhere in New York, Jewish children were under the double compulsion of securing an extraordinary amount of protection from their parents and erecting unusually strong defenses against them to preserve their relation to the present. The result was that certain elements in the personalities of the children remained almost statically identified with their parents while other elements were so sharply divorced as to make for excessive conflict. In Brownsville—and this, I think, was true of Brownsville especially—the struggle between children and parents was almost purely on a physical and practical level. Intellectual and spiritual independence came easily to the Brownsville child—too easily, perhaps, so that it was never really acquired and always undervalued. But the right to breathe freely, to use one's arms and legs and voice forcibly, to own personal possessions, to take up residence away from home—all these privileges had to be conquered inch by painful inch. Brownsville's parents, unsure of their tradition and how to transmit it to their children, could not do battle in the realm of the spirit; but they devoted correspondingly more energy to the bitter struggle for mere physical obedience: be on time to dinner, go to school, go to bed, stop hollering!

Meanwhile, all the street life of Brownsville fought against them to develop in their children the most immediately necessary qualities. The weak were simply despoiled of all rights and privileges and every shred of self-respect. Pity, charity, remorse were nearly nonexistent among Brownsville's male juveniles, and even the weakest of the underdogs would rather have had his face pushed in the mud than be made the object of such mawkish feelings. The incredible Brownsville intolerance of weakness and ineptitude often brought out the necessary qualities by sheer compulsion. And, indeed, I have often thought, perhaps with some of the crustiness typical of those whose early experience has been rough, that the reformist epithet "underprivileged children" should be reserved for the offspring of the wealthy and genteel—it is they who are deprived of the natural endowment of children: the rich physical life, the concealment from adults, the instinctive awareness of the lawless, unacculturated state of man. How can anyone finally accept the restraints of society without resentment unless he has experienced something like the opposite? And how can any society recreate its institutions unless it obtains from somewhere a glimmer of what lies beyond them?

There was also a solidarity among the boys that was quick, instinctive, and very often heroic. Once, when I was about eight years old, I went adventuring on the BMT elevated lines with two boys who were slightly older than I. We had used up our money and had waited on one of the platforms so long that we thought no trains were coming and decided to cross the tracks to the opposite side. My friends hopped up on the other platform easily. I tried desperately and couldn't make it, and was still stubbornly and stupidly trying to clamber up when a train roared over the horizon. I would have been ground to cinders if one of the other boys had not leaped down and simply shoved me up on the platform while the other pulled me. He then clambered up a cinema second ahead of the train. It was quite an exhibition of agility, the result not so much of courage or nerve as sheer, unhesitant animal instinct.

The peculiar thing was that nobody thought such acts in the least praiseworthy, or expected or received gratitude for them. I was in this case absolutely furious with the boy who saved my life because he had had the temerity to think I wouldn't have made it without help, and both the other boys baited me vindictively for my clumsiness for days afterwards.

On another occasion we were all playing "follow

the leader" on the roof of a six-story building. We were prancing ostentatiously but cautiously near the edge when one of the lesser wits of our group, a boy we called "Abie Kabibble," stumbled and started to fall backwards off the roof. One kid grabbed his sweater. The sweater tore and there was a wild scramble and a series of grabs and Abie wound up hanging from the roof by one hand while two of us held the other and the rest held on to whatever portions of his clothing they could grasp and to each other. None of us ever did figure out how we got him back up without going over the edge ourselves, but we did.

About a week later one of the kids who had helped to rescue him fast-talked Abie into betting a dollar on his ability to hack off his own finger at one blow with a knife from a butcher shop in which he did odd jobs. Abie lost the bet by a shred or so, but came so close to winning that he had to be taken to a hospital for repairs.

"We are all much more simply human than anything else," Harry Stack Sullivan wrote some time ago, and since the statement was probably meant to apply to psychiatrists and schizophrenics, it will serve, I hope, to de-emphasize the writer's necessary exaggeration of the uniqueness of what he has seen. There were, indeed, dark nights in Brownsville, nights when we ran or hid in secret places, acknowledging no law but our own, hurling each other and being hurled against the concrete from every possible angle, caught in an endlessly tormenting, endlessly exhilarating game with little or no human knowledge we found acceptable to light our way into the future. But so it must have been in many another corner of America, cut off as ours was from a working central culture, from any principles of authority and conduct sufficient to contain life as it is really lived and guide us into the age when animal exuberance would be inadequate, when we would need something more and would find instead only a blank wall that spins us like balls back into the youth we should have long since outworn.

V *Earl Raab*

"There's No City Like San Francisco"

"*There is no city* like San Francisco," the
Jews of the Golden Gate say with some conviction. But
they say it in two different ways. Some say it happily,
with an expansive smile. Others say it drily, and sadly
shake their heads. As is usually the case in such matters,
both are probably right.

The almost universal experience of any visitor to
San Francisco is nostalgia-at-first-sight. This is normally
the kind of reaction reserved for small villages tucked
away on some by-road in a farming country with an
ancient pitcher pump in the square, an ambling popu-
lace of about five hundred, an atmosphere of more or
less live-witted serenity—and a single national origin
and cultural heredity. San Francisco's population is
three quarters of a million. It is the commercial and
banking center of the West. It is a polyglot city that has
been heavily infiltrated by a dozen nationalities. Withal,
there is no mistaking its village air of friendly order
and homogeneity.

There is the pitcher pump, deliberately, in the form of the rheumatic old cable cars. There is the serenity, in good measure: sidewalks that are wide and fit the people loosely; greens and flower banks, and little flower vends on every third corner; streets that dip and bob like a merry carnival coaster; and a population that rushes only when it has some place to go.

Of course San Francisco considers itself a sophisticated and gaily flavored town ("Bagdad on the Bay"), but there are few physical evidences of upstart vulgarity and self-conscious bohemianism such as mark many modern American metropolises. Thomas Mann (in concert with others) has called San Francisco the most Continental city in the country.

San Francisco is a genteel city. San Francisco is a poised city. San Francisco knows where it's been and where it's going.

Confronted with it, what East-weary mortal can resist nostalgia?

And what Jew will not sigh just a little longer than the rest?

There are fifty-five thousand Jews in San Francisco, and not even the historic traces of a ghetto. There is a Jewish community that has been called, with reason, the wealthiest, per capita, in the country. There is at the same time a startling poverty of anti-Semitic tradition. San Francisco, for cities of its size, is the nation's "white spot" of anti-Jewish prejudice.

In near-top-level social and country clubs there is Jewish membership and even charter membership. Gentlemen's agreements are quite uncommon in its quality residential sections, old or new. In filling public and quasi-public posts, there seems to be no trace of a policy of exclusion or "quota" or even discriminatory hesitation. At times Jewish citizens have concurrently held the presidencies of the Chamber of Commerce, the Community Chest, the Board of Education, Art, Fire, and Harbor Commissions, and many other appointive and elective posts; it is a situation that cannot be duplicated in any other city with a 6 per cent Jewish concentration.

Of course, "anti-Semitism" is not a word without meaning in San Francisco. The Jewish Survey and B'nai B'rith Community Committee handles anti-defamation matters, and across its desk every day the usual reports pass in light but steady flow. An employment agency whose cards are marked parenthetically "No J's," or "Blonds only." Private cooperative housing ventures that won't include Jews. A sidewalk altercation where someone turns out to be not only a "damned —" but a "damned Jewish —."

There is, then, a steady incidence of employment discrimination and of petty uglinesses, but they are relatively infrequent and without pervasive quality. So far as the city and its institutions are concerned, the Jew is a first-class citizen. It may well be that he can live in San Francisco with a greater degree of personal dignity than in any other large city in the country.

The attractive face of San Francisco, and the attractive status of the Jewish community within it, have common causes. The histories of the city and of its Jewish community have developed together along a shared course.

In 1848, of course, San Francisco was a mule-stop. When gold was cried and the West exploded, and San Francisco became the center of new wealth and of wealth-seekers, Jews were there with the first wave. They were, in the main, immigrants from Germany, although there were many from England, France, and Alsace-Lorraine. The second surge of Jewish pioneers in the early 50's contained some East Europeans. They came the hard ways, the only ways, across the hazardous continent or over the Isthmus. During the High Holy Days of 1849, services were held in a tent on the old Embarcadero near the waterfront.

While the mass of the forty-niners went scrabbling into the hills for gold, there were surer fortunes to be made in the city. One Jewish immigrant landed with his baggage in '49 and immediately invested a hundred dollars in stationery, which he sold in front of a hotel at 500 per cent profit. After a short interlude of playing a piano in a honky-tonk for an ounce of gold and a "grab" (literally a handful) of silver, he bought a store and began buying up trunks from gold speculators anxious to get into the hills. Selling these again, he made five or six thousands in seven or eight weeks. Soon, dozens of boxlike little stores were set up by his fellow Jews along the sprawling streets, heaped with hard-to-get clothing and merchandise shipped by friends and relatives in the East.

Other Jews played a part in the creation of the financial institutions on which San Francisco's economy was to rest. They turned banker, money broker, exchange dealer. Names like Davidson, Priest, Dyer, Glazier, and Wormser were identified with the giant financial transactions that became necessary with Europe and with the East. The London, Paris, and American bank was founded by the Lazards. The Seligmans helped create the Anglo-American bank. The directorates of a half-dozen other mushrooming banks bore Jewish names. Jews became leading realty brokers, founders of engineering enterprises, and manipulators of the grain exchange.

Further than that, some of these Jewish immigrants had brought with them uncommon strains of culture and education and qualities of leadership, and many of them plunged immediately into civic life. Samuel Marx was made United States Appraiser of the Port of San Francisco in 1851 and Joseph Shannon was County Treasurer in the same year. In 1852, Elkan Heydenfeldt and Isaac Cardozo were members of the state legislature, and Heydenfeldt was also Chief Justice of the state supreme court from 1852 to 1857.

The San Francisco *Herald* in 1851 struck the note of respect that was to be characteristic in generations to follow: "The Israelites constitute a numerous and intelligent class of our citizens and conduct themselves with great propriety and decorum. They are industrious and enterprising and make worthy members of our community."

From the beginning, the Jews were conspicuous for their sense of community. The first two welfare organizations in San Francisco were set up by Jews. In 1850 the Eureka Benevolent Society was organized to help the needy, and it still exists as the Jewish Family Service. As the little clothing stands turned into large department stores, and the money counters into financial empires, the Jews—feeling an understandable kinship with the city—began to make large financial contributions to the general community life.

This tradition, as well as the tradition of civic participation, has persisted until today. A startling number of the pools, parks, libraries, museums, and halls that are available to the public at large bear familiar Jewish names, aside from the many institutions that are administered under Jewish agency auspices but are nonsectarian in character (such as the very new and splendiferous Maimonides Hospital for chronic ailments, which serves a specific community need). Even the more private support of the cultural institutions of the city by the Jews has been too frequent to escape public attention—the music critic of the *Chronicle* recently reported that he had been informed that about 40 per cent of the deficit of the San Francisco symphony orchestra is written off by three Jewish families.

The fact is that the Jews in San Francisco have never been cast in the role of "intruder." This was historically impossible. There was no aristocracy in California in 1849. There was only a rag-tail gang of money-hungry pioneers, of heterogeneous origins, welded together into a "frontier brotherhood" community. As the "first families" became incrusted, they became incrusted necessarily in amalgam with the "first families" of the Jewish community.

The Jews aside, San Francisco has maintained a degree of tolerance for minority groups that has not obtained in other cities along the coast. (Notoriously: Los Angeles.) One is prompted to speculate on the reasons for this, not only partially to explain the relationship between San Francisco and its Jewish community, but also to explain something of the nature of the Jewish community itself.

San Francisco boomed in 1849 and it has not had a really serious boom since. It was built on California gold and Nevada silver, and settled down as a financial and commercial center. It has never changed its basic character. The recent great industrial eruptions in the West—with their accompanying invasions of "barbarian hordes" from the East and the Midwest and the South, and their extensions of eastern power and influence—which have boomed and burst cities like Los Angeles and Oakland, in the main by-passed San Francisco, and were reflected only in its increased prosperity as a financial center. Indeed, San Francisco is physically not capable of much expansion along industrial or population lines. It is a compact city, bounded on three sides by water, and on the other by a number of small communities jealous of their identity. It has been estimated that, just by virtue of physical limitations, San Francisco's top population would be around a million. As a matter of fact, the artificial surge in population which San Francisco experienced as a result of wartime activity has in large part already been dissipated. (At the end of the recent census, policemen and firemen were dispatched by frantic city officials to ring doorbells in an attempt to find untallied citizens and bring the census figure somewhere near the special 1945 figure. But, alas, almost a hundred thousand estimated people had flown the coop.)

San Francisco is thus a middle-class, white-collar city. (It has the highest average percentage of office-building occupancy and the greatest telephone density in the country.) It is also a city whose top social and economic layers have remained fairly well preserved. As a result it has a conservative cast, with accompanying overtones of unblurred tradition and general *noblesse oblige*. (To be sure, it has also had a rather violent labor history—notably the general strike of 1934. But since San Francisco is not, like Detroit, a city of industries with a large industrial working class, its labor history has had surprisingly little effect upon the "tone" of living.)

All this has worked, of course, to preserve undisturbed the status of the Jew in the community. It has also worked to preserve the internal structure and character of the Jewish community itself. The Jewish population has increased, along with the general population, not by spectacular leaps, but by normal accretion. And the Jews attracted to San Francisco have generally been those who would not tend to disrupt the community's basic character. There have never been in

San Francisco, for instance, the job opportunities that would encourage a mass influx of Eastern Europeans of the first generation. (The garment industry is small-sized with about an 8 per cent concentration of Jewish workers. There is no other Jewish "proletariat" to speak of.)

There are many who claim, however, that the favorable position of the Jew in San Francisco is not just a derivative of the history and nature of the city, but also of the "historical position" and "astute leadership" of the old Jewish families who have maintained their identity and influence over several generations. This claim certainly has some truth. On the other hand, it is also true that out of this "historical position" and "astute leadership" by the older Jewish families there has developed a deep-rooted set of conflicts and a Jewish community on the verge of schism.

This schism is not so notable for its actual violence or disruptive effect, or for the number of people involved, as it is for its symptomatic quality and its implications for American Jewry in general. The history of the conflict is not just a petty scrap for power (which it sometimes has all the earmarks of being), or a local fight for "democracy," or an ideological dispute on this or that specific; but it seems ultimately a reflection of sharp differences in approaching the fundamental problems of Jewish identity in America.

There have long been people who felt privately or semi-privately that the Jewish community was "moribund," that Jewish life as such was "marginal," that the organs of Jewish expression in the city were muffled and misdirected, that Jewish community organizations were not representative, that leadership needed changing.

When these critics talk about the "leadership," they

know exactly whom they mean: certain members of the old and influential families who have firmly held their rein on community organizational life, and particularly on such agencies as the Survey Committee which long served as the *de facto* public relations body for the Jewish community. But when they talk about "autocracy," they are not always clear as to exactly why, if the dissidents were in large number, no remedial action was ever effectively attempted. The explanations run variously that: the leadership was entrenched; the leadership had the money and the facilities; the atmosphere was "such as to smother" any creative activity; the body of the community was mired in a long tradition of uninterest in Jewish matters; they themselves had developed no effective leadership. Always, however, for a full explanation, it seemed necessary to add a mysterious ingredient, sometimes referred to as the San Francisco "x" factor. (Someone postulated that if a half dozen Jews of similar background, Jewish intensity, and ideology, were settled three in Los Angeles and three in San Francisco, they would be found to be very different groups in outlook and activity after five years.)

The catalysts of Hitler and the State of Israel brought these latent elements to a boil.

In 1943, when the extraordinary horrors of Nazi genocide in Eastern Europe reached a publicity peak, mass meetings were conducted everywhere in this country. In San Francisco, preliminary deliberations stretched over two months. A modest conference was at first suggested and it became clear that the "traditional leadership" as such was reluctant to sponsor a mass political meeting of an obtrusively Jewish nature that had no precedent in the city's history. A provisional committee was formed and a call was sent out for representatives. A reported fifty-three organizations responded.

A prominent section of the traditional leadership, including the Survey Committee, refused to participate, personally or organizationally. On June 17, 1943, at the Civic Auditorium, more than ten thousand people packed the hall to hear Thomas Mann, Eddie Cantor, and others.

Shortly afterwards, two prominent Russian Jews, Solomon Michoels and Itzik Feffer (the latter has since been "liquidated"), were sent to this country by the Soviet Union, then our "staunch ally," to "bind up the American Jews into one anti-fascist bloc in common with the Russian Jews." They were received by public dignitaries and by Jewish communities at large meetings throughout the nation. Again, and with the Soviet stigma lending them added conviction, the "traditional leadership" declined to lend support to a mass San Francisco reception. Under the same sponsorship as the previous meeting, the Civic Auditorium was again filled to capacity on August 31, this time for the two Russians.

The impact of these successes, and the emergence of some earnest young men of leadership caliber, led to a round of discussions and conferences on the possibility of reconstituting organizational life in the community. A United Council was formed by the "new coalition" of organizations to provide some channel for "representative community expression." This left the community in deep breach. A number of dismayed individuals immediately pressed for a compromise between the two camps. There ensued a brief period of labyrinthine political activity and a compromise Association of Jewish Organizations (AJO) was formed, to include all the elements of the community.

But, lo and legerdemain, when the smoke cleared, the AJO was revealed as an organ of traditional policy and of traditional leadership, and the cries of "aristocracy" and "no representation" were undiminished in vigor.

There is a lot of political over-the-fencing about if and why and how the AJO is "undemocratic by constitution and intent." (Example: Should the Welfare Fund have representation, as it now does, for every 125 members, giving it a balance of power, although there is no voting constituency and the delegates are appointed "from the top"; if not, what about the people who would not otherwise be represented and, "Where would you get a hall big enough to hold a vote of the Fund membership anyway?") And there is some question of how the "opposition," claiming to represent the "popular" sentiment, could not exercise enough control in open convention to scotch the "undemocratic" provisions of the AJO in the first place.

But the central fact was that against the first major attempt to unseat them, the Old Guard firmly maintained their role as the community leadership.

In 1948 a picket line was set up in front of the British consulate to protest the British refusal to allow refugees to debark in Palestine. The Survey Committee promptly dispatched a letter of apology to the consulate, disavowing the demonstration. A representative of the irate picketers wrote a letter to the public press, disavowing the apology.

In the fall of 1949, several "Where Do You Stand" and "You Are Not in Exile" anti-Zionist advertisements were paid for by the American Council for Judaism and were run in the press. The Survey Committee tried to dissuade the Council from this step, offering to publish, in lieu of the ads, a brief statement of policy under the name of the Survey Committee. The Council, however, felt that their ads should run, which they did. The Survey Committee published its own statement, anyway, "in the interests of Jewish public relations in San Francisco." This statement embodied an attack on Ben Gurion and the late Daniel Frisch for remarks that they had made concerning the responsibilities of American Jews to Israel.

This incident again brought to a boil those people who felt that the Survey Committee was: (1) in effect, acting as the public voice for the entire community, (2) in this capacity misrepresenting the community to itself and to the world at large. (The Survey Committee calls itself "the duly organized and recognized agency for public relations in the community.")

Out of this latest occurrence, delegates from forty-odd organizations in the community elected a working committee of about a dozen to discuss again the problem of community organizational life. This committee is currently functioning, although not in what might be called a violently activist atmosphere. (Remember the "x" factor.)

Whatever the various merits or demerits of the contending parties in the present situation, partisan polemic should not be allowed to obscure the Jewish concern of the Old Guard.

To say, as many do, that its component members are fearful of anti-Semitism, is to say merely that they are Jews. To say that out of this fearfulness they would not be averse to a withering away of the Jewish community as such, is simply untrue: they have spent too much time, money, and sincerity on the preservation of that community. To say that they subscribe to the "craven" theory that "Jews out of sight are Jews out of mind" is untenable: they have not followed the logic of that pattern.

"The leadership," one of its spokesmen says (and rather piqued about having to say it), "has never acted out of fear or truckling. Quite on the contrary, it has always shown particular courage of conviction in following a line of thought. . . ." That line of thought is really a kind of political philosophy for special groups in an American community; they should not unnecessarily duplicate civic functions, nor intrude on the community with their internal problems, nor, for their own sake, engage in public relations activities which will unnecessarily offend the general community.

Of course, the leadership's definition of "good public relations" has always been shaded by their general political complexion, which is naturally conservative and often strongly Republican. "Mass meetings and mass pressure," they insist, "can serve no useful function in San Francisco, and can only militate against the group that uses them."

The leadership points to its successful technique in handling anti-Semitic incidents as a blueprint for proper public relations behavior: "Once we have the facts, we contact the offender in man-to-man fashion—the American way. We explain the danger of prejudice, the unfairness of indicting a whole group, the harm it can do to a free American society."

Several years ago a local radio station was broadcasting the program of a well-known anti-Semite. There was a movement afoot to prevail on all the Jewish clients of the station to cancel their advertising. The Survey Committee quelled this movement, and instead called on the proprietor of the radio station who, after discussion, canceled the contract.

"I'm canceling this program," the station owner said, "because you came to me in a decent way and presented a decent argument. Had you moved in by threatening my business, I'd have fought you all the way."

When a bus driver used offensive language, the

Committee called quietly on the personnel manager; when the temples were smeared with Columbian slogans, and the culprit's membership in a local church was traced by a private detective, they approached the priest; when a real estate concern acted out a discriminatory policy, they met with the owners in conferences lasting more than a year before convincing them, in all logic, of the error of their way.

There can be no question but that this kind of diplomatic approach to anti-Semitism in-the-fact has worked effectively to date in San Francisco.

As for the internal life of the Jewish community, the leadership thinks of it largely in institutional terms and is proud of its accomplishments. Certainly, in the general, there is no look of impoverishment. The orphans' home, equipped with cottages and "mothers," is a showpiece, generously endowed. The residence home for Jewish working girls is complete with all the extra-curricular facilities that might be desired. There is a home for the aged that is described as a "veritable hotel." The Community Center is huge, thriving, and unstintingly equipped.

Critics (some of whom grew up in the East) certainly have no quarrel with these activities so far as they go—but they don't think they go far enough. They feel that the leadership (and community thinking) has been too exclusively concerned with considerations of a public relations policy, on the one hand, and of a welfare community on the other. These critics point to the disparity between the tremendous sums that are generally spent on philanthropic projects and the almost negligible amounts that are allotted to such projects as Jewish education. They also deplore the paucity of activity directed towards underlining the historical mission of

Judaism and the historico-religious ties that bind Jewry to Jewry everywhere.

What they are in fact pointing up and objecting to and being frightened by, is the apparent trend of a large (and the particularly "San Franciscan") section of the community, and its leadership, to slip away from the traditional moorings of Jewish life, to loosen its Jewish roots, and in the process eventually to blur and devitalize Judaism itself.

This kind of trend, insofar as it is a by-product of Americanization, has its evidences all over the country, but nowhere else does it involve such a large portion of the Jewish population. Nowhere has it kept such clearly defined lines or been less obscured by "recent generation" leavening. Indeed, such leavening has served, more than anything else in recent years, to point up "the trend."

In defining the various segments of the Jewish community, the synagogues serve as the most convenient and the most accurate (though always approximate) focuses. Temples Emanu-El and Sherith Israel have the largest congregations in the city, a combined total of about twenty-five hundred members. They are the Reform temples, and both had their origins in the pioneer year of 1849. (There is some disagreement about which was first.)

In these congregations all the lay leaders and the famed "leadership" of the community are found (when they can be found in any congregation). Temple Emanu-El has the preponderant number of first-family and wealthy-family names in the community. Its social character has remained more stable, having acquired less of the foreign (to San Francisco) element, and fewer of the "nouveaux." Symptomatically, almost all of the local members of the American Council for Judaism are affiliated with Emanu-El, almost none with Sherith Israel. One rabbi has said: "Just as America will be the last citadel of capitalism, so Temple Emanu-El will be the last citadel of the kind of thing that Isaac M. Wise and Elka Cohen and Voorsanger stood for."

In general, the diminution of ceremonial intensity in religious life that has characterized the Jew (and the Christian) in America, is particularly noticeable in San Francisco. And there has been a general (not official) stretching of the Reform philosophy at its most radical points. Some of the city's religious leaders feel that many of those who have maintained their affiliations with the temple could be very happy in a church named, say, the American Mosaic (or Monotheistic) church, where people who believed in Moses' One God could convene to make their simple devotions, renew their faith in the moral tone of life, and where their children could attend Sunday school.

Culturally, this segment of the population has lost its basic contact with the historical language and literature of Judaism. Hebrew education is barely existent. And the European accent is, of course, completely gone. One of the more prominent members of the community tells this story: At a private affair he was attending in Los Angeles, a number of men around the table burst into strange song. "What in the world are they singing?" he asked. He was astonished to hear that they were singing Yiddish songs. That sort of thing, he said, could never have happened in San Francisco, or at least in that large part with which he was acquainted. It says a great deal that shortly after the American Council for Judaism was formed in 1943, fourteen hundred of its twenty-five hundred national members were San Franciscans. (The local membership has dwindled since.)

The rate of intermarriage is probably greater in San Francisco than any place else in the country. This is an inevitable result of the relative freedom of social movement. One old-timer named, offhand, children of five rabbis who have intermarried in the past. It is only necessary to read the social pages of the press over the months to get a comparative index. However, it is widely believed that intermarriage has passed its peak, and that the rate will not appreciably increase.

The really significant fact about all these various aspects of Jewish life in San Francisco is by and large the naturalness and matter-of-factness of their development. They are not marked by evidences of self-hatred, Jewish anti-Semitism, fear, hysteria, or other minority neuroses. The most remarkable fact of San Francisco is not the vanishing (or shrinking) Jew, but on the contrary, the insistent Jew—the Jew who insists on being a San Francisco Jew despite the historical (and geographical) distance from his ethnic origins, the thorough Americanization, the complete lack of ghettoization, the social mobility, the freedom of wealth, the mutations in religious thought, and the relative isolation and absence of pressures. Even those who have disaffiliated, formally or effectively, from religious congregations, or are strictly "High Holiday men," insist vehemently on their Jewish identity and engage in the active leadership of the Jewish community.

This may seem strange in an area where the sentiment is strong that "Jews are members of a religion and nothing more." But one man said: "Of course I'm a Jew. I'm a Jew by religion. Is a Jew not religious because he doesn't go to temple every Friday night?" There is an overwhelming emphasis on the ethical texture, which men like this feel is unique to, and inherent in, the Jewish religion: *rachmones* or a deep-felt (not just formal or ideological) compassion for fellow men. This, along with a personal devotion to One God, they feel is the essence of the Jewish religion, and they know they are Jews because they feel it and live by it and believe in it.

Yet, on the occasion of Israel's fight for independence and its constitution as a nation, many of San Francisco's anti-Zionists were profoundly affected, and the tone of the whole community shifted perceptibly. As a matter of fact there has been recently in the "integrated circles" an intensification of religious life, as there has been in the rest of the country. This has been reflected in temple attendance and activity. And of the recently installed rabbi at Temple Emanu-El, one of the Conservative-Orthodox rabbis in town said: "He is, if anything, a more intense Jew than I am."

There are also two fair-sized Conservative congregations in town—one of which can still understand an address in Yiddish—and a scattering of Orthodox. Influenced by the same historical circumstances as the older settlers, but on a smaller scale, these people generally consider themselves integrated civically and socially into San Francisco. There is little evidence of intermarriage in their ranks, but there is a tendency for them, with the accumulation of time of residence, position, and influence, to move over to Sherith Israel, the next step on the ladder to Emanu-El. And some of those who maintain their affiliation elsewhere have liked to send their children to temple Sunday school so that, as one rabbi said, "little Sarah might grow up with and catch the eye of some little San Francisco scion."

There is, community-wide, a relatively small synagogue attendance and—compared with other large cities—a relatively light preoccupation with Jewish affairs at large. (Although, again in pattern, the Welfare Fund in San Francisco has had the reputation of having a higher percentage of contributors in relation to the population than any city but Boston.) One member of the community seriously offered as a partial explanation of the generally limited amount of synagogue activity the fact that San Francisco had such fine weather that people weren't so disposed to go to meetings or services. But considering the climate of Palestine, or at the very least Los Angeles, it would seem that the predisposition to apathy owes less to the temperature of the air than to the tone of the community.

The vocal critics of the present leadership of San Francisco's Jewish community are centered mainly around several hundred people who feel strongly about traditional Judaism and world Jewish affairs. They aren't interested in excommunicating those whose personal Judaism has taken a different turn ("They are mostly good men. They have done fine things here. But because of their background they are out of step with Jewish life. A Jewish community cannot flourish without its traditions, its historical and cultural references. . . .") so much as they are interested in making their own influence felt, sponsoring activity along more traditionally religious and more Zionist lines. They feel that a different leadership would give a different, "more specifically Jewish," complexion to the community, and this is what they hope to achieve.

The "Old Guard," for its part, is not anxious to relinquish any more of the office of leadership than it has to. It is clear that they feel that it is not they who are "out of step" but their critics, who fail to recognize that Jewish life must mean something different to third-generation American Jews from what it did to their ancestors in the ghettos of Europe.

"Majority" is cried on both sides but there has been

no counting of noses. (In any case, most of the noses of the community wouldn't be twitching excitedly in any direction.) At this point, "unity of expression" does not seem possible or, by any democratic standards, desirable.

It does seem, however, that in certain areas the disputants are becoming more amenable to cooperation. In 1948 the AJO held a meeting to greet Reuven Dafni, West Coast consul of Israel, and everybody came. Dafni wrote a letter to the AJO stating that he was gratified in the understanding that it was the "first time" that all the elements of San Francisco had so gathered. More recently, all the groups worked together against the Mundt-Nixon bill.

A prominent "both camps" man in town said: "Give us five or ten years more and all this bickering will have been reconciled." He is probably over-optimistic, but the gap in general is not so great as it was ten years ago. San Francisco is less isolated. No matter how neat its own back yard may be, it is no longer so easy as it once was to ignore the untidiness of the outside world, or to resist its pressures. The younger generation, in all classes, has teethed on Hitler and Israel and modern war. It is less certain of the righteousness of the *status quo;* it is more perplexed about things in general, and more consciously interested in its Jewishness in particular, than were its fathers and grandfathers.

The over-all character of San Francisco's community seems to be in for some "pendulum" change, however slight and however temporary. But come what may, the bulk of the Jews of San Francisco, neither vanished nor concerned with themselves as laboratory specimens, will merely thank the Lord that in whatever fashion they find it necessary to practice their Judaism, they are doing it in San Francisco.

VI *May Natalie Tabak*

My Grandmother Had Yichus

Aladdin had a lamp, the Rothschilds had money, someone's uncle had a candy store—my grandmother had *yichus.* It was as substantial as a stock of merchandise, yet magical and mysterious as the words "open sesame."

When I was very young, my mother died and her mother came to Chicago to live with us. It was from my grandmother that I learned Yiddish—and yichus. It was Big Bill Thompson's Chicago then. Our mayor had somehow destroyed or confused time for us, and we Chicagoans were desperately determined not to bow to the yoke of English tyranny. The watchword was: "All men are created free and equal." Every Chicago child was a defender of the weak, provider of the needy, and fighter for freedom. Our ancestors and our guide for living were the Minute Men, William Tell, and Sir Galahad. In the midst of all this my grandmother introduced yichus.

Yichus was everything. The possessor of yichus

could see through false appearances, as Beauty saw beyond the Beast to the Beloved. In the face of any and all trials, poverty and riches, success or failure, yichus enabled you to conduct yourself with modesty, dignity, courage, and grace. It also imposed certain obligations: to behave with gentleness, courtesy, charity, and love toward everyone. Not for personal gain, that would be useless; the calculating older brothers were turned to stone by the King of the Golden River. Yichus, at the proper moment, revealed and rewarded the true worth of people and things.

My grandmother, I am sure, had never heard of Sindbad the Sailor, yet her tales convinced me that without yichus Sindbad would never have been "selected" for his adventures. Joan of Arc, Barbara Frietchie, Esther—all obviously had yichus. When a little later I read about Becky Sharp, I understood her behavior—no yichus. All the Knights of the Round Table, on the other hand, obviously had it. No one ever said so, and it was not necessary for me to think about it. I just understood it, as I understood that the world was round.

Other matters were also decided automatically by yichus. When my grandmother returned to New York with us, many people came to our house whom I had never met before; through the years, I was to hear their status discussed in detail. Some were considered undesirable. Pincus, for instance, was a *cham*, an illiterate, who had sneaked into the house through the back door by marrying a person of yichus. Such marriages were not unusual in this country where value had lost its meaning. Young Maxwell was a "shoester" and the son of shoesters. I already knew better than to point out to my grandmother that the unfortunate wretch had two college degrees. To my grandmother he was and would always remain simply a man who had no yichus.

Why? Quite simply: his father was no scholar, his grandfather was no scholar, his great-grandfather—the less said about him the better. It followed that even if Maxwell had gone to school, he had not done so because he was interested in learning for its own sake, but because he expected a profit from his investment in study. That made him a shoester.

Being a shoester—need I add?—had nothing to do with working on shoes. In this case the shoester taught French at Columbia. Conversely there had been famous rabbis who supported themselves and their families by cobbling. These men were not shoesters. Their thoughts were profound, their conversation learned and eloquent, their manners charming, and—they had yichus. In our house it never mattered, either for good or bad, how a man earned a living, or how much wealth he possessed. A doctor might sit in respectful silence while a buttonhole-maker held forth. Indeed, it is only now that I am very much older that I know he was a buttonhole-maker. In those days, all I gathered was that he was a learned man who had yichus, and was therefore listened to with respect.

Occasionally someone would show up who had plenty of yichus, but was nevertheless a fool. He aped the style of the learned and was said to be ignorant and pompous. Yet no one ever exposed him, and his inanities were never interrupted. His vain display was interpreted as an effort on his part to show respect for the scholarship of his ancestors by imitation. The company, therefore, showed its respect for that same scholarship by refraining from the Talmudic allusions and scholarly puns with which they would have hastened to put him in his place had he been lacking in yichus. In effect, the be-yichused dolt was treated with an almost tender tolerance, as if he had been the victim of an accident, say a twisted knee, or had a handicap, like a humped back. *Nebach a nahr.*

Recently my Uncle Hiram wrote a biography of my Uncle Barney. He dedicated it to my Uncle Sol, whose financial assistance made the publication possible. The dedication reads "To Kotin of California." Now "Kotin of California" is a trade name, well known in the dress industry. The dedication shocked me. Not only was my California uncle being addressed by a surname, but by a trade name. The book might as well have been dedicated to Coca-Cola or General Motors. In our house to introduce a man by his surname was equivalent to saying: here is a man who is nobody. A kind of John Doe or Joe Doaks. They call him Doaks or Levine because no one knows who his family is. (One can guess what they must be like.) Anyone who *was* someone, even if he were an old man, would be presented as Reb Tevyeh, son of Hershel, grandson of Michael. It was immediately apparent that here was a man of consequence. This eighty-year-old man had yichus. In mentioning his name one was remembering his grandfather. It was that simple.

Someone would pick up a child and ask: Whose child is this? No one thought to say, here are Hannah and Hank, the parents. Instead, it was always: he is the grandson of So-and-So, or even the great-grandson of So-and-So. My own grandfather had died in Europe long before I was born. Yet whenever we came to New York and met people at my grandmother's I was invariably identified as my Grandfather Michael's oldest grandchild.

Yichus was everything. My grandmother might grant that on rare occasions a man who appeared to have no distinguished rabbinical forebears had become an important scholar on his own. Trapped, she never went so far as to state flatly that appearances were deceitful and that *really* he was the descendant of a distinguished line. But by sighs and shrugs she did her best to intimate that if all could be told (sometimes the man might be dead three hundred years) yichus would be found not alien to him.

Gentiles, naturally, were foredoomed to a sort of second-class scholarship at best. With enough brains and application they might master a learned trade such as medicine or engineering. But *true* learning, the Talmud or philosophy, would forever remain incomprehensible to them. Of this my grandmother was convinced, and no amount of argument could alter her conviction. Triumphantly, I would confront her with the name of a great non-Jewish scientist, and give her an account of his accomplishments and of the honors and recognition he had received. My grandmother would respond by questioning the value of his contribution. If that could not be broken down, she would then attempt to prove that the scientist's discoveries were merely the restatement of the work of a Jew.

Take radio, for instance. Centuries ago the Talmud mentioned "radio" as a means by which one can hear voices from afar. My grandmother proved this by showing me an article to that effect in a Jewish newspaper. Don't ask me what it all meant, but there it actually was. If the claim of plagiarism failed, she would undertake to distort the great man's name to show that it was originally Jewish. Somehow this device filled me with particular fury, and the few times my grandmother proved to be right I refused to admit it. When every other explanation failed, my grandmother darkly hinted that for a long time people thought the child Moses was a goy—a nobody—child of a *shiksa* princess.

Sometimes, moreover, it seemed, the soul of a great rabbi might be returned for devious reasons to the world in order to teach him and mankind humility. This informed soul might appear sometimes in the child of a family lacking in yichus or even, though this was very rare, in a goy. It was never a mediocre scholar who was thus produced. He was always a *zaddik*, a genius—and easily recognizable. By this means certain individuals, who happened to have appeared in unlikely walks of life among the communicants of other religions, were granted a special exemption by my grandmother, since their origins were lost in mysteries known only to God and the angels.

Having dismissed everyone lacking in yichus, my grandmother could afford to be completely democratic. As I grew older I had friends of many groups and many religions. So far as I was ever able to see, it made no difference to my grandmother whether the girls I brought home to meals or to spend the night or a week-end were white, Negro or Chinese, Catholic or Mohammedan. Once she had mastered her disappointment at their lack of yichus, she treated them all with equal cordiality and hospitality. A Negro girl used to come with a Hindu boy. Both of them seemed too thin to my grandmother and she would worry about them. Whenever they visited our house she would provide in abundance the foods the Hindu permitted himself to eat, and she prepared special rich dishes for the Negro girl. To her all the races of the world, save one, were all the same—goyim. People—good, interesting, human—but not even Jews—and without yichus.

Her graciousness to these friends and her utter indifference to their financial or social position tended to lull my socialist-Jeffersonian militancy about the equality of all men, yichus or no yichus. And then I would bring home a well-dressed, brilliant Jewish classmate with excellent manners, only to note suddenly that my grandmother's thin lips had entirely disappeared and that her manner had become quite altered. I would become uneasy and at the first chance would rush her off into a corner. "What's wrong now?" I would demand belligerently.

"That I should live to see the day when Michael's grandchild associates with a vulgarian, the daughter of a *grobe yung*."

"What do you know about her father?" I would cry. "He's a fine educated man, a lawyer."

"American education—a lawyer. A social climber, you'll see," and my grandmother would retire to her bedroom, bitter over the downfall of Michael's house.

Filled with rage, I would return to my friend, my innocent attachment spoiled. And sooner or later it would turn out the girl was affected, or her father told dirty jokes, or her grandfather was illiterate. In the end, no doubt, she married for money.

What a nose my grandmother had for yichus! A fine car would drive up and a boy in evening clothes would come in to take me to a prom. Before anything else, he had to be presented to my grandmother, who somehow or other could only be located on these occasions in the kitchen in an apron, peeling a token potato. We never discussed this, but the potato peeling was obviously some sort of test of the essential good breeding of a new rich friend—just as a new poor friend was somehow always greeted in the living room with great ceremony, and a new clean headkerchief. If the newcomer found favor in my grandmother's murderously critical eyes, she would rise and greet him.

"He has an *edele ponem*—a cultured face," she would say to me in Yiddish. "Ask him who his ancestors are." Blushing, I would ask the boy, who knew not one word of Yiddish, The Question. My grandmother confidently waited. Invariably, her judgment was vindicated: he would produce at least two rabbis.

My grandmother could even spot a kind of goyish variety of yichus—this never meant money or an old family, but an ancestor who was a poet, or a historian, or a scholar. In time, my friends learned to bring my grandmother the name of a worthy ancestor as one brings a box of candy.

My grandmother refused to speak English in the presence of a Jew. To me this was another grievance. She spoke Russian and German rather well and a couple of other languages adequately. (These she had learned in Europe in order to conduct a business to earn money to leave her rabbi husband free to study.) Our Anglo-Saxon neighbors were all her friends. They exchanged roots and garden cuttings with her and always inquired about her respectfully when she failed to appear in the garden or street for a day or two. She could not have been so intimate with them had she not spoken some sort of English. But we in the family could never catch her at it. I am convinced that she regarded English and all other languages except Yiddish as good enough only for goyim and the mundane communications it was possible to exchange with them. Not for Jews. Slowly I came to realize that except in Yiddish she could not pepper her speech with the allusions and parables which her yichus and her responsibility to us demanded of her conversation with another Jew.

My father had become an atheist as a boy, when he had believed himself an anarchist. We grew up with the impression that religion was a matter of taste. But because my grandmother was the oldest and the most easily hurt, we observed at home all the most Orthodox practices. Every Seder my father conducted the services as if every detail were infinitely sacred to him. In restaurants he might eat pork regularly, but at home, even in my grandmother's absence, he would never put cream in his coffee after meat. In his later years, he has become a chain cigar-smoker, yet he has never smoked on the Sabbath in her presence. It became a custom for my grandmother to disappear after the Sabbath meals, presumably to take a nap. This is a silent acknowledgment that my father might be too tired to take a walk around the block while having his smoke. She never returns to the living room without a good many coughs or much loud talking. This gives my father the opportunity to get rid of his cigar butt. Thus his comfort is respected and her honor not impaired. I cannot say exactly what this has to do with yichus, yet this Sabbath ritual has always seemed to me to have some connection with it.

"What happened to the little girl with the dancing thievish eyes?" my grandmother once asked.

"She married a writer."

"A writer? Good. What does he write?"

"He has a successful play on Broadway. It's a comedy." Then I explained what a comedy was and how the plot of this one went.

"Very interesting," said my grandmother. "It sounds like an easy way to make a living. But you say he is a writer. Now tell me, what does he write?"

I tried to explain that plays, even such plays, had to be written, and that the people who wrote them were, in America, called writers. Impossible to make her see the point. This was not writing. Writing had to do with "learning," it was a serious, even a divine pursuit, and no man whose ancestors had devoted themselves to study would consider himself a writer because he manufactured trifles in order to earn some money.

That any cultivated household could conceivably not feel honored to welcome me, the granddaughter of Michael, her husband, never occurred to my grandmother. Thus I was trained to regard myself as a desirable member of any valid society. The possibility that I might be excluded or discriminated against because I was a Jew simply never entered my mind.

Instead of being concerned about the Jewish problem, I spent years insisting to my grandmother that *she* was intolerant, and that my Gentile friends were fully as good as I. I was so occupied with trying to get her to accept them that I never realized until very much later that perhaps they might have had similar difficulties trying to convince their parents that their own yichus was not compromised by me, a Jew.

As the years went by yichus assumed a new and unfortunate significance for my grandmother. It became a consolation, a protective mantle in which she could wrap herself and feel immune to the new ways and values that were freezing hers out. Many of the older people had died, and their children talked of strange things: how a business deal had been put over, how much their cars and fur coats cost, the poker hands they had held, the hotels and restaurants they had visited. Against all these wonders my grandmother could only assert the value of yichus, more and more desperately it seemed. Would she become the sole grim custodian and proprietor of yichus, like some ancient Southerner still treasuring his hoard of Confederate money, confident that some day it would recover its full value? Gone was the time when my grandmother dealt with the vulgar with light self-assurance. Now she fought them with bitterness and contempt, as if she sensed her inevitable defeat. Worse still, she now bragged of her yichus. It was pathetic, as if a king assured you that he really had a crown, and made of real fourteen-carat gold.

Came the summer's day in the country, when I broke the news to her that I was going to get married. My "friend" had gone for a walk and I was standing with my grandmother in the parlor of the old farmhouse we had been visiting for years.

"He's well educated," I explained. "A writer." My grandmother took on her most remote look and said nothing.

"He has no money," I went on, hunting around for likely references, "and will probably never earn any."

What more could she ask? Still no response. "He has contributed to a philosophical journal," I said hopefully.

Still silence. It was time to play my trump. "He reads and understands Hebrew."

"Who is his father?" my grandmother demanded in a dead and hopeless tone.

"A man who has taught his sons Hebrew," I said proudly. "And he goes to synagogue."

"Have you told his father who you are and what your yichus is?"

"Not altogether," I said evasively.

At this point the subject of our discussion walked in by the porch door.

Standing very erect, hands stiffly at her sides, eyes staring straight ahead, my grandmother launched into a recital of her yichus. She told him, without preliminaries, about my Grandfather Michael, about his father and his father's uncles and cousins, grandfathers and great grandfathers, where they had studied, who had ordained them. She did not ask whether he understood what she was talking about. Slowly and in orderly detail she went through the list as if she were replying to some immense questionnaire. Before she had finished I was faint with humiliation.

Then my friend spoke. In broken Yiddish, but with equal solemnity, though I detected an occasional glint, he began an account of his grandfathers *on both sides*, their uncles and cousins, his great grandfathers and their uncles, the famous commentary of Rabbi So-and-So who was his maternal grandmother's first cousin. Casually he mentioned the celebrated interlineations of Rabbi Thus-and-So, who was simply his father's great-uncle. Surely, my grandmother must have known or at least heard of his maternal grandmother, familiar to everyone as Raisel of the Yeshiva. Yes, my grandmother had heard of her and of her accomplished uncles. Together, she and my friend pursued this line through a few centuries.

Then my friend switched to his paternal grandfather. These relatives were *really* interesting and important. Alas, they were also more numerous. In each generation they spread out over the yeshivas of Europe like a swarm of praying mantes, studying, writing, leading their communities, leaving a heritage of eternal wisdom. This uncle had a grandfather on his mother's side and an uncle on his father's side. That nephew—. The entire tribe of Jacob seemed caught in the net. All rabbis and all of the highest.

My friend had been cheerfully following the prolific and tireless branch into medieval Spain when I suddenly became aware that for a long time my grandmother had said not a word. I glanced quickly at her. She was still standing, looking out into the distance. But there was a slump in her figure. All at once I felt very sorry for her. The history of the Jews takes a long time to tell. "Perhaps," I interrupted, "we ought to sit down."

My grandmother awoke promptly to the opportunity I had offered her. She pulled herself together, and —rather severely, I thought—said to my friend: "Remember, my son," she said, "remember that yichus isn't everything. What really counts is what a man is, himself. Yichus is not everything."

VII *Wallace Markfield*

Seventh Avenue: Boss and Worker

He started west from the Lower East Side and then reached a point beyond which he could not pass; this was Seventh Avenue and he settled there. Twenty or so years ago the firm name on his business stationery was simply Sam Katz, but today it is Ess and Kay. He likes the models and the office girls to address him as "Mr. Kay"—especially in the presence of out-of-town buyers.

He maintains an ornate office near the showroom, but there is nothing he hates more than the fact that he is compelled to spend so much of his time behind the desk. For no matter how long his cutter and markers have been with him, he cannot trust them. He carries a load of anxiety, wondering whether remnants are being sold under his eyes, suspicious of any employee who leaves at the end of a day with a bundle under his arm. No matter how busy he is with customers, there always comes a time during the day when he must walk nervously about the cutting-room floor, looking almost into the hands of his cutters, fearful lest he say too much, since their union is strong. Sometimes he will stand with the marker, watching him chalk the patterns on a long rectangular section of cloth. A sudden spasm of economy, and he will pick up an odd piece of chalk from the floor with a hurt look in his eyes.

Between him and the marker there is war, though never a word is exchanged. Standing over the table, the boss lifts a pattern, searches about on the cloth till he places it at a point that will gain him another few inches of material. Almost scornfully the marker will shift it to the original spot, slapping the heavy cardboard down as though it were a pinochle hand. This is a symbolic challenge, wherein the marker dares his boss to assert superior knowledge of the trade. If once again the boss picks up the cardboard pattern to slap it down with redoubled force, he is reaffirming his own judgment, taking full responsibility for the change. Tentatively he reaches toward another pattern, but this time the marker ignores him, places his hands in his apron pocket, taking the pose that means he will walk off the floor at any moment if the ritual is continued.

In his shop there is no role the boss aspires to more than that of *paterfamilias*. When the children of his employees are married or Bar Mitzvah he will send down for schnapps and cookies. He himself may come to the ceremony, but even if he is not there, his check usually is. During lunch hour, for example, he will often walk over to the shipping table where the men are seated playing rummy, and deal himself a hand. It is like a meeting of a burial society or a family circle, till the hour ends and work begins again. Then newspapers are thrust aside, the machines turned on again, and the transition from *landsman* to wage-slave takes effect. For in the garment center the boss translates the Calvinist doctrine into his own terms—the worker by his very nature bears a load of sin and must never be praised. No matter how honest is a man's work he will seldom hear a word of commendation, nor does he expect it. Cutters who never lift their eyes from the table, doing their job with the neatness and precision of the experienced artisan, are sneered at, compared with some real "mechanic" who always works for a rival firm. Even if it has been a good day for the boss and he is cheerful, he must walk unsmiling into the cutting room.

Remembering his own origins at the sewing machine, he likes to believe he could still sit down and run off seams and pockets at a faster clip than any of his operators. But that is as far back as he cares to go. Recollections of the ghetto, the tradition of learning and Hasidism, the patriarchal family unit—all of these sentiments fall away when the boat docks and the immigrant is cast out from the steerage to assume full status as a "greenhorn." Before his first dinner in the New World is even finished, his older cousin is demonstrating the art of the piece-worker in the small room behind the shop. In the months that follow, if all goes well, he sends passage-money to his family, and soon, if his children are old enough, their hours after school are spent sitting with him, helping with the piece-work.

Phylacteries remain untouched in the morning, laid temporarily aside for a more material security, for a goal that can be achieved only by amassing a load of frugality and self-imposed suffering at a faster pace than the workers who sit at the machines next to him. The pattern is simple—first to learn the trade, lay away every penny that can be spared and even more joyfully those that cannot be spared, and then the slow wait for the "break" that will make a small business possible. Almost ruthlessly does he set himself apart from every remnant of the old culture. Especially does he scorn the *luftmenshen* whose nostalgia for the old heated arguments and longwinded Talmudic dissertations serves only to set off the sadness of their lives as they sit in coffee-shop and synagogue.

Then, when the "break" finally materialized, the garment man often found himself in the strange position of employing some of his old friends, even close relatives. Here the ties were definitively severed, and gradually another factor crept in. He, the manufacturer who had sensed what counted in this new world, could look only with a smugness that approached scorn upon fellow Jews who seemed to accept their lot as workers. It was not only that they were Jews without money, but, more pathetically, they were Jews without *chutzpah*. In business he adopted a *proste* attitude—a dollar was a dollar, let somebody tell him different. There was no point in disguising the fact that he was out for "number one," and he neither expected nor showed mercy.

He found that the success of one season would not necessarily avert a disaster in the next. There was no certainty in the trade, and just holding his head above water required absolute mastery of the art of "hustling." If he managed to get a large order, the delivery of the goods he needed was never on time; if he had a dozen samples made on a buyer's promise, another house had produced the same model at a cheaper price; if he was stocked up with woolens at the end of one season, gabardine was the big hit for the following year. Always on the verge of putting over a deal that would place him on Easy Street, he found himself defeated again and again by the sheer anarchy of an industry where your own shipping clerk can be quietly getting set to steal your best designs and open his own shop. A strange fatalism pervades the garment man's thinking, as in the story of the manufacturer who cannot procure woolens. Suffering from insomnia over this, he is told by a psychiatrist to try counting sheep. One night he dreams happily that he has gathered all the sheep he has counted and sheared them by the thousands, thus solving his problem. But a few hours later he wakes from a horrifying nightmare and moans—"The dirty dogs! I got all the woolens in the world, but do you think they'd let me have some linings?"

Basically his survival had little to do with business ability. He was a poor bookkeeper, a spineless bill collector, knew next to nothing about modern production methods or cost accounting, but, like a Hollywood producer, he depended less upon organization and efficiency than upon sales and ideas. What he sought was a certain tone, a style, a quality—in short, *shmaltz*. Shmaltz was the ability to look at a dress model that flopped three years ago and turn it into this season's big number simply by adding a few sequins to the bodice. Without shmaltz, he might have the most spotless of reputations, employ the best designer in the industry, use only the finest materials and handwork, but he might just as well declare himself bankrupt and place his assets under his mother-in-law's name.

The last step toward his full emergence as garment man came with the advent of the unions, when he found himself hiring Irish and Italian strikebreakers. The mechanism had begun to function at full capacity, clogging his ears and shutting out Peretz's plea—

> *How can a man strike his brother,*
> *How can a man mock his brother's tears?*

But he soon found that bringing racketeers into the industry served only to create new problems. Sometimes the move was countered by the unions with other gangsters or, more often, militant squads of workers known as "educational committees." And as time passed, ironically enough the gangsters themselves became unionized, and attached themselves to the bosses like bloodsuckers. In the end, the only way to shake them off was to accept the less threatening claims of the union.

The union leaders were wise to all the dirty tricks in the game and had their own brand of *"prostkeit."* Volatile and dynamic, and fully as shrewd as the manufacturer, they browbeat him into at least a tacit acceptance of the fact that the welfare of the worker was more than a platitude that took money out of his pocket —it was a problem of industry as a whole. They set out to prove to him that with good management and rational planning, the American consumer might be educated into becoming the best-dressed citizen in the world. Across the conference table this idea was drummed into the boss by organizers, walking delegates, top-rank officials, till it almost seemed that to fight the unions would be equivalent to fighting the progress of American capitalism.

And as the unions came to dominate the industry, the old days when a man could set himself up with a little capital, three or four machines, his father-in-law as the designer, and call himself a manufacturer were over forever. The average wage, which before the first war was under twenty-five cents an hour, is now almost a dollar an hour. Today the boss finds himself cordially welcoming the business agent into his office, eating lunch with him, even recommending him to his own tailor for suits. And as it has turned out in many instances, not only is he forced to accept the union, but he might find himself going to it for favors, using its production men, time-study experts, and merchandising analysts.

But even though the union has pardoned the manufacturer his former sins, he still enjoys a vicarious piratical image of himself (mostly imaginary) as an unscrupulous "operator," someone who can fake his books and outsmart a competitor with the best of them. He likes to recall the old turbulent days of the industry, when private detectives used to "ride shotgun" on his trucks, when he was "palsy-walsy" with gangsters. (Two of Lepke's boys used to get their suits by him whole-sale.) Walking up Seventh Avenue he is able to spot a gangster from three blocks away, and if you seem impressed he will walk over boldly and ask him for a cigar. "God knows," he reflects later over the cigar, "he's a thief and a murderer and a bum—but you should see the apartment he keeps up for his mother in the Bronx!"

But despite what warmth and color his world retains, he cannot rid himself of a sense of insecurity. With another Jewish manufacturer he has no qualms about following the codes set down by a vindictive God of Business, and he will press him to the wall over a penny-a-yard difference on a hundred-yard order. But in his occasional dealing with the *goyim* it is a different story, and often, under the heading of "good will," he takes a loss that would normally make him wince. With the Gentiles he can never be quite at ease, for he is always fearful that the mask of graciousness may slip off and disclose their private image of him—a Fagin with a tape-measure. He is always, at bottom, in the position of that Jewish millionaire who invited his parents for a cruise on his new yacht. Proudly displaying himself in his "captain's" uniform he looks to them for approval. "Look, Sonny," says his mother, "by me you're a captain, by Papa you're a captain, but what are you by the captains?"

He can create no business dynasties that may be passed on to his children, for he too is infected with the disease of the Jewish middle class, and only those of his sons who are so poor in school that they cannot become professionals enter the business. If he has a daughter, he resigns himself to the fact that he must "buy" her a professional. His attitude towards this transaction is likely to be ambiguous—as one manufacturer said upon the day his intended son-in-law was to graduate from medical school: "Nu, so today he is a Buick!"

He takes pride in contributing to such organizations as the UJA and subscribing to full-page ads in charity journals. Sometimes he pretends annoyance over the fact that his name appears on virtually every "sucker" list, but no matter how pressed for time, he always manages to spend fifteen minutes conversing with telephone solicitors, secretly proud that someone recommended him as a "contact." When it comes to a theater benefit, he is always the first one approached, and he takes tickets for the Second Avenue musicals which he swears he will never use. But, as his wife points out, for a good cause it doesn't hurt to show his face, and besides, Menasha Skulnick is still good for a few laughs.

Lately he has taken to attending *shul* frequently, doing his best to pass it off as a mere social form. But somehow, if there is a new wing to be added, or some refugee yeshiva students who need a home, he is the first to contribute. On the High Holidays he bids heavily for the privilege of placing the Torah inside the Ark, and when he *davens*, without even straining himself, he can drown out the combined voices of the cantor and his choir.

II

A cutter for thirty years; since he's been in the garment trade, he's promised himself a little chicken farm some place near Lakewood, and for the last twenty-five years he has been taking orders for fresh butter and eggs to be filled in the future. But time passes, and the closest he's come to the fresh green earth is the little cemetery plot he pays for through his lodge. *"A kaptzen bleibt a kaptzen"*—("A pauper stays a pauper.")

He is grateful to the union for the fact that his craft status has been strengthened year by year. But such projects as the workers' educational program, which go beyond strict trade union activity, leave him with more than a few doubts. He feels little desire to return to school or see his union compete with the colleges, and the idea of a cutter learning economics, taking lessons in painting, or attending poetry classes seems frivolous. On the other hand, if he is a member of the ACWA, he is proud of their recent "womb-to-tomb" plan of workers' benefits. He deposits his savings in the Amalgamated Bank and fills out an application for an apartment in an Amalgamated housing project.

For the past few years he has been a little in awe of the manager of his local, who has perhaps eaten luncheon (at twenty dollars a plate) with Henry Wallace, or shaken the hand of Bernard Baruch. Walking into the local office, he gazes respectfully at the autographed photos, stares at the leather upholstery, the commodious oak desk, the large murals covering the walls, and remembers the old lofts that once served for offices, the days when the only visible equipment was one or two broken-down typewriters and an old Mimeograph ma-

chine. Twenty years ago there was always a possible
excuse to offer the shop chairman who came at the end
of the week pleading for dues; today, the union's almost impersonal systematization permits no such dila-
tory practices, and he knows that his union book, perhaps the most important single document he carries in
his jacket pocket, must have the small stamps pasted
in twice a month.

When union elections come, he votes straight down
the line to retain the old leadership. To the cries of
"bureaucracy!" from the "left" opposition he responds
with a tolerant smile, as though humoring a fractious
child. When he does attend a meeting and listens to the
perpetual challenges and issue-raising of the "left-
wing," he feels even more secure—after all, every union
must have its own little *communistlach* who can be
threatened with excommunication or serve as the butt
of good-natured jokes. For his part, he is always willing to match wisecracks with them, for Karl Marx
or no Karl Marx, they can never prove to him that a
summer at Grossinger's is not better than a summer
at Coney Island.

The recent influx of younger men into the garment
houses raised certain problems for the older worker
like himself. After the war ended, the union, as any
large-scale enterprise, faced the problem of taking care
of its own. It set up a regular system by which veterans
could be taught the trade, apprenticed, and, after a
probationary period in a shop, fully enrolled in the
union books. For the older worker, what was particularly astounding was the idea that anyone, especially
a young man, could conceivably enter the clothing trade
of his own volition. Union membership, which twenty
years ago was predominantly Jewish, is now giving way
to new groups—Italians, Puerto Ricans, Spaniards, and

occasionally Negroes. Observing this, the garment worker is made more than a little insecure. (After all, would *they* be so generous to Jews?)

He is shocked to see the Italian workers taking their children into the shops and teaching them the trade: how can a father deliberately take his son from school and make him into a worker? Like the manufacturers, his ambition is to achieve a middle-class position which will insure his children against ever having to know the inside of a shop. So closed off and separate does he make his working life that it is not unusual that fellow workers who have labored across the table from one another all their lives should have seen each other's children only three times—at circumcision, Bar Mitzvah, and marriage. The occasional visits a child may pay to the shop are marked by uneasiness and mutual embarrassment.

Though on the whole the garment worker wants no contact with his family when he is at work, this does not mean that the events of the working day are held back from them. At home, over the dinner table, he creates his own myth. His tales of early hardships go beyond the usual description of sweatshop conditions and the horrors of piece-work. They reveal a peculiar quality of Jewish melancholy, as though the garment worker conceived of himself as paying through the nose for some unremembered sin, for which the price of atonement is an irrevocable doom to the status of a worker.

In his stories the cutter appears upon the scene as a youth, energetic and hopeful, and then finds suddenly that he has grown gray and old, that his best years have been irretrievably lost to the boss, that at least one of the occupational diseases has caught up with him—hernia, heart trouble, or ulcers—while the boss grows younger every day. And is it any wonder, he will ask, as he lays his working life across the dinner table, after starting out in the old days with the *messer*, the long knife that tore out your *kishkes* against the material? Coloring his memory of that period is always the story of some act of aggression that ends with his waving his knife or shears before the frightened eyes of the boss, tossing his apron at him, and stalking off the floor. And there is the description of the racketeer who once managed his local, the secret dangers undergone before the "Hitler" was driven out. (Will I forget how, he should rest in peace, Kornfeld had his eyes stabbed out by the gangsters?)

Long since has the cutter discarded the *messer*, but the shears remain his personal property, though he has less and less use for them except to cut occasional "singles." But he keeps them oiled and sharpened, for in the cutting room it is only his apron and his shears that belong to him. Continued sharpening of the shears make the cutting edges narrower and narrower, and eventually useless. It is against these edges that the cutter measures out his life.

For despite the changes that have come to the clothing industry, he knows that he is still the traditional *shneider*, who, if he knows his craft well, may come to be honored with the title of "mechanic." Garment-making remains a hand industry that has been only partially mechanized, and he still does the same things in very much the same way. He still walks back and forth the length of the thirty-yard tables with his cutting machine—miles every day—while behind him comes the entourage of bundle-tier and button-puncher, and even as he finishes up one section, a team of pullers has already set up the next table for him.

At work, conversation is limited, save for an occasional *kibbitz*. Most of the talking is done during lunch hour in the streets outside the buildings, where the men pair off and exchange their views on every conceivable topic. Between twelve and one the streets of the garment center become a kind of proletarian Bourse known as "The Market," where you can take stock of conditions in other houses and present rumors concerning the trade for verification or denial. Often there are heated political discussions, with the participants ringed by a wall of onlookers as in Union Square.

And since every garment house must have its *philosophe*, its one intellectual alienated amongst the philistines, where else would he be found declaiming but in the streets? This man's working day is spent mourning the passing of a golden age of writers. He will make clear to you the fact that the hacks who are in charge of the *Forward* can never force him to change his style. If you are unfortunate enough to be collared by him, he will draw out of his hip pocket a sheath of Yiddish poetry and read it aloud—sometimes revising as he goes along—with appropriate gestures: a sigh, a slow mournful nod, clenched fists. On week-ends he frequents the Café Royale and is on the best of terms with the leading Yiddish writers. He lives under the shadow of Peretz and Mendele, and he curses Sholem Asch for selling out. Union meetings he never attends, and more often than not, as far as his work goes, he is a "butcher." But, if ever he makes a serious mistake, the other men will cover up for him. He carries his lunch to the shop and generally, as he is declaiming, holds up a sandwich in one hand. For him there is only one certainty—that his kind is fast disappearing, with no replacements coming up.

Finishing his lunch off with an assorted bag of fruit,

the *balagula* or presser leans against anything that may partially remove the weight of his body from his feet. It does not matter whether it is a hydrant, a hand truck, or a carton—he spreads himself out on any part of the sidewalk and remains fixed. When he has thrown away the bag he does not stop to speak with anyone, for he goes off to search for sunlight. No matter the weather, the *balagula* never wears a jacket. He is the genuine proletarian of the garment world, traditionally generous and "*gezunt vie a ferd*"—"healthy as a horse."

The "Market" is characterized by an extreme restlessness, a frenzied attempt to cram everything into the lunch hour. Bookmakers mingle casually with the crowd, taking bets; good designers are besieged by salesmen attempting to seduce them with fantastic offers into fly-by-night firms. Around the corner, the side entrance near the freight elevator is the shipping clerks' territory. They remain in the lobby during lunch and wash down the morning with Pepsi-Cola, shooting crap with the elevator operators and the truckmen. The shipping clerk is the transient of the garment trade, emerging at the end of June with the last images of high school graduation still in his eyes, trying—if he is ambitious —to put away a few dollars before the college term begins in September. He may belong to a small union that remains virtually powerless against the mass of shipping clerks who cannot be organized. For who can define his duties? If he is not tying packages he is carrying piece-goods into the cutting room, if he is not loading the salesmen's samples into a cab he is rearranging stock, and if nothing is left there is always the floor to be swept or the cloth-ends to be folded. His working day is a perpetual search for the moment when a cigarette can be lit, for no one knows when the fire inspector may pop in, or when the boss may wander with an assumed casualness into the men's room to assert the democracy of the bladder.

But "The Market" cannot be confined within the limits of the streets. It flows over into the cafeterias, where kosher and *treif* exist side by side, where the busboys hover about ready to remove a coffee cup while it is still half full. For the garment worker there is nothing easier than to move through the packed aisles balancing a roll, a piece of Danish pastry, a cup of coffee, and one of the Yiddish dailies. As soon as he sits down he leans the rest of the chairs against the sides of the table, glaring with hostility at any unknown who may foolishly expect to take a seat. And by the time he has started breaking off small chunks of the Danish to dip into his coffee he is joined by two or three associates, and the table passes automatically into their hands. They are conscious of their status as steady customers, and unashamedly protest if they are given two slices of rye bread instead of the customary three, and manifest true dignity as they demand an extra pat of butter. Nor do they temper their scorn of the new counter-man who dares add this to the check.

Delicatessen is a sin to eat in a cafeteria, but they cannot resist such other Jewish delicacies as *kashe pirogen*, which however invariably fail to please them, since, after all, even if it did taste like something, for what they paid for one portion their wives could make enough to feed the family. Leaving the cafeteria, it is part of the ritual for the garment man to grab a handful of toothpicks at the cashier's desk, faithfully dropping them into his jacket pocket where they decompose till the suit is sent to the cleaner.

He hurries back to the showroom, for it is during lunch hour that most of his friends and relatives drop in for the "wholesale" transactions, which of course seldom appear on the books. Wholesale in a garment house is divided into two categories—"goniff" wholesale and "absolute" wholesale. "Goniff" wholesale is for distant relatives, those that can be left to the tender mercies of the salesman, who usually splits the difference with the garment worker. "Absolute" wholesale is for the *very* immediate family, and part of the ritual involves the garment worker's swearing by his life that he isn't making a penny for himself. Not only does he bring the designer over, but the head salesman and even the boss, who must all swear that the fit is superb and the price is right. (Just stand like a *mensh* so the shoulders won't droop!) By means of some mysterious mechanism, no matter how the customer wavers, a purchase is made just before lunch hour ends, and the garment worker goes back to his machine promising himself that *positively* this is the last time.

Resting in his modern apartment in the Bronx or the two-family house in Flatbush, the garment worker today feels himself a proletarian aristocrat; he has forgotten, or perhaps chosen to forget, the radical tradition of trade unionism. To him the very idea of being a good American is bound up with the idea of being a good trade unionist. Once a seasonal man, uncertain of the number of months he would find himself working during the year, he is today protected from the perils of the labor market by the union, whose statisticians watch all trends, keeping themselves a season ahead of him. The union is the bridge between his own handicaps as a worker and his sense of participation in American society. And whether he likes it or not he is in politics, even if it is only to the extent of showing up at a rally or a conference by order of the manager of his local.

He no longer sees his boss as the "capitalist cock-roach" of the sweatshop days: the typical cartoon in a union paper would show a foreman carrying a prostrate employee into the boss's office: flicking his ashes over the rug, the boss says coldly, "Well, if she's a piece-worker, give her the afternoon off"; another cartoon shows the boss standing over an operator who has just run a sew-ing machine through his finger and benevolently saying, "Don't worry, Harry, I'll get somebody else to finish off the dress."

Today the garment worker no longer need fear the boss of the Art Young or Redfield cartoon. Instead, the boss, as the garment worker conceives him, is simply another human being who must be taught by stalwart trade unionists that his best chances for success lie in a closed shop and a union label. If the manufacturer de-viates from this idealized image, it must be demon-strated to him not only that he is helpless against the union, but that his attempts to evade union rulings are wholly irrational. For the manufacturer, no matter what his vices, is still a Jew. The farther he has strayed, the greater joy is there over his return, and, like Irving Davidowsky in Asch's *East River*, at the eleventh hour he will always sign with the union and become recon-ciled with his people. It is the basic acceptance of this myth which lends a peculiar warmth and color to the garment world, distinguishing it from the rest of Amer-ican industry.

VIII *Morris Freedman*

The New Farmers of Lakewood

About sixty miles from New York City, in the flat, unspectacular pinelands of central New Jersey, there exists what would seem to many a double paradox: a new community of Jews who are farmers and also intellectuals. But perhaps it is no paradox that Jewish farmers should be intellectual ones.

The first Jewish chicken farmers settled in the Lakewood area some twenty-five years ago. They were no more than half a dozen, all immigrants, and they had strong ties with the Lakewood Jewish community of hotel-owners and small businessmen; with the years they expanded into chicken breeding and direct egg- and poultry-selling, more or less leaving "simple" farming behind.

In the late 30's, there began a small-scale exodus from New York City to the farms. Some had been soured on the city by the depression years; others sought security and a pleasanter life in a "return to the soil." One farmer's wife, whose life has been by no means easy, told me of her early feelings: "I would go out in the morning," she said, "and breathe my own air, scoop up my own soil, touch my own trees, and pass my hand slowly along the walls of my own house."

These settlers ranged remarkably widely in their occupations: there were clerks and small shopkeepers, garment workers, high school and college graduates who had never worked at all, civil service employees and ex-WPA workers, lawyers, social workers, psychologists, businessmen, salesmen. Although a few of the newcomers were to some degree Orthodox and some were strongly atheistic, most were simply indifferent to their Jewishness and, coming from a city with a great Jewish population, perhaps almost unconscious of it.

In the late 30's and early 40's a number of refugees joined the settlement. Although the costs of buying and operating a farm in the area have risen meteorically, new persons are still coming out, though in much smaller numbers. The Jewish Agricultural Society provided impetus to both waves in the form of advice and occasional financial aid.

At first the arrivals of the late 30's tried to graft themselves onto the older community centered around West Farms, off the Lakewood-Freehold road. But this older community, composed largely of middle-aged persons, was oriented more toward the conventional European-urban way of life, precisely one of the things some of the young farmers had hoped to escape. The gulf between the two groups was sharply defined when it was agreed that business meetings at the West Farms Community Center, having to do with eggs and poultry, would be conducted in English but social affairs in Yiddish. After a while, none of the new settlers attended the parties and banquets and lectures, and it was not long before none went to business meetings, either.

The core of the intellectual community is made up of about twenty families, the faithful membership of the discussion group, the oldest communal activity. These twenty families are all active members of other groups such as the co-ops and the local parent-teachers associations, and thus have close relations of some sort with perhaps more than two hundred families.

Whenever I visit the community, I stay with my friends Erik and Margaret Nappa. I had known Erik from before the time he had left our high school to go into farming.

Erik came to the area in the late 30's with his parents, when he was seventeen. The family had come from Germany in 1929 and was immediately hit by the depression. A candy and stationery store proved frustrating and profitless, and Erik's father, Leo, became a clerk in a carpet factory. At one time the parents considered going back to Germany (this was just before Hitler achieved power), but Erik dissuaded them. As it happened, he was in the midst of reading the Tom Swift series and didn't want to leave America until he had finished it.

In 1937, an opportunity arose to buy a farm cheaply and with a relatively small down payment. By redeeming a life insurance policy and inducing five fellow workers to borrow two hundred dollars each and lend the money to him (the five stood security for one another), Leo Nappa managed to scrape together the thousand dollars needed for the down payment plus legal fees. The farm had a small four-room bungalow and a two-story chicken house with accommodations for twelve hundred chickens. Erik left high school in his last year and with his mother attended to the farm, while his father continued to work in the city to provide a small flow of money, coming out on weekends.

I visited them during their first winter and I remember it vividly. Chicken farming then had advanced little over ancient methods. Daily, Erik had to carry water to the many scattered fountains on the range for the growing chickens. (Today, pipes buried in the ground perform this work.) All night long during February and March, snatching moments of sleep, he had to patrol the brooder houses where the baby chicks were kept warm under kerosene-fired heating hoods: if one of the fires went out, the chicks would pile up in one corner in an attempt to keep warm, and all those at the bottom of the heap, sometimes as many as two hundred, would suffocate, while those that survived would never be any good as layers because of the chilling they had suffered. Once Erik fainted from exhaustion. (Improved heating facilities and automatic safety devices control this hazard today and night patrols are no longer necessary.) The house itself had no central heating, and when the small kerosene stove broke down, as it often did, the family went to bed fully dressed. An outside pump supplied water.

Setbacks were frequent. Yet the farm slowly prospered. In the early 40's, Erik's parents were able to help him buy his own farm, a small place with no house about a quarter of a mile down the road. Erik lived in the feed room, using an outhouse, and proceeded to expand the chicken house and clear the overgrown land to provide a range for young chickens. About this time, refugees from Germany had begun to settle on the farms, and Erik met and married Margaret, who had got to Lakewood from Germany by way of a concentration camp in France and stopovers in Portugal and Spain. They built a neat four-room stucco bungalow. Three years ago a larger farm was offered for sale across the road, and although the house there was considerably older it was also much larger. Erik sold his own farm and bought the larger one. By that time the Nappas had a son; they now have another boy.

Erik's parents live along a winding road that cuts through tall pines. Their farm appears suddenly, surmounting a gently rolling, carefully landscaped lawn. The low white stucco dwelling is seen first, and behind it a long two-story white clapboard chicken house.

On my most recent visit, I found the farm considerably altered from what it had been shortly after the war. A two-story garage in front of the main chicken house had been extended to double its original size. Across the cleared land to the left were several groups of one-story, long white stucco buildings. The house had been entirely remodeled: a large pine-paneled living room with a fireplace had been built onto it, the kitchen and bath modernized in the best style of the magazine advertisements, the bedroom extended, and much new furniture bought. On the small porch stood a full set of white wrought-iron furniture and a glider.

Erik's father showed me around the new farm with quiet pride, now and then recalling how things had been in the early days. In the feed room, an elevator had been built to hoist the hundred-pound bags of feed to the second floor. The enlarged upper floor of the garage had five good-sized rooms for a farm worker and his family. In the basement of their home, a tremendous and ingenious machine sorted eggs according to size. I recalled how I had helped to weigh each egg individually.

"Before," Leo Nappa said, "I could never take a day off. Chickens, of course, work all the time. Now I can take several days or even a week off every year and not worry too much. My worker takes care of things."

The farmers are highly conscious of their independence and strongly maintain their individuality: I remember the violent arguments that used to break out over such a matter as whether wet mash was superior to dry mash for feeding growing chickens. But when cooperation was necessary for something desirable, there was never any hesitation about everyone pitching in. When chickens are full-grown, for example, they have to be taken off the range and put into the chicken house. The transfer is always made at night, when the chickens are asleep, or at least sleepy, and in the course of the transfer they are vaccinated and have opaque "spectacles" put on their beaks—the spectacles make it impossible for the chickens to see straight ahead, and thus keep them from pecking at one another. All this is a job that requires several hands, and each farmer calls upon his friends to assist. Throughout the whole process of catching the chickens, carrying them in crates, releasing them, vaccinating them, "specking" them, the farmers manage to keep up a steady flow of political and philosophical argument. It was partly to organize this peripatetic argumentation that the discussion group was started.

Among the charter members of the group were Bobby and Lillian Primack. They are in their twenties, and childless. Ever since the two came out to the farm nine years ago, they have been living in an attachment to a chicken house that on other farms usually serves as a feed-storage room. This annex they have divided into three little rooms. The living room, into which Lillian led me after we exchanged greetings, is about ten feet square. A reproduction of Picasso's "Woman in White" hung over the couch, while smaller reproductions of Hals and Renoir were on the other walls. A bookcase along one wall was jammed with books. The floor was bare concrete. In the bedroom were a plain double bed and a piano piled high with more magazines and books and music. A cubicle of a kitchen and a closetlike bathroom completed the living quarters. When the plumbing occasionally breaks down, Bobby and Lillian visit the Nappas to take showers.

After Bobby came in, I went out with him while he collected eggs. "When we first came out here," he remarked on the way to the chicken house, "there was only that wooden building you remember." He motioned behind us. "Our capacity then was about a thousand. We've since added several rooms. Now we have about a seven thousand capacity." I asked what that meant in terms of income. "Well, you figure roughly from a dollar and a half to three dollars profit on a chicken a year. But," he quickly added, "few farmers actually can put that money in the bank. Right now I owe about thirteen thousand dollars that has to be paid in the next four months, not to mention long-term debts. Then there's the continual building of one sort or another. Some day, I hope, we'll be able to afford a house."

We went into a room cluttered with feed bags and squat wire pails, some empty, some partly filled with bright white eggs. Bobby picked up an empty wire pail, called out softly "chick, chick, chick, chick, chick," opened the wire gate to the first room, and motioned me to follow. The plump white hens scurried away at our approach but turned to form a nervous semi-circle, red-topped heads bobbing forward and back as though controlled by puppet wires. With their red or yellow opaque plastic spectacles, they looked like a fantastic congregation of Hollywood-type schoolmarms. Bobby turned to the two rows of metal boxes on the wall and began taking out eggs, one, two, three at a time, and putting them into his basket. He kept up a silent count, his lips muttering every so often as he paused while talking.

"The discussion group started about five years ago," he told me. "Most of our first meetings were on political subjects and attendance was small. But after we more or less talked ourselves out on politics—that is, when we all knew where we stood and that we probably couldn't budge one another—we branched out. First we started on literature. We prepared the early lectures ourselves. Lillian read several of Shaw's plays and a biography, and then talked about him. We have had talks on Joyce, Dostoevsky, Mann, Faulkner, Stendhal, modern poetry, and so on.

"As more and more people joined the group, we went into other fields and began inviting speakers, usually authorities of one rank or another. We offered them nothing except ourselves as audience, a night's lodging if they wanted it, and travel expenses. Most of them took nothing at all, but were actually pleased to come to talk to us, perhaps only to see what kind of freaks we were. (Lately we've been able to pay a small fee.) We've had Clement Greenberg on art, for example, a number of editors, teachers from the New York colleges, and a whole collection of social workers, psychiatrists, and psychologists from New York. Right now we're going to have a man from Princeton down to give us a series on genetics."

Bobby objected to my describing the participants in the discussion group as "intellectuals"—the word carried for him an air of professionalism and slight affectation. "The meetings," he said, "obviously mean a lot to everyone, if not purely for intellectual reasons, then for social ones. After each of the meetings, which are usually rotated from house to house, the hostess of the evening provides coffee and cake. There have been times in the winter when a dog-team and sled would have been better equipment to travel some twenty miles than an automobile loaded with about six of us, all carrying shovels to clear away snow or dig us out of ditches. Once it took one couple four hours to get to a meeting. Our smallest attendance has been about a half dozen; our largest, on a psychiatric subject, close to a hundred." Once they spent several sessions taking up the question of Jewishness, using Sartre as a jumping-off point.

The farmers have become much more conscious of their Jewishness since moving out here. It is a troublesome paradox to them that while all of the activities they participate in are "nonsectarian," and while none of them is definably Jewish by religion, custom, interests, or language, nevertheless only Jews make up the discussion group, the nursery school, and to a large extent even the egg and feed cooperatives. Their business affairs keep them in close and continuous contact with their Gentile neighbors, and the farms themselves are so widely scattered through the area that few find themselves next to other Jewish farmers. Yet their social, cultural, and intellectual lives fall into what seem to be familiar Jewish patterns, even if the contents are not specifically Jewish. Most of the homes have record libraries containing the conventional classical symphonies and concertos and the folk-song recordings of Richard Dyer-Bennet and Burl Ives. Lately, Jewish folk songs have been added in a few homes. Their reading, when it isn't of the standard works in psychiatry (Freud, Horney, Stekel, Reich), is concentrated on "great books," usually the classics of the 19th century and some of the little-read but good works of today. Their taste in art hovers between the sentimentality of

Saturday Evening Post covers and the assembly-line reproductions of the museums and the little frame and art shops; there are early Picassos, for example, but no Mirós. Except for psychiatry, they are not especially identified with the avant garde culturally, but neither have they become fixed in their attitudes; they are very willing, even humbly willing, to have their tastes widened; and they are usually aware, if only vaguely, of the latest intellectual issues of discussion.

Few have changed their fundamental attitudes toward the question of Jewishness since coming out. Some have become more tolerant of religion, but no one near the hard core of the discussion group has made a flicker of a movement toward formalized belief and away from the characteristic vague atheism. Most do not in any way observe the Jewish holidays; some are not even aware of them; few plan to have their sons Bar Mitzvah. Around the Jewish holidays, there is a surge of Jewish feeling that remains amorphous and dissipates quickly. The group is largely indifferent to Zionism, except for one or two members who are mildly nationalistic.

COMMENTARY is a favorite magazine. Contributors and editors have frequently addressed the group; articles have provided subject matter for meetings; one group member set forth some of the farmers' problems about Jewishness in a letter that appeared in an early issue of the magazine (February 1946). These mainly concerned their children, who were reaching school age. The articles with a religious overtone and the "Cedars of Lebanon" section, remote from their interests and experience, are least popular; the speculative articles on the nature of Jewishness, factual reports, and the essays in "From the American Scene" are most popular.

All in all, there is a good deal of ambiguity, not to say confusion, about their attitudes. One night after dinner, I was startled to hear a sudden emotional defense of strict Orthodoxy by one woman whose sons were not circumcised by a *mohel* and who obeys none of the dietary laws. In general, the members would like to consider themselves, at least on the broad social level, as typical integrated Americans (in the fullest "white Protestant" sense) with no distinguishing marks; yet their way of thinking and living does stamp them as different, and the fact is that they are rigorously set apart from any portion of the Gentile community.

Before one Christmas a strained atmosphere developed on one of the school boards when a Jewish member suggested that the exclusively Christian character of the holiday be toned down in deference to the sensibilities of Jewish students. This particular situation was resolved when it was decided that the school would indicate the variety of celebrations that go on during this period among many different groups. One of the psychiatrists (non-Jewish) associated with the nursery school suggested that the Jewish community should observe Christmas in the traditional American way—tree, carols, and all—since there was no point in making the children conscious of a difference that seemed to mean nothing to their parents. Some families did just that. Erik Nappa, for one, cuts down a pine tree and sets it up in the living room every Christmas for his children.

The most organized demonstration of anti-Semitism, or at least anti-Jewish exclusiveness, in recent times (during the 20's the neighborhood KKK had burned crosses on the farms of newly arrived Jews) occurred during an election for the local board of education. For years, about twenty or thirty people had chosen the body. One board member had held office for fifty years; most members had no more than a grade school education. After it felt more or less established, the Jewish community decided one year to run a progressive candidate, a person who happened to be exceptionally well qualified for such a position—and Jewish. Although the Jewish candidate, if elected, would have been only one member in nine, the Gentile community turned out three hundred strong to defeat him. (Jews have since been elected to the board.)

Of course, much of the opposition to Jews may be no more than the usual resentment of the natives (some with ancestry going back to colonial America) toward newcomers, or of stick-in-the-mud rustics to smart-alecky city slickers. The Jewish farmers have revolutionized chicken farming in the area (merely by going at it according to the recommendations of state and federal advisers) and have always held as their physical ideal the bounteous American life as exemplified by the slick-paper magazines. While the Jewish farmers, for example, converted to central heating as soon as they could afford it, some of their Gentile neighbors are still getting along with a coal-burning stove and a kerosene heater.

There is also much evidence to indicate that the wall between Jews and Gentiles may be neither solid nor permanent. I spoke briefly with the Jewish president of one of the local parent-teachers associations, a strikingly handsome, tall woman, with none of the characteristics of manner or speech occasionally ascribed to Jews but at the same time with no thought at all of ever denying her Jewishness. She is the elected head of a mixed body and reported no evidence of anti-Semitism in her experience. As for social mixing, her comment was that she could have as much of that as she wanted. (It is fair to note that in surrounding cities, such as Freehold, Jews whose roots in the community go so far back as almost to be invisible without gene-

alogical research—and who are usually rigorously Orthodox—serve in high municipal positions and are prominent in semi-social organizations like Kiwanis and the
Rotarians.)

It is hardly possible to overemphasize the effect
the Jews have had on this area. Before they came, egg
production was a minor, hit-or-miss, often subsidiary enterprise of the local farmers, carried out on a marginal
basis; now it's a scientific, mass-production business.
One man, a refugee, soon after he came to the area
built a two-story, scientifically ventilated chicken house
embodying every latest advance. He soon sold this farm,
and went on to build an all-steel, hangar-like chicken
house that attracted visitors from miles around, even
one pair from Russia. It's hard to say whether this was
a successful venture—steel has not come into general
use for chicken houses—but at least it illustrates the
trail-breaking ardor of these farmers. One member of
the discussion group invented a new type of spectacles
for chickens. A few members of the group were among
the first to try out a new breed of chickens developed
not long ago by Henry Wallace (oddly enough, they lay
pink eggs). Some of those who tried out the new breed
did so partly out of a sentimental interest in Wallace; at
the time I was there, the experiment seemed not to be
a success.

This spirit of enterprise and experiment has so far
been largely confined to the Jewish community, and
the old-fashioned farmers, in danger of being squeezed
out, are naturally resentful. But the cleavage between
Jews and Gentiles goes considerably beyond differences
in farming techniques.

The history of the nursery school is most illustrative. When the school was organized, the parents went
enthusiastically from door to door seeking community

support. They met one rebuff after another. Even ministers were distant. One minister's wife enthusiastically volunteered to serve as nurse, but soon after, with no explanation, withdrew. Youngsters of non-Jewish families were extensively sought after, but none was enrolled; one Gentile boy attended for a short while but left abruptly.

For a while the nursery school board considered giving up the "pretense" of being nonsectarian and closing on Jewish holidays, when attendance was low. And just recently, the board of directors decided that Jewish holidays should in some way be "observed." Little parties have been held for the youngsters, and some of the history of the holiday explained to them. The board provided reading material in Jewish history for the non-Jewish full-time teachers. This innovation is not, however, a substitute for the traditional American customs and symbols for certain holidays. Thus, matzos may be eaten along with non-kosher chocolate Easter bunnies, and the Christmas tree decorated and carols sung simultaneously with the lighting of Chanukah candles.

Much of the opposition to the nursery school can be explained on grounds other than anti-Semitism. Part may be the result of an undeveloped notion of what nursery schools are for; part is the result of the school's extremely progressive character, which has given rise to some weird rumors about what the little boys and girls do together; part is a simple opposition to the fact that the head teacher is Negro. But in addition, there appears to be something fundamentally involved in the nature of the nursery school itself that may be close to the source of the general alienation between the Jewish farmers and the Gentile community.

The school constitutes a kind of temple dedicated to the children. There is no enterprise the farmers have gone into with more open, whole-hearted, and aggressive enthusiasm. Everyone—including childless couples, grandparents, and parents of alumni—supports the school, and it has become in many ways the very center of their lives. Nursery school banquets, dances, plays, the periodic educational lectures, attract a large attendance, with many coming from inconveniently outlying sections. There probably is not a person in the community who hasn't contributed time and energy to add to the property of the school in the form of curtains, playthings, and equipment. (After some tough sledding, the nursery today owns its own building and grounds in Farmingdale.)

The children themselves love the school. I went along one morning with Erik when he drove his son to school, stopping along the way to pick up the children of two neighboring farmers. When we got to the school building, the kids burst out of the back of the car and scattered across the lawn and up the steps into the school with shrill shouts of anticipation. (Incidentally, a good many of the Jewish families already have two children and a few have three, which seems to be the number most are driving at—though one family was planning on six the last time I spoke with them. It is interesting also that this area was the first in this country where Dr. Grantly Dick Read's theories of "natural childbirth," set forth in his book *Childbirth Without Fear*, were put into practice, though this was perhaps fortuitous: one of Read's earliest American disciples practices in the neighborhood.)

The children's education is something the farmers will not compromise about. When they were seeking a teacher, the best-qualified applicant happened to be

Negro. Although the parents well realized they were taking a chance in antagonizing the community, they nevertheless didn't hesitate a moment to hire her. Today, in the opinion of experts who have visited it, the school compares with the most enlightened nurseries in the world, like the Bank Street School in New York and the Summerhill School in England. An active mental hygiene clinic, with a social worker and a consultant psychiatrist, is attached to the nursery. For a long time, a psychiatrist came down once a week from New York and mingled with the children during a regular session, reporting her observations and making recommendations to the board and teachers. There are regular educational meetings at which the parents are addressed by experts in various fields; a recent visitor was A. S. Neill, the famous director of the Summerhill School. Through the influence of the school, modern concepts of child-rearing have infiltrated the most old-fashioned homes and even, to some extent, the schools in the surrounding community.

But all this enthusiasm for the nursery school, and the devotion to their children it expresses, epitomizes one of the factors that keep Jew and Gentile apart. I think it may fairly be said that the Gentile farmers are not ready to understand this powerful—perhaps exaggerated—concern for the needs of the young. To non-Jews, it probably appears as just one more example of the newcomers' irritating compulsion to be "up to the minute"—and the resentment it arouses is probably not so much anti-Semitism as a generalized anti-intellectualism. The inability of the Jewish farmers to fit themselves to the established ways of the surrounding community makes it probable that the alienation of the two groups will continue for a long time.

National Jewish organizations are beginning to corral some of the Lakewood farmers. A B'nai B'rith chapter in Lakewood has held meetings patterned on those of the discussion group; it even had the same speakers several times. A newly activated Reform temple has grown with remarkable speed, in spite of the somewhat scornful reactions of the more radical members of the community. One appeal made to them has been on the basis that religion can be a "unique intellectual experience of the highest order." The rabbi is young and anxious to meet the needs of his congregation. Addressing one group gathered in the temple, he remarked: "We'll have to work together. For me, you are my first congregation; but for most of you, I am your first rabbi."

Although there are probably other important reasons, I think the farmers' concern with psychiatric theories, amounting at times almost to an obsession, is deeply tied up with the overwhelming responsibility they feel towards the psychological health of their children. Surely no other community of farmers in the country can claim the distinction of having supported—and handsomely—two psychiatrists, one specializing in children, the other in adults. Indeed, so extensive was the demand here for psychiatric help at one time that several new psychiatrists settled temporarily in the area. Not a person in the community remained untouched by the vogue, and it was odd to hear the farmers classify each other in psychiatric terms: Reichian, anti-Reichian, partial Reichian, Horney-ite, Adlerian, orthodox Freudian, those who were anti-psychiatric altogether, and so on.

With some, the enthusiasm for psychiatry was superficial, the result of skimming through the particular master's works or hearing one lecturer; others allied themselves with a particular school as the result of treatment (one hears of no cases of unsuccessful therapy); still others read and thought in the field with an intensity and probing intelligence sufficient to astonish some of the expert lecturers who came down to talk to the group.

At least partly, I think, the psychiatric atmosphere emanated from the gulf between the generation born and raised in America and their European-born parents. The same source of disturbance, of course, may be found among urban young people (who, as we know, tend more and more to deal with it on the analyst's couch). But the farmers were affected differently—or at least more clearly—perhaps simply because they were thrown together so intimately that their difficulties become sharply visible, and psychiatry itself became a thing of communal concern; and, perhaps more important, because many of the younger farmers were closely tied to their parents, who live either with them or not far away.

Is the community a happy one? The evidence is ambiguous. Certainly, few leave it. Even those who fail at farming are likely simply to shift to another way of making a living associated with farming, such as delivering eggs to consumers in New York or fuel oil to the farmers, and remain in the area. One man still lives in the same house and commutes daily to New York, some two hours away.

Yet, in spite of their evident loyalty to the way of life they have established, there is a spirit of unrest among the farmers. The preoccupation with psychotherapy seems excessive. A good number of the marriages are not happy ones. Rarely relaxed, the farmers accept few events about them matter-of-factly. Whenever I have visited the area, I have found the group intensely and rather painfully taken up with some recent occurrence, discussing the participants and their motives and the general morality of the thing with a thoroughness and subtlety that often shaded off into an amorphous Henry Jamesian kind of analysis superior, perhaps, to mere gossip, and yet, in its persistence, not less expressive of mutual tensions. The very fervor with which the farmers pursue knowledge (perhaps too often confused with the *dernier cri*) may indicate a frustration not superficially evident. I have heard the father of one of the younger farmers, himself very successful as the result of a single-minded devotion to egg production, remark that if his son and some of his friends, not notably successful as farmers, had put as much energy into their farms as into their intellectual discussions they might long ago have achieved a good measure of his own success. But of course it may be that these young farmers are finding self-fulfillment precisely in this division of interests—certainly that is what many of them would claim.

It might be claimed also that the surest sign of psychic health in our time is, after all, an extreme self-consciousness combined with a practical impulse to improve those specific details of living that have been found wanting. There are, surely, many signs of health in the Lakewood community. Most of the farmers have remained sufficiently skeptical (in the best humanist sense) about their allegiances to be able to listen with particular interest to speakers opposed to their pet theories. And finally, it may be significant that some of the most ardent and knowledgeable believers in psychiatry have not submitted themselves to therapy, feeling no need of it—a fact that may indicate either a clear understanding of the proper place of psychotherapy or, of course, merely a hidden "resistance."

Without sentimentalizing, it may be said at least that the members of the community find it a useful and desirable social organism. Perhaps the ultimate test will be the children now in its nursery school.

IX *Donald Paneth*

I Cash Clothes!

The shops of New York City's second-hand clothing dealers crowd the bottom of Elizabeth Street on the rim of Manhattan's Lower East Side, in the block below Canal Street. The block is quiet, despite the insistent echo of heavy trucks rumbling noisily across Canal Street's uneven cobblestones; the Fifth Precinct, which polices the Bowery and Chinatown, is near the corner; the small shops nestle in low, ancient brick buildings, and their proprietors buy frayed suits, coats, and trousers from old-clothes peddlers and sell them to Midwest and Southern outlets. The peddlers are as shabby as the clothing they bear. They are old men, Jewish immigrants from Russia and Poland, who have shuffled through the city, clutching wrapped newspapers, crying, "I buy! Cash clothes!" for thirty, forty, fifty years. The peddlers are poorly dressed, and many need a shave. They are poor men.

Henry Getoff is an old-clothes peddler. He canvasses neighborhoods—Washington Heights, West End

Avenue, Jackson Heights, the Grand Concourse—for old clothes, calling, "Buy cash! Buy!" He carries a tightly folded newspaper ("This is the sign I buy," he says) and brown wrapping paper for his purchases. It isn't an easy business. He works in all weathers, is unable to take a vacation, is constantly liable to arrest for making unnecessary noise, and his earnings are unpredictable. "It is a lot of walking," he says. "And nothing extra in money. Just enough to get along."

In the neighborhoods, housewives know him. When they hear his familiar cry, and they have clothes to sell, they lean from apartment windows and call, "Hey, mister!" From them, Getoff buys a vest for a quarter which he resells for fifty cents, a suit for one dollar which he resells for two-fifty, a topcoat for three dollars which he resells for five. He buys only men's clothing, women's styles shift too quickly. Before he buys, he carefully examines each garment for torn linings, moth holes, cigarette burns, and damaged collars. "Makes no difference if it's old and dirty," he says. "But it must be in good condition. Those that aren't we call wrecks. Junk peddlers buy *them*." Near mid-afternoon each day, Getoff leaves for the market, the crowded row of shops on Elizabeth Street, where he deals amiably and rapidly with two dealers, whom he knows particularly well. On a good day, he sells them twenty-five dollars worth of clothing. "The dealers know me," he says. "And I know the dealers. We know what everything's worth. We don't try to fool each other."

Getoff, a short, stocky man, sixty-two years old, differs in appearance from most peddlers. His clothes are clean, he doesn't need a shave, and his face is unlined. His hair is gray though and closely cropped, his mustache is small and fuzzy, his eyes are alert and intelli-

gent. He speaks English hesitantly, but capably. He has
been an old-clothes peddler thirty-nine years.

He is a businessman without office, inventory, or
records. He has a neat card with his name, address, and
phone number, his hours of business are 9 A.M. to 4
P.M. with special evening appointments. He has many
regular customers. "I have customers twenty-five years,"
he says. "I never lose a customer—unless I don't like
him. I buy from the people in a nice way. I always try
to satisfy them, and if they forget something in
the pocket, I return it. In business, big or small, you
have to be honest." Getoff emphasizes that he is his
own boss. That is important to him. When he arrived
with his wife in the United States from Russia in 1913,
he was employed for a week as a clerk in a grocery
store. A religious man, he prepared to leave the store
for synagogue early Friday evening. The shopkeeper
said to him, "What's the matter with you, Getoff? Are
you a greenhorn? In America, you don't stop work for
synagogue." He quit the job abruptly, and since then
has been self-employed.

Each weekday morning, Getoff leaves his Bronx
home on Fulton Avenue, opposite Crotona Park, and
selects a neighborhood to canvass; depending on his
impulse it may be in the Bronx, Manhattan, Brooklyn, Queens, and even Long Island or New Jersey. He
walks slowly through the neighborhood, along avenues
and down side streets, backtracking too, for five or six
hours. "I like to walk," he says. "I like the fresh air."
As he walks, he swings his wrapped newspaper, scans
apartment windows for customers, and calls, "I buy!
Cash clothes!" Or, "Buy cash! Buy!" All old-clothes peddlers carry a newspaper as a trademark. "Apartment
houses are very high," he explains. "A customer may
not hear the call, but she will see the paper. So she

149

knows the old-clothes man." In every neighborhood, Getoff is friendly with a shoemaker, a tailor, or a druggist, with whom he can leave his package of clothes, as it becomes too heavy for him to carry easily. "Some peddlers must walk with the package," he says. "They are not acquainted with all the people as I am." Two or three times a day, he calls his wife at home for phone messages she may have received for him. "I call her from the road," he says, "like a doctor calls his nurse."

In his quest for customers, Getoff is confronted with three business hazards: the weather, the police, and the holdup. Rain and snow are bad for business. "That's what you call the miserable days," he says. "Housewives don't like to call the man from the street. She has a nice carpet, or little children who might catch cold." In the past ten years, Getoff has been arrested five or six times for making unnecessary noise, but he has always been able to pay the one dollar or two dollars fine, and so has never passed a night in jail. Once, a policeman on Washington Heights gave him a summons for hollering before 9 A.M., and when he appeared in court, he pleaded guilty, but with an explanation. "Your honor," he said, "I leave my house at nine, and I take two trolleys to the Heights. It takes me half an hour, maybe three-quarters. I could be on the Heights at nine?" The judge dismissed the case. The holdup is actually the least of the perils, but Getoff fears it the most. He has never been robbed, but he knows several peddlers who have been beaten for their money, a few dollars. So whenever he receives an evening call from someone he doesn't know, he asks his youngest son, Louis, to call and check and make certain the offer to sell is legitimate.

Getoff scrawls the last name and address of reliable and productive customers in a battered vest-pocket notebook. His customers are mostly business-men—"Working people don't sell old clothes," he says —and he has known many of them twenty or thirty years. "One customer by the name Sobel lives on the Concourse," he says. "Very nice people. He's manager in a big concern. It must be a nice salary: they live nice and educate their children nice. Another customer lives in a hotel on West End Avenue. He's a rich man, a manufacturer of men's suits. I buy from his daughter too. One woman in Yonkers I know thirty-five years. She treats me like a brother. When I come, it's 'How are you, Getoff? Take your coat off. Sit down.' She recommends me to many people."

Although he is obliging, he often has small difficulties with his customers. They may recommend him to a sister or cousin whom he may dislike, but to whom he must be as pleasant as possible: he cannot offend a good customer's relative; or a woman will bargain relentlessly with him, demanding a price he cannot pay. He has a formula for coping with her. The clothes she offers may be worth twenty dollars, but she asks fifty dollars, and since she would simply shrug if he offered the true value, he proposes thirty-five dollars. "Go on! Go on!" she yells. "Take a walk!" A week later, Getoff calls back, and she remembers him: she has already spoken to three more peddlers, who refused to buy, and perhaps quarreled with her, and she is willing to lower her demands. "All right," she says. "I'll take thirty-five dollars." But, now prices are off, the market is down, and Getoff says twenty dollars—which she accepts reluctantly.

When he refers to his customers, whom he likes to observe and analyze, Getoff customarily divides them into two groups: woman and *woman*, man and *man*, rich people and *rich* people, boy and *boy*. "Old people

from the other side who have money think they're
somebody because they're rich," he says. "They look
down on you. They show they don't like to deal with a
peddler. Then, there are *rich* people with education.
They give me a chair and on a hot day a cold drink.
They have feeling. They have consideration. A boy is
twenty years old. He talks to me nice, he doesn't get
excited. A *boy* is thirty-five. Maybe, he's not so bad, but
he gets excited. This is in him already. He's an old
bachelor, and he's got too much on his mind—why he
didn't marry. Probably he's disappointed."

Getoff leaves the neighborhood with his package
for the market about 2 P.M. At Nos. 5 and 9 Elizabeth Street, the peddlers have lockers in which they
keep the clothes they are unable to sell immediately.
9 Elizabeth Street is a store with an unwashed window and two signs: "Restaurant—Home Cooking" and
"Tailor—All Repairs." Inside, the store is long and narrow and dimly lit, the wooden floor is bare and dirty,
a long, narrow counter for resting packages is at
the right. Nearly one hundred lockers crowd the walls
from floor to ceiling. They are deep, two feet by two
feet, and rent for one dollar to three dollars a month;
the lockers nearest the ceiling are the cheapest. The
tailor and restaurant, with four tables and a perpetual
pinochle game, are in back.

Peddlers crowd the store in the afternoon. Activity
is intense with much movement and loud conversation
in Yiddish and English. In a corner, one peddler offers
another peddler a suit. "This is a good suit," he says.
"Sharkskin." "I give you two dollars." "Two dollars?
Ha! I take it home with me." "OK, two-fifty. Your own
brother wouldn't give you more. Would I fool you?"
"Listen, what the hell's the matter with you? If you
want it, buy it—at a fair price. If you don't want it, I

don't feel bad. I sell it." At a locker, a short, pudgy peddler sorts clothing as he comments hoarsely to his neighbor about a mutual acquaintance: "That guy is a crook. I know him. He's no good for nothing. He's crazy. Him with all his money. He works Saturday, he works Sunday, he works Yom Kippur. Big shot! He oughta be on Fifth Avenue. I don't talk to him no more. He can drop dead for me." Near the door, a tall, stooped, grumbling man, an alcoholic from the Bowery, a block away, attempts to sell a ragged garment to a peddler. "Look at that label," he says. "That alone's worth fifteen cents. I hate to tell you what I paid for this shirt originally. Eight dollars. Eight dollars. And now I can't get fifteen cents for it. But I could buy a suit or coat here cheap as hell. For fifty cents a suit that I could pawn for two dollars. I know. I've done it."

Getoff is friendly with most of the peddlers, and speaks to them while unwrapping his clothes, before going into the market; among them, the timeless question is, "What've you got?" This is what they talk about. "One peddler," Getoff says, "I used to go partners with, and split profits. He's mine age. He comes from Poland. I would have the money. He would have the customer. I appeal more to women than him. We're still friends."

The tight row of dealers' shops—the market— crowds the street outside 9 Elizabeth. "The market was here when I came," Getoff says. "And I know peddlers ninety years old, who have been here sixty-five years. They say the market was here when they came." Getoff sells his clothes to two dealers, who operate small, cluttered shops, where clothing is piled on high, huge shelves; in the fall and winter, he sells them winter suits, top coats, and shoes. (Summer is the slow season with little to buy and sell.) One of the dealers is sixty-five years old, he comes from Vilna; the other is fifty-eight, he comes from Kiev. "They're plain Yiddish men," Getoff says. "They have a nice family. Plenty of money. They deal nice." They remodel and clean and sell the clothes that they buy to retailers from Detroit, Cleveland, Des Moines, Dallas, Atlanta, Savannah, Birmingham, where they are sold eventually to farm and factory workers.

Henry Getoff, old-clothes peddler, was born on July 16, 1887 in Lubin, Russia, a small, hilly city of twenty thousand in the Ukraine. He was the son of Tuba, a religious, charitable, simple woman, and Louis Getoff, a friendly, unexcitable, good-natured flour dealer. Getoff had two brothers, Zalman and Jacob, and three sisters, Fanny, Bella, and Ida; they lived in a stucco, three-room house on the edge of Lubin, near a small lake, where townswomen washed clothes and fetched water, and boys like himself fished and boated and swam. "It was quiet and pretty," Getoff says. He studied the Bible and Talmud at a small school in Lubin from his sixth to his twelfth year, and then looked for work. "In the little city there was nothing to do," he recalls. "I went to Kiev." From fourteen to twenty-one, he traveled about the Ukraine, from Kharkov to Odessa to Kiev. "I was in all kinds of business," he says. "Different business every year." In Kharkov, he sold flowers; in Odessa, he worked in a shoe factory and was a rope salesman; in Kiev, where he lived five years, he owned an appetizing store, which sold prunes, salmon, figs, dates, white fish.

"Kiev was wonderful," he says. "A clean, beautiful city with factories of all kinds. I felt nice in Kiev. It was something new and interesting. In a shop window on the widest boulevard was a solid gold lion—an advertisement. In all of Russia, I never saw such. Just in Kiev. Also, businessmen made a good living. Some Jews had permits to live there, but small people like me had a politician. I paid him one dollar a week for a certain paper." But life in Kiev was not entirely pleasant. In 1904, when he was seventeen, he was one of two hundred Jewish men and youths who fought a pogrom mob; a pistol bullet wounded him in the neck, and he was hospitalized three months. "Boys were men in the old country," he says. "Life learned us quickly. We supported ourselves. Not like in America, where a boy may be good in school, but nothing else."

When Getoff was twenty-one, he returned to Lubin and avoided conscription in the Czar's army through the intervention of a physician. "He was a family friend," Getoff explains. "And the head doctor for conscription. He did a favor, and overlooked me. He was an honest man. He took no money." Then, Getoff married Bessie Platkin, a young baker's daughter, whom he had known as a child. "Business in Russia was not good," he says. "It was bad for Jews. There were always pogroms, and you couldn't go to the university. Only rich Jews could live in Moscow or St. Petersburg. This makes me come to America." He and his wife sailed in 1913 from a Latvian seaport aboard an old German freighter, jammed with seventeen hundred immigrants; his sisters, who married, and his brothers, who went into business, remained in Russia, and he hasn't had a letter from them since 1938. The transatlantic voyage in rough seas took twenty-one days. "I will never forget how bad it was," he says. "We were all seasick terrible. Everyone was praying the ship shouldn't go down."

In New York, he stayed for two weeks with an uncle in the Bronx, on Third Avenue between 173rd and 174th Streets two blocks from where he now lives.

He worked a week in a grocery, and meanwhile met an old-clothes peddler, who told him, "You're a young man; better to be in my business. It'll keep you out in the fresh air." "I didn't want to work in the garment shops," Getoff says. "The pay was too low. So I went in this business." He then attended night school for three weeks to study English. He enjoyed the school. "They teach the foreigners so good," he says. "They learn us to read, to talk, to everything. They explain the people very nice. I see it was a mistake—I should go at least a year in school. It would be better for me. But, I was a married man; my wife didn't like to be alone at night."

Getoff liked the United States too. "I was happy," he says. "The difference was day and night. Russia was miserable, but here children went to high school, Jews were doctors and lawyers, you could open a shop wherever you want. It appeals to me very good." He became a citizen in 1935. As a peddler, he learned quickly: he became acquainted with dealers' needs and prices and he slowly acquired customers about the city. He would stop people in the street, and ask them if they had any old clothes to sell; if they didn't he would give them his card with his address. He didn't have a telephone then; his customers sent him postcards. "When I was starting," he says, "I used four or five dealers. I didn't know the value of clothes, and when they gave me a price, I didn't know if it was right. My dream was that I should be a dealer, but I never could collect enough money to open a shop."

Though he needed business, Getoff never worked on Saturday, when he went to synagogue, or on Sunday, when he might be arrested for hollering on the Sabbath. He took his religion seriously, and regularly attended Friday evening and Saturday morning services. "I was religious when I was young and now I am the same thing," he says. "There is a God. I believe in it. God is whatever I see—rain and snow and earth and mountains. Who could make it but God?" In 1917 he and ten friends formed the Congregation Sabbath Observers of the Bronx; today Getoff is vice-president of the congregation, which has sixty members, its own synagogue, and two small cemeteries in New Jersey.

In 1918 and 1924, his two sons, Hyman and Louis, were born. "My father was very giving," Louis says. "He didn't have much, but he never held back anything. When it snowed, he built snowmen with us in Crotona Park, and every night he played checkers with Hy, who usually lost. Pa was good at checkers." Getoff insisted his sons should be educated. Hy was graduated from City College and New York University's Law School; during the war, he served in army intelligence on New Guinea, and he is now an attorney in Los Angeles. Louis, who was an army sergeant in India, also attended City College; he is a clinical psychologist, studying for his doctorate at Columbia University.

Getoff's wife, a short, stout, gregarious woman, recalls that the old-clothes business was never particularly lucrative. "It's a bad business for money," she says. "Sometimes, I'd yell at him: 'Henry, you are a dope. Why are you in such a business? It's lousy rotten.' Afterwards I would feel bad. He is a good man." Getoff earned the most money during the 20's when he sold sixty or seventy dollars' worth of clothing a day; now thirty dollars a day is excellent. "Now is worse than after the first war," he says. "China used to take fifteen million old hats a year. No more. Turkey, Russia, Bul-

garia, Hungary used to take also. But no more." During
the depression, people didn't sell old clothes, and Getoff was continually in debt to loan companies. "My father wouldn't consider relief," Louis says. "I tried to
explain to him the obligation of the state. But he
wouldn't listen." To simplify business, Getoff installed
a telephone in 1934, and at first his wife wouldn't answer it when she was at home alone; "I was green," she
says. "I was scared of it." In 1936, to stimulate business, he started to send postcards to families who published obituaries in the New York *Times*. He didn't
like to collect clothing from bereaved wives and children, but it was a source; finally, the technique spread,
and in 1942, when a woman in his apartment house,
whose husband was killed in an automobile accident,
received a dozen postcards from old-clothes peddlers,
he decided to abandon it.

Thirteen years ago, he spurred another change, a
permanent one, within his trade: he helped organize
the Used Clothing Dealers Association, to which one
hundred and fifty peddlers—all of those in the city—
now belong. "We needed an association to benefit peddlers," he says. Members pay twenty-five cents a week
dues and the association retains a lawyer, pays court
fees, and lends needy or ill peddlers up to two hundred
dollars. Getoff is a trustee and chairman of the loan
fund, and twice a month on Thursday evenings he attends a board of directors meeting at 96 Clinton
Street. The board ordinarily considers routine business:
a request for a loan, a proposal for a banquet, the collection of dues. But recently it faced a new and unex-
pected problem: the charity racket, in which an individual obtains a "permit" for five dollars from certain
yeshivas, and rings doorbells for contributions of old

clothing, which he pawns or sells. In January one hundred and fifty peddlers held a protest meeting. "Some yeshivas do not care," Getoff declared angrily at the meeting. "They have the five dollars." And a month ago, he met with several yeshiva rabbis, who said, "This is unbelievable," and assured him they would investigate.

In his trade, Getoff is known as "The Professor." Peddlers respect him as a leader and as the father of a lawyer and a doctor. He is serious, quiet, energetic, and assiduous. "He is a medium nature," his wife says. "Not bad, not good. He gets excited when I ask for more money. But he's not stingy—he doesn't have it. He is a good husband: he doesn't look on other womens, and he's kind. He doesn't play cards, but he likes his schnapps. He gets high on all the Jewish holidays." And although he is essentially quiet, he is expansive at parties, weddings, and dinners, where, with the provocation of schnapps, he may make a speech, dance, or sing a Hebrew song.

When he leaves the Elizabeth Street market at 4 P.M. each day, he takes the Third Avenue El home to the Bronx. "My trade is all right," he says. "I made a living. I raised my children. Now, young people are not becoming peddlers. This generation doesn't like it. Maybe the next will—if it doesn't, the trade dies." Getoff's five-room apartment, overlooking Crotona Park, is small and cluttered. "But, it's comfortable," he says. "A home. This is the best pleasure." He eats simple suppers, enjoying soup, meat or chicken, and potatoes most; he doesn't like dairy foods. In the evening, he rests. He has low blood pressure, but he refuses to see a doctor. "When it's my time to go, I'll go," he says. He reads the Jewish *Day* and *Morning Journal*, but he no longer reads Sholom Aleichem, Tolstoy, or Gorki; he sleeps instead. Nor does he walk after supper, as he used to, and on a warm, sunny Saturday or Sunday, he likes to sit quietly in the green park opposite his house. "I am not a lawyer or a doctor," he says. "When it is Friday already, I am tired."

X

Harry Gersh

"Kochalein": Poor Man's Shangri-La

In the good old days when my great-uncle Zissel came to America (circa 1904) the word "fix" had two distinct meanings. If you "fixed" a house or an umbrella, you built it up. But if you "fixed" a person, then it was just the opposite—you tore him down. Is it any wonder that my great-uncle Zissel had trouble with English?

But Fetter Zissel and his generation bided their time. As soon as they had settled down a bit in America, they gave "fix" another meaning. In a way they fixed "fix." They built it up, so that the verb was no longer a threat to living persons. As in: "She went to the country to fix herself."

I have always felt that their deep faith in the healing power of the country was in some way connected with our mothers' passionate worry about eggs. In our house (in yours, too) an eating egg—very, very different from a baking or cooking egg—had to be rushed into the icebox within twenty-four hours after it was laid or you could get poisoned. Nature's foolproof packaging miracle, and it wasn't good enough for mama. (That it remained in the icebox for four or five days didn't matter.) Mama had a conviction about color, too. Wyandottes, Plymouth Rocks, Barred Rocks —whole families, divisions, generations of chickens lived to no purpose—they laid brown eggs. Definitely not for human consumption. But in the country you got fresh, white eggs. You could eat them before the cackle died out. A little smelly and dirty, but in the country that's healthy.

And milk. To a growing boy nothing tastes worse than warm, bubbly milk fresh from the teat. But it's healthy—Pasteur to the contrary notwithstanding.

Air. In the city every vagrant breath of air is evil. Any air in motion is a draft—an immediate threat of pneumonia, influenza, pleurisy, and *lung-untsindenish*. In the country you go outside in a half-gale, with the dew thick as sour cream, half-naked, to enjoy fresh air . . . fresh from the North Pole. That's healthy. A *meshugas*.

Yes, a lunacy indeed, but in the old days reserved strictly for rich people. It cost money to go to the country and who had money? But the yearning for the unattainable therapeutic Mountains remained in the Jewish breast, and in due course from the womb of time came the *kochalein*, the poor man's Shangri-La, where he, too, could "fix" himself, like any millionaire, almost. . . .

Scattered through the Mountains since my great-uncle Zissel's time, it was not until the 30's that the kochalein flowered into the big business it is today. Child from its beginnings of the shrunken pocketbook, the decade of the Depression was its opportunity. Suppose stocks plunged downward and the dresses hung

customerless on the racks, a man must still fix himself
—indeed all the more reason. . . .

Today the kochalein population exceeds that of
summer camps and hotels combined.

I know this fact because I recently overheard a
well-known hotel owner admit it, in an argument with
a kochalein entrepreneur.

The hotel man had been citing a long list of il-
lustrious inns and equally sumptuous summer camps,
their history and loyal following.

"Hotel people are hotel people," the hotel man
contended. "Your kochaleiniks are just people who
can't afford a hotel. Give them a few dollars and a taste
of a hotel and they'll never go back to you."

The kochalein owner was wily. "How many rooms
you think in all the hotels and camps in the Mountains?"

The hotel owner deliberated. "Forty thousand."

"*Nu*, and how many kochalein rooms you think?"

The hotel owner bit. "Twenty, twenty-five thousand."

"All right, so I'll agree with you," the kochalein
landlord said. "Forty thousand hotel rooms and twenty-
five thousand kochalein rooms. Now tell me, how many
people live in a hotel room and how many in a kochalein *shtall?*"

That was the end of the argument. It takes
a shrewd man to run a Catskill hotel. He had established the figures, now he had to accept the conclusion.
Anyone knew that in kochaleins, as compared to hotels,
you have twice as many people in half as many rooms.

To those who know it best, the word "kochalein"
means "crowded." "Cook by yourself"—but live together. And what a together!

The price of a hotel room is determined by the

number of people using it. But once a kochalein is rented—it is the same money if mama and the kids come up alone, and it is the same money if the whole family comes along. So one can afford to be a sport. For the Fourth of July week one has brother Jake and his family as guests and two weeks after that Joe and his kids. It sounds very nice, "Come up for a couple weeks to my summer place."

So kochaleins are crowded. That holds for deluxe accommodations, semi-deluxe, ordinary, and subordinary. The differences in classification have to do with how many people use the same bathroom and whether there are private or community facilities for cooking. (It's more trouble, but a lot more fun, if everybody uses the same kitchen.) These classifications, it should be noted, are for researchers only. By common consent of rentiers and renters alike, no kochalein is ever spoken of except as "strictly deluxe."

There are all kinds of sub-classifications, too. But kochaleiniks are not interested in words. They come to fix themselves.

Towards the end of winter, any winter, ads appear in the metropolitan dailies. Something like this:

"BUNGalows, hskpg apts, all impvmts, all spts, 75m N. Y., reasonable."

It's all abbreviated except the reasonable. Uninitiated kochaleiniks sometimes argue about those abbreviations. But it doesn't do any good. If the landlord couldn't win arguments he couldn't stay in business. Not that business, anyway.

I heard one such argument last summer. The potential renter was being a bit critical of the housekeeping potential. The landlord was not amused.

"My own wife keeps house like this," he said. "How many maids you're expecting to bring up?"

How about the "all spts"?

The landlord had a ready answer. "Sure, we're all sports here." When the customers still insisted on specifications, the landlord was not embarrassed. "So what's missing? Polo and horse racing? Such sports we aren't."

That renter must have been an outlander of some sort. He should have known that the sports list at a kochalein is standard—pinochle, mah-jongg, gin rummy, and back-biting. The 75 miles from New York is not too inaccurate. So it's 91 miles from George Washington Bridge. Which means that during the season, in a good, fast car, with a hungry New York City taxi driver at the wheel, you can make it in six hours and twenty minutes.

"Reasonable"? Well, really, what's reasonable these days?

As soon as the ads appear the customers come up to look. They may have spent the last ten summers at the same place and still they come to look. That's a funny thing about kochaleiniks. Some things they never learn. Each year, when they leave, the landlord tells them of next season's wonders. The new swimming pool, the new refrigerators, the new sinks and stoves. And each year the same overflowing brook, the same overflowing refrigerators, sinks, and stoves. But each year they come to look.

First to come up are the cautious souls. They come early, sometimes before the ads appear. They come because they know that the good places go early. And maybe the owner hasn't figured out what kind of a season it will be and will let the first one go cheap. They're silly.

In April and May the second group appears. They just happen to be passing by on a picnic and so they stopped in to take a look. No one is fooled. These middle-of-the-roaders hope that the landlord is getting worried about the lateness of the season, or maybe he's getting soft-hearted, or maybe he has only one left and wants to close his books. They're silly, too.

The gamblers come in June and even early July. They figure that if there is anything unrented this late in the season, they'll pick it up for peanuts. They're just as silly as the rest.

After renting, the next step is moving. There are three groups here too. These groups divide up according to children. One week before school closes half the renters arrive. Their kids are smart—so what if they'll miss a week? And anyway, what can they learn in the last week?

The day after school closes the other two groups come up. The families of the really smart kids—you have to work at being smart—and the households of the not-so-smart ones. Why should you take a chance just for five days?

As for transportation, there are cars, trucks, taxis, station wagons, limousines, and a peculiar vehicle known as a hack. Hacks are 1928 model Cadillacs, Lincolns, or Packards, the biggest sizes made. They appear only during kochalein season. The rest of the year their owners spend in Florida. They can afford it.

The luggage compartments of all bulge with trunks, suitcases, handbags, satchels, Gladstone bags, and old-country wicker *kezinehs*. Strapped on the roofs are baby carriages, playpens, cribs, mattresses, and high chairs. Crushed into the front seat with the driver are the adults—the children ride precariously in the rear on a mound of bedding, dishes, coats, food, and toys.

Police in the back country roads used to do all right with such charges as overloading, freighting without a license, obscuring the driver's vision, and other assorted infractions. But even the police can stand only so much. In one town on Route 17 the officers admit they hide during the first two weeks of September and the last two of June. It isn't worth it, they say.

Arriving at their home-away-from-home, the kochaleiniks unpack while the landlord stands by. He is there to forestall complaints. The newly arrived householders now see that the new bed (guaranteed) was not moved in; that the mattress (absolutely) is the same one they rebelled against last summer; and that the sink (I give you my word) is still rusty. If the landlord waited until mama had the whole list in her head and came looking for him, he'd have trouble. This way, as she calls out her complaints one by one, he escapes trouble with the same answer.

"Don't worry, we'll take care of it as soon as you're settled."

In a kochalein the settling process takes until August 1. After that you're thinking about going home. Obviously, then it's too late to do any major repairs or changes. As for next season, he'll have it all fixed up by then.

To fix yourself and the kids (that's the reason for all this, remember?) you need food, air, and loose clothing. The air is already there and the clothing you start loosening on the way up. So food becomes important.

The first days' meals are no problem. In the load of furniture, clothing, and kids there was a long paper bag. The poundages vary from kochaleinik to kochaleinik, but the ingredients are standard: a dozen large rolls, a pumpernickel, a pound of corned beef, a half pound of pastrami, pickles, mustard, sauerkraut, sour tomatoes, bagel, lox, cheese, and a large smoked white fish. It's quite satisfactory. When this is gone, about the time the husband leaves to go back to work, the real struggle to keep alive begins.

This struggle with the elements takes a good part of the time and thought of the female kochaleinik. (In kochalein country the local farmers and food purveyors are part of the elements.)

Milk is easy to come by. For not a penny a quart more than you pay in the city you can get fresh, whole, country milk. But healthy.

Eggs and chickens are no problem. The landlord or the farmer next door has a few chickens. The eggs are so fresh they're still stuck with feathers and dirt. Once a week, on Thursday or Friday, the local *shochet* comes to kill the chickens with due ceremony. And who needs chicken except on Friday night?

Vegetables, home grown, and staples, city imported, are available from the landlord's own store. It's not really a store. The landlord is the first to admit it. It's a service to the renters run—almost—without profit. The vegetables are good, vine-ripened. They come from the farm down the road. By some peculiarity of capitalist economics they cost just a little more than the same vegetables—picked, packed, and shipped to New York—bought at a high-rent greengrocer's.

The landlord explains it this way, "But this is fresh picked. All the vitamins. It's not worth a penny more?"

Sure it is.

Meats are a bit more complicated. To get kosher meat the women have to go to the Village. (In the Mountains it might be a bustling city of twenty-five thousand with six five-and-ten-cent stores and two movies. But to the kochaleiniks it's always the Village.) The butcher will deliver a phone order but what kind of a *beryeh* will buy a piece of meat without seeing it cut and weighed? Who can trust those butchers?

Twice a week the women go to the Village to shop. Probably they need only two lamb chops for the baby, but they go to shop. In the butcher shop they meet all the other women from all the other kochaleins, all in to see a piece of meat. While they're there they step into the ten-cent store, the department store, and the specialty shoppe to price that shorts and halter set.

Preparing the food involves the real heartbreak. The facilities are limited, the children are underfoot when they should be outside, and four miles away when they should be eating. And there are too many women anyway. The competition is terrific.

This kitchen in one kochalein is in a great, over-built farmhouse. The place is big enough to feed a large hotel. But it has more cooks. It serves fifteen families. Against opposite walls are two rows of stoves, seven on one side, eight on the other. Over each stove is a cupboard. The third wall has five sinks and against the fourth are food closets from floor to ceiling. Each food closet door has large staples with burglar-proof locks. Down the center of the room runs a large work-table. The layout, with some minor differences, is fairly standard.

At breakfast the kitchen is almost seemly. Breakfast depends on so many factors—the age of the children, the weight of the mother, how simply exhausted she is, and what did she do last night. Lunchtime varies too. And anyway, did anyone come up to the country to spend the day in the kitchen? The kids won't sit still long enough to eat a hot meal. The store carries several well-known brands of salami, baloney, and wurst.

Suppers follow a weekly pattern. Monday isn't so

bad. The mothers are tired from the weekend and there's always something left over from Sunday. It doesn't spoil in one day. Tuesday, some energy returns and hot meals appear. Wednesday is movie night in the Village. And when it's hot what can be better than sour cream and farmer cheese? Thursday you eat lightly because tomorrow is Friday. On Friday—the men are coming—all week they ate in restaurants, you don't know what *chazerei*—and there's only two days to fix them up.

On Friday it starts after a hurried lunch. Fifteen women assisted by assorted older daughters and female relatives working over fifteen stoves and five sinks. Plus a recapitulation of the week's events, mama's favorite recipe, and that Mrs. Field down the road. As an overtone, each cook deprecates her own *meichel* while all tied up inside trying to outdo her neighbors.

The job is harder than it appears at first. The competition. Friday night these women all have chicken because the *shochet* comes only once a week—and once a week you need chicken, no? Fifteen different ways of preparing chicken, each way better than the other fourteen. It's impossible in the city—in the country, in a kochalein kitchen, it happens.

There are other niceties and excitements on Friday in the kitchen. That's the day for healing old wounds, ending established feuds—and starting new ones. Fifteen female cooks and at least fifteen female helpers—it's impossible.

Mrs. Miller has just pulled the innards out of a chicken and she runs to the sink with her hands held far out in front of her. She wants wash water and she wants it fast. (The only drawback to killed-on-the-farm chicken is that it comes complete.) The first sink she gets to, they're all taken, is the one where Mrs. Berg is carefully running cold water through a sieve filled with *lokshen* for *kugel*. Mrs. Berg cannot stop this process because if she does the *kugel* won't have the proper crispness on the outside and the proper softness on the inside. Mrs. Miller, however, can't wait because her hands are so dirty and smelly she'll get sick. That's enough to start this week's feud.

The words that start the imbroglio are unimportant. They depend on the chronological age of the participants, their ages relative to each other, and their respective social strata both at home and in the kochalein. (Mostly the kochalein is a sound democratic force, a leveler, with divergent social and educational groups meeting on an even plane. Mr. Berg is a cloaks operator, Mr. Miller is a candy-store owner, Mr. Levine owns a dress factory, and Mr. Goldquist is a doctor.)

The Miller-Berg feud is on. When Mr. Miller and Mr. Berg arrive that Friday evening they are at a loss. All last weekend they had played pinochle and all the way up on the train they had discussed pinochle. Now their wives get mad if the men as much as look at each other.

On Mrs. Berg's left is Mrs. Blatt. Two Fridays ago they had a misunderstanding about accidentally spilling some hot chicken fat over some cold tomatoes. Since then there had been a cold, voiceless haughtiness between them. But tomatoes are tomatoes and a *kugel* is a *kugel*—right is right. So Mrs. Berg explains the whole thing to Mrs. Blatt. Mrs. Blatt is properly sympathetic. She remembers a ruined *kugel* herself.

For all that the dinners get cooked—and well cooked. At seven they are simmering redolently on fifteen stoves awaiting fifteen work-weary and restaurant-starved husbands.

Men going to the country for a weekend pack according to a peculiar pattern. Their clothes they carry in packages, while their suitcases bulge with treasure from the delicatessens and appetizing stores. Blame the landlord—he doesn't hold with food from the city. It's not that he minds losing the business, but bringing food from the city is a personal reflection on his prices and quality. City food brings mice, too. The landlord's displeasure is important when it comes to small repairs— the rent is already paid. So the lox and corned beef ride in the suitcase.

When the men have paid their three dollars a head for a three-mile ride from the station they look for their wives in the line of women on the porch. It's not always easy to find your own wife right away. The clothes always differ from last week's ensemble, and are unfamiliar anyway.

The men wash and change into slacks and sport shirts, the dining room fills up, and the festivities begin. (Mr. Green doesn't change into a sport shirt. He wears a white shirt and tie all weekend. There's a Mr. Green at every kochalein.) It's a close fit in the dining room on Friday night. The old customers are near the windows and near the kitchen. The new Mrs. Litwin, it's her first year, is over in the corner. Mr. Litwin is inconsiderate. First he complains that by the time his wife brings the soup it might as well be cold borsht. Then he complains that it's so hot in his corner that everything tastes fried.

The decibel level in the room is high. Fifty per cent adult women noise. Forty-nine per cent piping children noise. And one per cent "yes," "hum," and "uhhuh" from the men.

After supper the men drift outside and lower themselves onto the porch rockers. In the dark they surreptitiously loosen their belts. If their wives have really outdone themselves, they open the top pants button. The women and children—that is, those children whose parents believe in the *potch* and *frosk* method of raising children—clear and wash the dishes. A half hour of the clean piney air and the men are ready for the evening's entertainment.

At an unspoken signal they drift back inside to the dining room. In a few moments the tables have been rearranged and two large poker games, six pinochle sets, three gin groups, and one persistent mah-jongg game are going. One foursome plays bridge. They don't really belong.

Shortly after the games are started the windows are closed against drafts. As the night progresses the cigarette, pipe, and cigar smoke solidifies. At twelve there is a break for coffee, tea, and cake. Of course, there's always some *balagoleh* who demands a thick sandwich. The refreshments do not interrupt the important business of cards. But eventually they all go to bed; you sleep well after a day in the country.

Saturday night's entertainment is different. It's a peculiar fact, but with all the space in the Mountains, ninety-three per cent of all kochaleins are within walking distance of a hotel or summer camp that has professional entertainment and a dance band. One explanation is that the rent of kochaleins is determined in part by the quality of this nearby—and free—entertainment. One enterprising entrepreneur even used it in his advertising. But that's misrepresentation. He couldn't guarantee entrance.

In the old days—at least eight years ago—hotel owners didn't mind the Saturday evening visitors. True, they took all the front seats at the show, they filled the bar with beer drinkers and discouraged the Scotch drinkers, but it helped to have some men around. It looks bad when most of the couples on the dance floor are women. But like all good things, it was overdone. This explains why high-priced, high-entertainment-level summer places are more closely guarded than Fort Knox. It doesn't help, though. Koch-aleiniks are smarter than guards.

This perennial struggle has been known to precipitate serious diplomatic incidents. There are two fine camps up in the Mountains within a mile of each other. One belongs to an international union, the other to a school. The school camp, open to anyone with the steep price, is known for its shows. It is, therefore, surrounded by a stout wire fence and patrolled by private guards.

One summer Saturday night the union president, a frequent visitor to the White House, walked over to the neighboring camp. His union and the school were quite friendly, and he knew the manager of the camp personally. A private policeman, complete with Sam Browne belt and large pistol, stopped him at the gate and asked for his registration card.

"I'm the president of the union over there," the labor leader explained.

"Can't get in unless you're registered," the cop answered brusquely. He knew all, or almost all, the dodges of kochaleiniks.

"But I'm Phillip Philipson, president of the union," the visitor cried angrily.

"I don't care if you're the President of the United States. You can't see our show for nothing." The cop was a Republican.

They say that Mr. Philipson hasn't visited his friends since.

Too bad the union president didn't succeed in getting in. He would have found most of the adult population of the dozen kochaleins in the neighborhood calmly watching the show—many of them members of his own union.

How they get in is a secret. Some know the right combination of dress and manner to awe the cop. Some have boats cached away and know of secret landing places. There are even claims that kochaleiniks train their children to open secret holes in the steel barricades. But mostly it's a secret. And when the camp owners discover the latest loophole, the visitors invent a new one. For every new defense there is always a new, more powerful offense.

Although the kochalein comes alive to the husband only on weekends, it still goes on during the week. In his absence, it fixes his wife and children. Most important are the wives, in kochaleins as elsewhere.

Some wives take the whole-summer-in-the-country idea seriously. They shepherd the kids through planned activities, play games with them, sit in the sun, and go swimming. The first year they even bring their tennis rackets along. This kind of progressivism is accepted by the other women with knowing smiles. They were young once themselves. But can you live and bring up children with books?

As for older and wiser women, either they play mah-jongg when they should be taking care of their children, or they play the latest variation of gin rummy until long-after-they-should-have-been-in-bed-already. For casual dress, bathing suits are worn. But the bathing suits cannot be of knitted cloth. They must be of woven material. I think they're called dressmaker suits. For more formal occasions they wear shorts and halters or slacks and halters. Usually the ones who wear slacks should wear shorts and the ones who wear shorts should stay home.

The conversation is pretty stylized, too. "Did the baby go from baby foods to junior foods and why doesn't my Leslie eat like your kids." "David got the same spots after eating tomatoes as your Philip got from peaches." "I could never use Birdseye diapers on my babies. They have such tender skins."

In between there's always a youngster who comes crying because he lost his toy or because he didn't lose his toy.

Saddest denizen of the kochalein is the husband on vacation. Two weeks of ease and comfort and not another human being around who even cares how the Dodgers are making out, or who can intelligently meld a pinochle hand. He gets up early because the kids are in the next room and the walls are paper thin. Fourteen days in the whole year when he can honestly sleep late, and he has to spend them at a kochalein.

During the day he wanders about looking, he doesn't know for what. Nothing is as it should be. In the evening you can't get a *News* or *Mirror* for a dollar and in the morning there's some kind of skinny paper with a strange name. He plays with the kids for a while but there are too many of them, and you can't slap someone else's kids. So he goes and talks to the landlord about the price of new sinks. As if he cares.

In the afternoon he tries to take a nap. It's easier to sleep in the zoo. Later he wanders into the kitchen for a glass of tea to pass the time away. Once inside the door, once he hears the noises of thirty women preparing dinner, he rushes out. It's a long time till Friday when the rest of the men come out.

Lately some of the progressive mothers have introduced new "improvements." In one community they now have weekly "cookouts." It's for the kids. And the kids weren't happy before they invented "cookouts"?

First they badgered the landlord into building an outdoor grill. Now he has the job of providing charcoal for the fire. In mid-morning of cookout day the women start gathering before the grill. As soon as they are all gathered they break away to bring half their belongings to the cookout. They bring most of what is in the icebox, also tables, chairs, silverware, and dishes, plus things to keep the children quiet.

For years these same women sterilized bottles, toys, and everything that went in or near their kids. Now they drag them through the cinders to the cookout.

No one knows how to build a fire, so either there's a roaring furnace that engulfs everything on the grill or a puny little flame that won't even warm your hands. And while the fire is abuilding the kids are underfoot and half inside the firebox. Why don't women ever get ulcers?

Main cookout dish is hamburgers. Very healthy when cooked on an outdoor grill. These hamburgers, we would have you know, are made of the finest beefsteak chopped. Unhappily, they are charred black on the outside and dripping raw on the inside. But in the country it's healthy.

From all this you guess that the march of progressive education and scientific child upbringing is beginning to be felt by the world of the kochalein. The cookout is only a harbinger of aberrations to come, novelties that if continued will wipe out the whole *geshmak* of kochalein living. For either you have kochaleins or you have Dr. Gesell. You can't have both.

XI *Milton Klonsky*

The Trojans of Brighton Beach

When my grandfather was alive he could walk up and down six thousand years as though it were a little narrow room; for him, all history could be contracted to the span of memory; and, since the Jews were the People of History, the memory of each one was a monad which represented the history of all. The time was always now. When anything happened in the house or the neighborhood, he could fish up a correspondence from the Bible at the drop of a line. If you asked him a simple question he would answer by a parable; and all his questions were usually rhetorical, like God's own. The Greek philosophers thought of God as an Engineer or an Architect, and the Christian theologians as a Judge, but the Jews made him One of the Family —and I think the God of the old days must have been like him, a brooder in dark corners, minding everybody's business and keeping himself aloof, jealous, stroking his ego like a beard. *Olav hasholem.*

Anyway, my grandfather's insight was true in at least one respect: fifty centuries after Moses my family still had traces of the old desert restlessness in their blood. Of the true breed of *luftmensh!* After living up in the air for a whole year, they would pack up the apartment like a tent and move off to a greener oasis, quieter, where the people are more refined, from Staten Island to the Bronx to Manhattan to Brooklyn (somehow by-passing Queens) so that with each shift I had to pull up my stakes in the gang and the neighborhood and start all over again.

By the time we finally settled in Brooklyn in the late summer of 1930, I had absorbed so much street savvy up and down town that I was already something of a Culture Hero, with new accents, new games, new angles. But with or without Culture—to be a new kid in a strange neighborhood is an all-day lonely drag. We lived in a lower-middle-class section of Brighton Beach dominated by one gang of kids, the Trojans, who would have nothing to do with me.

At first I didn't mind eating cold chicken by myself, since there was so much to see and do. From where we lived I could smell Coney Island in the daytime frying in its deep fat; and at night, of course, there were Wonder Wheels, Freak Shows, Arcades, Coasters, Whips and Reels in a blaze of neon down to the slums. On the other side was Manhattan Beach, "a community of prosperous homes and gardens," fronting on Sheepshead Bay, which was filled with fishing boats and yachts. Brighton itself was the middle-class axis of this seesaw, sometimes tipping its families up and sometimes down. And in those early days of the depression, when capitalism was afraid of its own shadow and there was nothing to fear but fear itself, I could sense the anxiety of everyone to keep his place on the balance.

Until the cold weather came, I spent the days hunting and exploring.

But nothing can be more barren than a summer resort in winter, especially when you're without friends. Loneliness drives you out of the house and back up again—"*Et faim* [*fait*] *saillir le loup des bois*," as Villon said, who knew what it meant. You can read the old books over once more, Bomba the Jungle Boy, Poppy Ott, Tom Swift, Baseball Joe, etc., but there's no one around with whom you can trade and discuss the fine points. You daydream. At night the "heys" and whistles of kids aren't for you. When you see them in school, or after school in the candy store wearing their blue flannel jackets with red blazon: TROJANS, there's no familiar greeting, only a scraping of curious foils—but their eyes glance you through and through.

Any move you may make toward rapprochement in this stage must be lightfoot, delicate, since at the least blunder in protocol you can lose face, or be tied with a nickname for years like a tin can to a dog's tail. They ignore you, they cut you out. And then the contumely of *nebichs*, mama's boys, and small fry! Your pride rebounds like a billiard ball wincing from buff to buff in angles of refraction.

But at last from hanging around so much, the day does come when one of the Trojans is missing from a punchball game and they need an extra man. If you're any good, you're in. And now that the breach is opened you learn their names, the same set as on any other block: of course a Peewee, a Fatso, a Lefty; and a Herb, Willie, Sy, Izzy, Delmore, Manny, Dave, etc. There's always a sissy and a tough guy, a wisecracker, a bully, a nice guy, a blowhard. All of them size you up more closely, watching the way you throw a ball and your style at the plate with questions in their eyes: Can they beat you up in a fight? Will you take their place on the team? These issues can be settled only after months of playing ball together and one or two fistfights. If you can beat up Willie, and Willie can beat up Sy, then you can beat up Sy and your rank is proven by syllogism—but still, the social equilibrium is so unstable that the sissy, whom everyone despised, might suddenly shoot up to a hero or the wisecracker lose his verve. Because I had acquired so much outside experience, I already had an edge sharp enough to penetrate the Trojan enclaves. Ulysses was needed no less than Hector. And when, for example, I introduced the game of slugball from the Bronx, my position became really solid, since any new game is a victory in the constant battle against big-city cramp.

The streets of New York must have been virgin once, artless and unenhanced. But, by our time, the vacant lots and fields where the kids used to play baseball and football had already been supplanted by five- and six-story apartment houses until there wasn't a gap for miles. Where and how to play what was a problem. Parks were crowded with mothers wheeling baby carriages, and the schoolyards were taken up by girls playing potsy and skipping rope:

> *One, two, three alarey*
> *I spy Mrs. Sary. . . .*

It was no use trying to drive them out of the yards by terror, they would run to the custodian on any provocation. There was only one thing to do: take over the street. The brickwork and moldings of buildings, stoops, abutments, cornices, rungs on fire-escape ladders, the squares of sidewalks, even sewer covers were adapted to some sport which was then given a set of rules and a name.

Slug-ball was so conceived. The day I first introduced it was a hot afternoon in August, and a few of us
were sitting around on the curb with nothing to do, wondering whether we should hitch a ride on the back of
a trolley to Prospect Park or gyp some candy from Ep-
stein's store on the corner when, suddenly, I remembered slug-ball. A smash! Unless the war has broken
the great tradition, the ball is still being slugged in
Brooklyn.

Slug-ball is played off the sides of apartment
houses on a court that is four sidewalk boxes in area,
with the cracks serving as boundary lines. As one of a
large family of games such as stoopball, boxball, hit-
the-crack, etc., which are enclosed and restricted by the
sidewalk, it demands an ability to maneuver freely in
tight Mondrian forms. Weight and strength are no advantage: only celerity, jump, a shrewd eye, and a quick
hand. The kid who knows how to slice the ball and to
cut corners with precision can trim anyone bigger and
stronger than himself.

In the country, positions would have been reversed.
But that is the difference between the City Character
and the Country Character, which is, really, a difference
in state of mind and disposition of soul. Between the
two there is a breach as wide as that which divides
Plato and Aristotle. The geometrical forms of the city
impress themselves upon the consciousness of anyone
who grows up with them; they impose a way of seeing
and thinking. But the country is natural, that is to say,
raw, contingent, unassorted and particular, and must
itself be informed by the mind. If a ball is hit on a
grass field it can strike a leaf or a stone and shoot off
in any direction; but on the street, against hard ce-
ment, the angle of return is determined strictly by the
angle of delivery, so that any kid with *chutzpah*, who

knows all the angles, can always come out ahead of the game.

We played hard with a will to win so strong it willed itself. Sometimes we became so engrossed by a punchball or a stickball game that night would fall without anyone's being aware of it, and only our fathers coming home from work cranky, on the El, or the cross yells of mothers from both sides of the street, frantic over dinner growing cold, could ever break it up. If any one of us tried to leave in the middle of a tight score, he had to fight his way out.

When the immie (marble) season rolled around in the spring, a fever of acquisitiveness would erupt over the whole neighborhood, and we would play for them by day and by night under the street lamps. We pitched them along the curb, letting nothing stand in our way, sometimes scooping through puddles of mud and even under parked cars. My hands would be grimy and warted from the gutter; I smelled of the gutter— but O the sweet stink of property! To fondle in my pocket the cool, round smug glass immies like cats' eyes, purple, green, orange, lemon; heavy reelies made of steel; transparent glassies; milkies as pure as the white of egg; to feel them there was a capitalistic joy that transcended and eclipsed the vulgar interests of Rothschild or J. P. Morgan.

Sudden passions for checkers, bottlecaps, political-campaign buttons, the tops of Dixie cups, would rise and fall like jags on the stock market. The currency didn't matter much since everything was redeemable at the street exchange, six bottle caps for one immie, two buttons for a checker, etc., depending upon the season and the fluctuations of supply and demand. Sometimes the bottom would drop out of the Dixie cup market, leaving those who had speculated in them with a stock of worthless cardboard. But immies and checkers were always secure. You couldn't go wrong with immies and checkers.

No matter what went on at the curb—immies, hopscotch, ringelevio, or slug-ball—they were all attacked by mothers who complained because they had to complain, and, even more, by the old ones, those *zaydehs* with embroidered *yarmelkas* and their white beards worn like orders upon their chests. They wondered whether we were Jews or a new kind of *shaygetz*. On a sunny day they would take down their chairs and sit out on the street, massive and still as Druids, rarely exchanging a word with one another, but watching us with their slow eyes. At such times we would always take care to go to the other end of the street, as far as possible from their Klieg-light scrutiny like the stare of conscience. But sometimes we couldn't help meeting one of them coming from the synagogue, and then we would all have to stand by sheepishly while he asked us questions in Yiddish about our mothers and fathers, how much Talmud we knew, etc., until he left us, shaking his head from side to side.

They cramped our style, these old ones. If we wanted to play a game which involved some roughhouse, like Johnny-on-the-pony—in which one side would line up against the wall with their heads under each other's legs and their backs up, while the other team across the street would take running leaps and pile down hard on top of them, trying to break the bucking pony—for such games we had to go out of the neighborhood. And even then we could never feel secure. If anyone were hurt the news would surely be blown like a cloud over every family on the block and a gray continual nagging would rain indoors for weeks.

Nevertheless, we couldn't give up these games.

Our text was not from Isaiah, but the Book of Kings. To the North were the Falcons: a gang of kids with names like Pat, Mike, Danny, Frankie. And to the South were the Wolverines: kids called Tony, Angelo, Pete, Rocky. When they burst out of their own neighborhoods and descended on ours, as they frequently did in rough gangs, we had to stand up to them.

Halloween was the traditional time for street fights. And the night before, we filled all the silk stockings we could find with flour, broke up crates and boxes and rubbed colored chalk on the slats of wood. In the morning when we met one another we compared our weapons, whacking them on the sidewalk and on fireplugs in anticipation. We were never disappointed, they always came.

"Here they come!" The street contracts like a heart. There on the corner, two or three Philistines, standing close together to pool their courage, survey the street. Behind them is the rest of the gang, the bigger and tougher kids whose faces we know from the past. Soon these too come from around the corner with a swaggering nonchalance. We exchange insults.

> They: (personal) Hey Moe, ya fadder sleeps wid ya mudder.
> We: (political-satirical) Hey Angelo, watsadama ya no lika da Mussoleen?
> They: (religious) Hey Ike, we got what da rabbi cut off.
> We: (the last word) Send it back to da Pope; he needs it.

Suddenly we are caught unprepared by a fusillade of prune pits which they had concealed in their pockets. We rush them, and they fall back. They rush us and we fall back. A free-for-all begins. And the hulla-

baloo arouses the whole neighborhood. Somebody's
mother opens a window and heaves out a pail of water
—*pishachts!* A butcher, leaving his store and his customers, charges out in his bloody apron to separate us.
Suddenly someone spies the blue coat of a policeman
racing toward us, and the alarm is CHICKeeeee! We
scatter.

It was all over in fifteen minutes. Later when we
emerged from basements and lobbies, still pumping for
breath, we sat down on the curb and crowed. We didn't
give a hoot for the interdictions and naggings and cur-
fews which would follow. In that first release of tension and sweet lift of gravity after battle, none of these
things weighed a feather.

When the Old Guard heard about it, as they always did somehow, they were triumphant—we were
growing up hooligans, bums, outcasts, Cossacks! They
painted a picture of our decline and fall stage by stage
down to the steaming fosse of Perdition, until some-
day we would be eating pig and pulling beards on the
streets of New York.

The issue between them and us was drawn. And
any kid who put on more than an outward show of religion was regarded as queer, on their own side. Our
fathers mediated, improvisionary patchers, trying to
play both ends against the middle. The dazzle of America was still so bright in their eyes, it blinded them to
what was happening on our side of the street. Although
it was their generation which had inverted the Messi-
anic hope of the Jews into socialism, they could still
not let go of the old ways. And who could have blamed
them if sometimes they mistook the vision of Elijah for
the figure of Uncle Sam with his glad hand, high hat,
and star-spangled vest? Confused, troubled, they were
pulled by the old and the new, but, as time was on

our side, they let us have our way which was more and more becoming theirs as well. And when *zaydeh* died, the old life he represented passed with him.

(His picture in a gilt frame was first hung in the parlor; but after a few years we found it didn't look "nice" with the new furniture, and so *zaydeh* was relegated to the bedroom. A Van Gogh print was put in his place.)

American holidays began to displace the Hebrew, just as American newspapers displaced the *Day* and the *Forward*. The Friday night candles disappeared, and the two distinct sets of ware, one for meat dishes, one milk, were washed in the same sink. I remember— I am ashamed—I would shush my parents whenever they spoke Yiddish on the subway or the street. Everybody knew that the more Americanized families had the jump on success, and who didn't want to be a success? Don't be a sucker. $ was the sign of the Good Life.

Of course, certain of the more important Hebrew holidays were still celebrated: Rosh Hashonah, Yom Kippur, Passover. When *zaydeh* was still alive and could fire the four great questions at us over the matzoh and the wine, the Passover had a holy zeal.

Then it was: *l'shana habaa b'ara d'Yisrael.*

But now: This year in Flatbush; next in Forest Hills.

For two or three days of the festival there would be nothing but matzoh on the table—matzoh meal, matzoh balls, fried matzoh, egg matzoh, whole wheat matzoh, matzoh plain, until the whole family was thoroughly fed up with matzoh in any form. We longed for our daily bread. And once, this was the turning point, I think it was my eleventh or twelfth year, I was secretly given money in the middle of Passover and sent to an Italian grocery a few blocks away to buy a loaf. To avoid meeting anyone I knew I plotted a long route to the store, and I even carried an old knapsack to hide it from the neighbors. Everyone on the block must have been doing the same.

It was the neighbors who had to be placated by a show of religion, the neighbors who minded everybody else's business; and as for God—he was a very distant relative who never visited us any more, in business for himself.

My friends and I were at that time attending the Talmud Torah in preparation for Bar Mitzvah. Three afternoons a week after school, we would sit cheek to cheek with an old rabbi who had a beard like steel wool, swaying and chanting with a copy of the Talmud open before us, he in his cracking bass, we in our rising treble. When things were going well, he would sit in his velvet chair, his eyes half shut, picking his great bearded nose with his little finger while he mumbled after us. But whenever the noises of the street pulled us away from the lesson, we were pulled back again by a rough rap on the knuckles or a cuff on the side of the head. We were glad to get up and get out.

The year of the Bar Mitzvahs—then we were alive! We were climbing the last hump of childhood. From an inner distance, we could hear the reverberations of sex growing closer and louder. Some of my friends were actually dressing up (no more knickers), and even—this was prodigious—giving up a punchball game to hang around with the girls. The girls themselves had known the exhilaration of heels and silk stockings long before, the little harpies, waiting to pay back the old grudges.

In that twilight period when the values of the adult world came into collision with our own, some of us surrendered to them entirely, others tried to compromise, and there were some who resisted until as late as sixteen, joining groups of small fry. For the first time, the family position and fortune made a difference in our own status. Even a touch of anti-Semitism came in—it did not pay to look too Jewish, especially for the girls. There was, also, a breakup of caste—the athletes felt the mace of power growing soft in their hands, while the rich, the smart, and the merely good-looking felt it stiffening in theirs.

I remember the whole time as a continual bazaar of parties and celebrations. Every other week, one after the other, I saw my friends rise up and declare their manhood while the rest of us sat in the back rows, apart from the relatives, giggling and throwing spitballs, with our *yarmelkas* slanted on the side of our heads at a sharp angle.

So then, we were admitted.

But where? For what had we been prepared? Certainly not for the ritual despair of our forefathers, the Wailing Wall, the lost Temple and the rest, although we knew we could never resign from the old contract with the past, our long history bonded by memory and always annealed in the present. But what was our point of view?

What, in short, was the angle?

A New York question, rhetorical, rebounding from its own answer! It was New York we were prepared for, and New York, half-Jewish, which took us in.

New York! Ghetto of Eden! We go back always where we come from, in memory, to and from ourselves. The things that made us what we are made you. With your five bright boroughs of a superlative quincunx and your streets laid out in gyres, diamonds, squares, and rhombs like those perfect forms which Plato thought lay in the burrows of the Mind and which Nature could only roughly approximate, to see you is an intellectual joy, to think of you is to be reidentified with oneself!

XII *Ruth Glazer*

The Jewish Delicatessen

When I was sixteen my father became convinced he would never make his fortune as a milkman and decided to give the free enterprise system a chance to show what it could do for him. Armed with a capital of some $2,000 scraped together from a meager bank account, loans on insurance policies, and advances from friends and relatives, he began to look about for a suitable business. Finally, after lengthy visits from the aforementioned friends and relatives bearing sound advice consisting mainly of shining examples from their own life stories, plus some complicated reasoning and intuitive thinking of his own, he decided to move out to a new community in Long Island and open "a real Jewish delicatessen."

Now, "a real Jewish delicatessen" in New York, where it assumes its most specialized form, can mean at least three different things. In this respect, New York and a few other old Jewish communities on the Eastern seaboard are unique. Nowhere else in the country does the delicatessen exist in its pure, pungent form, an entity built around the sale of ten meats. (Except perhaps in Los Angeles, where not long ago two such institutions were rumored to have been established to meet the needs of the Broadway émigré groups in Hollywood, tired of flying delicatessen in from the Gaiety.)

In Chicago, a metropolis with 300,000 Jews, you can get a hot pastrami or corned beef sandwich in eateries which call themselves delicatessens. But they are sad imitations. They even have a soda fountain in the front! In Washington, I have seen an attenuated delicatessen hidden away behind a grocery store. In interior New Jersey, you can get your franks and beans in stores whose main business is the sale of liquor. Reliable sources from the hinterland inform me that when the craving for salami becomes too strong to bear it is sometimes possible to have one imported via the kosher butcher in town. But there is cold joy in a salami sandwich eaten outside the steamy atmosphere of a New York kosher delicatessen.

My father, then, had his choice of three types of delicatessen. The most primitive is the *shlacht* store, generally found in the market sections of the great old Jewish settlements on the lower East Side, in Brownsville, and in the East Bronx. Now and then one will crop up like a poor relation on Upper Broadway or even the Grand Concourse.

Its essence is in its simplicity. Around the walls of what is generally a small square store are ranged open wooden counters. Suspended from hooks hang salamis, cold pastramis, rolled beefs, and bundles of frankfurters. On the walls are a few shallow shelves containing a meager supply of the traditional accessories—beans, ketchup, some crackers, sometimes soup. The proprietor stands in the midst of this dominion using now one counter, now another, depending upon the location of the particular meat called for. The main attraction of these stores—for there is little of the warmth and geniality of the other types in this form—lies in their cut-rate prices, sometimes as much as one-half of the going rate. Generally the meat is "Jewish" but not kosher. A nice distinction, which has grown in popularity.

My father, though, had no taste for the rough and ready quality of the *shlacht* store. So he said the neighborhood was too "refined" for it. But another unspoken reason motivated him. Now that he was becoming a "businessman," he wanted a new, shiny, "up-to-date" store, something which by its opulent exterior would reflect the wealth and economic position he hoped to attain.

He passed on to consider the second, and major, variant—the kosher delicatessen proper. In the last twenty years it has seen many changes. But outside of superficialities like fluorescent lighting, refrigeration, and curved glass storefronts, it has deviated little from the pattern set down by some unknown progenitor, and it has shrugged off most of the advances of modern science. The food is still bad for the digestion, vitaminless and delicious. In the window is a steaming grill, warming knishes and frankfurters to be eaten on the spot. Then comes a diminutive beer bar, generally crowded with various extraneous items—cigar boxes or plates for the frankfurters—producing a very unbarlike effect despite the brass rail. Past the bar is a high combination showcase and cutting counter. In your ordinary *goyish* delicatessen the meat lies cold and pale behind the frosted glass of a refrigerated case. The customer points to a spiritless and limp roll of yellowish-gray meat and says, "Give me a quarter of a pound of liverwurst."

Contrast the kosher delicatessen! Facing a clear glass (sometimes, it must be confessed, not so clear) lies a succulent variety of rosy and warm meats in a never-varying order. You may visit every delicatessen in New York and not one will fail to have *first* in line its battery of ten or fifteen salamis, on the little raised platform facing the glass, ranged in three or four rows, one on top of the other; followed by rolled beef, the tongues, a few cold pastramis (for decoration, since pastrami is always served hot, sliced to order, from a steam box); the two trays of frankfurters—one of "specials," the short fat ones, one of the "regulars," the long thin ones; and finally a turkey. A smaller and rarer variety of frankfurter (extinct since the war) came in two sizes: the cocktail frankfurter, about as big as your thumb, and the "lilies," about half that size. "Lilies," research reveals, is short for "lilliputians." Sometimes the pans of cole slaw and potato salad are incorporated into this display. More often they are on the "back bar," the narrow counter behind the proprietor. Lying on the wooden cutting board is the inevitable corned beef which is always just about one half gone. And invariably on the glass-topped counter is a plate with small chunks of salami. In the old days the plate always carried a sign, "A Nickel a Shtickel." (A most convenient —and profitable—way of disposing of the ends of the salami, too.) This immortal rhyme succumbed during the war to the free verse of "Have a Nosh—10c." The poetic spirit of the industry was not to be quenched by this loss, however. A substitute slogan appeared all over the city right after the outbreak of the war: "Send a Salami to Your Boy in the Army."

While the delicatessen is to be found in neighborhoods of every economic level, the meats that are sold are luxury products. Even during the depression they averaged about a dollar a pound.

Mustard may be something you can take or leave, but in a work on the delicatessen store it requires some mention. To put it flatly, mustard is as necessary to delicatessen as—ham is to eggs, to revert to the American scene. Many is the customer who has come back mournfully to report, "The delicatessen was probably wonderful. But I couldn't even enjoy it. No mustard." Let me hasten to state here that the mustard which is given away free with every order is of a kind which is impossible to duplicate in any mere manufactured, bottled, commercial brand selling one million jars a year. And the storekeeper knows it. He can't say, "Oh, you must have had a jar around." There is no use evading the point. The corned beef, the pastrami, the tongue may have been the most succulent which ever left his store. But without mustard only the lightest whisper of its possibilities emerges. What is the secret of this mustard, its sharp, sour, delicious tang? A little cold pickle brine. Stirred into the crock of thick prepared mustard, its original function was to serve as what our genteel Shopping News ladies would call, genteelly, a "stretcher." But the unwitting originator created that for which men will fight. Haven't we all seen letters from the boys in the service saying, "All I want is a corned beef sandwich, and don't forget the mustard"?

Traditionally, mustard is distributed free with all purchases of delicatessen. The purchaser of a large quantity of meat will get a gill's worth in a little white cardboard box mysteriously labeled "Ice Cream." But even the customer who comes in for a quarter of a pound is not forgotten. He is given a "toot" of mustard. A "toot" is made of a square of waxed, mustard-color paper, which is twisted into a cone, filled with mustard, and then folded shut. Every delicatessen storekeeper makes his own with great speed and uniformity. I must point out that "toots" are made not only with an eye to mechanical perfection, but also with an eye to, shall we say, thrift. A little extra tug at the bottom of the cone before it is finished will reduce the volume by as much as 50 per cent.

The counter, though, is only one half of a real delicatessen establishment. The other half is the "restaurant." This is made up of a few tables and chairs, depending on the amount of room left after the counter has been installed. Originally marble-topped, the tables have attempted to improve along with fluorescent lighting and refrigeration. Now we see colored formica tops, and some elaborate establishments even use tablecloths.

But the kosher type of delicatessen did not suit my father, either. He had long been anti-clerical and was even known to have eaten ham sandwiches in his youth; and "anyhow," he said, "I don't want to have any business with rabbis snooping around my store to inspect whether it's kosher or not. I'd like to have a nickel for every kosher delicatessen that sells packages of bacon under the counter. Believe me, this'll be more kosher than some of those stores run by those *alte yiddlach* with *yarmelkes.*"

My father's third alternative, the non-kosher but Jewish delicatessen, is now probably the most numerous. This type differs, deliberately, in only the most subtle ways from the kosher delicatessen. It looks exactly the same, smells exactly the same, and the pastrami sandwiches lack neither juiciness nor flavor. But the neon kosher sign is missing from the window. For many years proprietors of this new type of delicatessen were in the haibt of substituting the word *wurshtge-*

sheft in Hebrew characters. This formidable word strung across half the window would seem to leave no room for doubt in the minds of the uninitiated that this was a very kosher delicatessen indeed. But, finally, in response to pressure by a group of rabbis acting on behalf of the kosher delicatessen storekeepers, a city ordinance forbade this practice as misrepresentation. The new terminology which is rapidly gaining favor in the trade is "kosher-style."

While the kosher delicatessens will serve only tea or soda pop in bottles as beverages, in the non-kosher delicatessen you can get coffee with cream, and butter on your bread if you insist on it. But the resistance by the proprietors has been fierce. In the six years that I spent behind a delicatessen store counter I rarely heard the cry, "Hot pastrami. Butter the bread." When it happened, we would ask to have the individual pointed out. My father, whose respect for tradition was very strong, would refuse to engage in such obscene practices, and would generally tell the waiter—"Give her a pat of butter, and let her butter the bread herself." Added to the display of meats in the *wurshtgesheft* is also a real roast beef (a non-kosher cut of meat). Most will not go so far as to include a ham, but I have seen even that in stores located in newer neighborhoods.

In earlier years the menu of the delicatessen was simplicity itself: franks and beans, any kind of delicatessen meat fried with eggs, sandwiches, and that aristocrat of dishes—a plate of cold cuts (consisting principally of hot meats). As time has gone by the list of dishes available from the kitchen now covers three or four pages of a printed bill-of-fare. "Delicious home-cooked meals, kosher style, like mother used to make" is a sign featured in most delicatessens today.

With the growth of the restaurant, various by-products of the counter which had formerly been sold at a discount found their way into the kitchen. Take tongue, for example. Tongue has always sold at a premium, averaging twenty-five cents more on a pound than the other meats. There is a very good reason. A beef tongue is perhaps three inches high for two-thirds of its length. It then tapers off to a thin point, perhaps a half-inch high. Whereas the meat in the wide section is light pink and fine grained, the tip is dark red and tough. Every customer who comes in for even a quarter of a pound demands, with justice, "center-cut." The problem was disposal of the tips of the tongues. It became customary to sell them to people who had dogs, at 10c a piece. But then some genius hit upon the omelette. Consider the difference between the frank "tongue and eggs, pancake style" and the ever so subtle omelette. In the former each slice of tongue gazes openly into the diner's face, its origins clearly discernible. But hidden in the folds and fluff of the omelette, the ancestry of the bits of meat is hardly so evident.

Since dairy dishes are not forbidden to the kosher-style store, a full selection of salads, fruit with sour cream, cheese and fish dishes is offered. All are served with bread and butter. But my mother could never get used to the idea of cutting a swiss cheese on the machine where a salami had lain but a moment before. After a while we all decided that we absolutely had to have another slicing machine—for the corned beef. We finally got one which was admirably suited for the purpose, tilted at just the proper angle to maintain even pressure against the blade and with a little trough for escaping juice. The "corned beef machine" was used exclusively to slice cheese. "You can cut corned beef so much better by hand," my mother would explain.

The three-decker sandwich is the newest addition

to the ancient art of serving delicatessen. While the old kosher delicatessens scorned to gild the lily, their imitators seized upon it as another means of keeping in step with the times. It must here be understood that whereas your ordinary three-decker American sandwich of toasted white bread is considered a frivolity for leisured ladies at Schrafft's, there is nothing more serious (or deadly) than a three-decker sandwich of three slices of good rye bread. Its sheer weight makes superfluous the delicate toothpick. The delicatessen three-decker is served, meaningfully, with knife and fork. Compare, too, the contents. While the toasted sandwich can rely heavily on vegetable matter like lettuce and tomato to expand it to a respectable height, the delicatessen three-decker, by custom, is all meat. Obvious combinations like corned beef and pastrami have been succeeded by complicated variations, culminating in four kinds of meats topped with lettuce, tomato, cole slaw, Russian dressing, and pickle, with an olive on top. Yet a rigid uniformity prevails even in this seemingly imaginative matter of combination sandwiches. Turkey, for example, is always combined with tongue. But these two aristocrats rarely mix with the heartier meats.

Trends indicate that despite the havoc a combination sandwich can wreak on the digestion (I have illustrated only the most delicate), it is on its way to supplanting the simple one-meat sandwich. The combination sandwich fits well with the elaborate modern interiors, which have eliminated the hot frankfurter and the knish. We have only to sit back and wait for the ultimate—"A Banquet Between Three Slices of Bread—50c." Or more probably, these days, $1.25.

To decide upon the type of delicatessen the neighborhood called for, my father took his own Gallup poll. He proceeded to visit the owners of most of the other

stores to discuss business conditions in general and the
possibilities for his own in particular. He then scouted
out the shopping area for a radius of several blocks to
see what competition he would have, measured the proportion of transient traffic to "home trade," investigated
the national, religious, and financial composition of
the neighborhood, consulted with local real estate men
and bank presidents, and finally made his decision. He
became the proprietor of a "kosher-style delicatessen."

While the economic factors were important, the
social composition of the neighborhood was the decisive factor pointing to the kosher-style form. Although
the population of the area was about 50 per cent Jewish,
there was a significant percentage of mixed marriages,
and an old established Christian community which had
already begun to look askance at the growing Jewish
group. It would be too blatant, there would be too
great danger of antagonizing the non-Jewish section of
the community, my father was advised by community
leaders, if he used Hebrew characters in his window
sign. And then the Jewish section of the community
was "modern" and "emancipated." They didn't care
about such things. My mother, who came from an Orthodox family, was appalled by the driveways leading
up to the main temple in the neighborhood to accommodate members of the congregation who arrived by
car for Friday night services. Besides a temple, the
Jewish community supported a large, modern, extensively equipped Community Center, where almost all
the social activity, secular and religious, was carried on.
Residents of the community were well organized, claiming branches of the Jewish War Veterans, Hadassah,
Young Israel, and various local Sisterhoods and Junior Leagues.

My parents were faced with the problem of handling that anachronism, the modern Jew. They were to satisfy his taste for traditional food in traditional surroundings without offending a newly acquired dignity and propriety. The metamorphosis of this particular *wurshtgesheft* was a reflection of some of the painful minutiae of social adjustment.

We had come originally from a rough-and-tumble neighborhood. Shopping for daily necessities was a wild adventure where she who did not elbow was elbowed out; and a stentorian voice able to make itself heard above the shrill ruckus in the markets was the mark of an experienced housewife. The comparative silence and orderliness of the stores in the new community amazed my mother. "They say good-morning to you," she reported after one of her first shopping trips. My father, who applied every driblet of information to the operation of his store, decided that he had better be careful in his choice of waiters. It is well known that a delicatessen waiter's sole function is to frustrate the hungry, intimidate the cautious, and rule the diets of his daily patrons whith an iron hand. Such a technique, felt my father, would not be quite appropriate for this neighborhood. So he proceeded to hand-pick a suitable staff. For his efforts there was little to be said, except that he got delicatessen waiters who, by definition, acted like delicatessen waiters. The one immutable institution.

Frequently the help in a delicatessen is augmented by members of the owner's family. A large business is generally run by two or three partners and their respective families are not called upon to help. But in a smaller, one-man store, everyone pitches in. As soon as the youngsters of the family are old enough to hold two "toots" in one hand and a ladle of mustard in the other, they are pressed into service. The next step, acting cashier during the dinner hour, is assigned to those sufficiently certain of their addition and subtraction. But being allowed to wait on trade is the real cachet of maturity. Learning to handle the meat knife with its fourteen-inch blade so that you can cut a slice of corned beef that is almost transparent requires months of practice. The trick of making sandwiches so that they look twice as thick as they really are calls for appreciable finesse. Carrying tubfuls of pickles or cases of beer from the cellar develops a respectable amount of muscle.

The values of coming from a storekeeping family cannot be denied. Besides, in this case, the obvious advantage of "all the delicatessen you can eat," there is a kind of education to be had from standing behind a counter learning to talk the language of other kinds of people. There is the discipline of the cheerful, friendly, public face. There comes first-hand appreciation for hard work, for the cut-throat realities of commercial life, and some understanding of the value of money. It produces, early, a maturity of demeanor. By and large, it is not at all a bad prep school to leaven the abstract tendencies of the incipient Jewish intellectual.

But the ennobling effects of part-time labor are not unmitigated. Businesses like the delicatessen are open seven days a week and sixteen hours a day, and working in the store sometimes becomes a substitute for home life. Frequently you will notice in delicatessens one table in the back, reserved for family activity. A few children may be doing their homework. One of the parents will be reading the paper or entertaining friends. But somebody is always behind the counter.

Until meat rationing forced delicatessens to close on Tuesdays, the one-man owner had two days off a year—Rosh Hashanah and Yom Kippur (kosher delicatessens did close on Saturdays, but reopened Saturday evening). The children of the family may be well provided with clothing and food, but their home is a dark place where they go at bedtime. Their meals, their spare time, their source of parental affection are all bound up with the store. These days as the investment in basic equipment has become larger, the one-man store has happily become more of a rarity, and the families of delicatessen owners may be seen as often as any others taking their ease on the sands of Miami Beach or crowding the lobby of Radio City Music Hall.

The variety of foods that made their way over the counter in my father's delicatessen store rapidly increased as word spread in the community that a Jewish delicatessen had been set up. The important word to our customers was not "delicatessen," but "Jewish." Uncertain, in a precarious world, of the articles of their faith, the Jews of the neighborhood could make one affirmation unhesitatingly. Jewish food was good. Requests for lox, sturgeon, whitefish, for sour cream, bagels, cream cheese, for gefilte fish and potato *latkes* besieged us, and were heeded. The store, recognizedly a symbol of traditional Jewish living, became a center for the dispensation of knowledge on Jewish cookery, too. On Passover women would come in to ask how to make *matzoh brei.* "My husband had some here, and he insists I learn how to make it." We closed on Jewish holidays, served matzoh with meals on Passover, and gefilte fish on Friday.

But the pull was not all in one direction. The Gentiles of the neighborhood regarded my father's store as a curiosity at first. They would come in at the urging of a Jewish friend and order "pastrami," pronouncing it in a way that made my mother giggle. Some wandered in by accident, thought it strange that we didn't have some staple like boiled ham, but would generally settle for something else. Undeniably the food was good, satisfying, but different. After a while it even ceased to be different. Without a tremor of strangeness, they would order gefilte fish on "fish night."

But assimilation in reverse was only a small part of the picture. How to satisfy those who asked for ham and cheese sandwiches, or bacon and eggs? How about those who wanted Christmas dinners in a Christmas atmosphere? What to do about the request for pork chops and baked ham? Here my father could not be so yielding. It was all right to feature clam chowder on Friday night, to hang some holly on the door at Christmas, to serve bologna and cheese sandwiches, as a compromise. Yet beyond a mysteriously fixed point he could not pass. His sympathies, principles and prejudices shaped the atmosphere of the store and left no room for the ultimate in forbidden food. Unkosher cuts of meat— roast beef, leg of lamb, yes. Meat from a pig, no. A lamentable rigidity of adjustment, perhaps. But he had gone as far as he could. The next generation could begin serving the hams.

XIII *Herbert J. Gans*

Park Forest:
Birth of a Jewish Community

In November 1949, I completed a study of the Jews of Park Forest, Illinois. The study had one especially intriguing aspect: under its very eyes—in the midst of answering questionnaires, as it were—Park Forest's Jews gave birth to a young, awkward, but unmistakable Jewish community.

Park Forest is a garden-apartment housing project located thirty miles south of Chicago. The project, privately developed, was started in 1947, when the Chicago housing shortage was at its height. The first tenants moved in on August 30, 1948, and for two years they continued to come in as new sections of the village were completed. By November 1949, there were 2,000 families—nearly 8,000 people—renting garden apartments at $75 to $100 per month. One hundred and forty-one of these families were Jewish. Of these, about thirty had not been in the village long enough to have met the other Jewish families; another fifteen were "mixed marriages," with both husband and wife having rejected any identification as Jews; and the remainder, approximately one hundred families (including a few mixed marriages), 5 per cent of the project, formed a fledgling "Jewish community."

The project naturally attracted the people most sorely pressed for housing: veterans with children. The men average thirty to thirty-five years of age, the women somewhat less (anyone over forty is generally considered old). Most of the men are at the beginning of their careers, in professional, sales, administrative, and other business fields. Although not long removed from the GI Bill of Rights, they were in 1949 already earning from $4,000 to $10,000 a year—most of them perhaps around $5,000. Few of the men, and few of the wives even, are without some college, and educationally, the Jews as a whole stand even higher than the rest of the Park Forest community. Ninety per cent of the Jewish men interviewed have college training, 60 per cent hold degrees, and no less than 36 per cent have graduate degrees.

The Jews of Park Forest dress as do the other Park Foresters, enjoy similar leisure-time activities, read the same newspapers, look at the same movies, hear the same radio programs—in short they participate with other Park Foresters in American middle-class culture. They observe few traditional Jewish religious practices; the village's isolation from synagogues and kosher food shops has probably discouraged observant Jews from becoming tenants, and brought problems to those few who did.

Not only do Park Forest Jews live like other Park Foresters, they live with them. Whereas most American cities have "neighborhoods" dominated by one ethnic group or another—in atmosphere and institutions if not in numbers—this is not true of Park Forest. Most Park Foresters live in what are called "courts"—*culs de sac* surrounded in circular fashion by twenty to forty two-story garden apartments. Each "apartment" is actually a house, built together with five or seven others into a single unit. Privacy is at a minimum and each court is almost an independent social unit. The Jewish families are scattered all over the village, and only rarely are two Jewish families to be found in adjacent apartments. Yet in just one year, a Jewish community consisting of informal groups of friends, a B'nai B'rith lodge, a National Council of Jewish Women chapter, a Sunday school, and even a Board of Jewish Education had emerged.

How did this happen?

From the very beginning it seemed to be important to Jewish Park Foresters to "recognize" whether or not any of their neighbors were Jewish. And the widespread labeling, in America and Europe, of certain Mediterranean-Armenoid facial features as "Jewish," plus the monopolization of certain surnames by Jews, has resulted in a stereotypical formula of recognition, used by Jews and non-Jews, which is accurate more often than not.

One early resident related: "I saw Mrs. F. in the court a couple of times. . . . I thought she looked Jewish. With me, there's no mistaking it. Then someone told me her name, and I went up to talk to her. Finally we talked about something Jewish, and that was it."

"Jewish mannerisms" were also used to establish, or at least guess at, the other person's Jewishness. "The woman across the street, her actions were typical New York, so we recognized them as Jewish immediately. . . ." People very skillfully explored each other through conversations, attempting to discover whether the other person was Jewish or not, and offering clues to their own Jewishness. "She's been told I'm Jewish, and I know she's Jewish, we haven't discussed it, but she uses Jewish expressions she wouldn't use in front of other people." Others turned the conversation to favorite foods: "It was a slow process, we told them what kind of food we like, corned beef, lox. . . ."

Many Jewish Park Foresters had known each other previously, had mutual friends or acquaintances elsewhere, or bore introductions from mutual friends to "go look up so-and-so when you get to Park Forest." The people with such previous contacts, however loose these may have been, quickly established friendships and often became "charter members" of social circles which then attracted strangers. In this respect, the Jews differ sharply from other Park Foresters, most of whom knew no one and had no "introduction" to anyone when they arrived in the village.

Barely had this informal network of friendships and acquaintances sprung up among the first Jews moving into Park Forest (it did not, of course, preclude friendships with non-Jewish neighbors—though these, as we shall see later, were rather different in quality from the friendships with Jews), when two formal Jewish organizations were set up—a chapter of the B'nai B'rith and a chapter of the National Council of Jewish Women. Both enrolled only about forty members—those who, for various motives and reasons, were "organization-minded," and those, especially women, who had no Jewish neighbors and wanted to meet Jews from other parts of the village.

Both almost immediately found a purpose: "doing something" about the Jewish children of the growing Park Forest community. And through them steps were

soon taken to establish the single most important Jewish institution in Park Forest: the Sunday school.

By June 1949, less than a year after the first residents moved in, the B'nai B'rith leadership had sketched
out the organization of a Sunday school as part of a
congregation—Reform or Conservative, it was not yet
clear which—to be established in the village. At a meeting with a delegation of women from the Council, however, the latter refused to help organize a congregation,
insisting that what Park Forest needed was a Sunday
school now, and a congregation later, perhaps. One
man said of the women: "They don't care for Jewish
values, but they recognize that they are Jewish and they
need a Sunday school because the kids ask for it. . . .
They want a non-sectarian school." The women, on the
other hand, accused the men of trying to take over the
community for their own political ambitions, of wanting a "Jewish Community Incorporated."

Eventually a steering committee of four men and
four women was formed to proceed with the organization of a Sunday school. While the administrative organization and the budget were being prepared, largely
by the men, the school's curriculum was left to a young
Chicago rabbi who had become interested in Park Forest. Quite unexpectedly to some, he supported the
women in their rejection of a congregation, and formulated instead a Sunday school that would involve the
parents in their children's Jewish education: "As we
train the children," he told the parents, "you will have
to train yourselves. . . . You'll have to move toward a
community center and a synagogue eventually. . . ."
The parents' major contribution would be to prevent
such inconsistencies as would be apt to arise from not
practicing at home the content of the Sunday school
curriculum.

At a meeting of parents there was a sharp reaction to the rabbi's plans. A large number of those present objected to the curriculum proposed; they wanted a "secular" Sunday school, one which would teach the child *about* Jewish traditions, but which would not put pressure on the parents to *observe* these traditions in the home. For the reasons that they did not want a congregation, they did not want a school that would involve them either. The committee resigned and a new committee was formed.

But exactly what type of "Jewish content" should be brought into the school, and how? The new committee did not have sufficient Jewish background to set up any kind of Jewish curriculum, secular or otherwise, and called for aid from a Jewish professional family that lived in Park Forest, the husband a group worker, and his wife a trained Sunday school principal. The group worker was finally successful in devising a formula that reconciled the two sides, and the basis of the reconciliation is revealing: "The children will not be taught that parents have to light candles; the children will be informed of the background of candles. . . . We're teaching the child not that he must do these things, we just teach him the customs. . . . Why, we even teach them the customs of the Negro Jew . . . and that the customs have been observed for many years, and are being modified."

In "Yankee City's" Jewish community* the conflict over the synagogue was between generations, the foreign-born and the first-generation American. In Park Forest, where almost everyone is native-born, the conflict over the Sunday school was of a different nature: it was between those who wanted what may be

* W. Lloyd Warner and Leo Srole, *The Social Systems of American Ethnic Groups* (Yale University Press, 1945).

called an *adult-oriented* community and those who wanted a *child-oriented* one.

The adult-oriented community is the traditional (but not necessarily Orthodox) one whose activities are focused around its congregation of adults, and in which the role of the children is to become Jewish adults and assume an adult role. The men who wanted a congregation, with its Sunday school, were thinking of such an adult Jewish community, training its children for eventual membership in the organized Jewish group. In a child-oriented community, the community's energy is focused almost exclusively around the children, around their problems and needs as Jewish children—but, of course, as the adults see these needs. Thus, the women wanted a school for the children and, as became clear, not one that would involve the adults in Jewish community life. The women feared that the contradictions between the traditional Jewish home, whose features are now incorporated in the Sunday school curriculum, and the American home, which embodies their primary present-day values, would lead to family tensions. So, although they wanted their children to learn about traditional Jewish life, they did not want it brought home.

Why, however, did the parents want the children to go to Sunday school at all? First, and quite important, was the fact that the children, in contrast to the parents of Park Forest, having found their friends within the court without concern for ethnic origin, would see their non-Jewish friends leave for school on Sunday mornings. As one mother explained: "Our kids want to get dressed up and go to church too. The Sunday school [the Jewish one] will give them something to do." A few children were actually sent to the Protestant Sunday school a couple of times, but the overwhelming majority of the parents found this intolerable, so the pressure from the children was translated into parental demand for a Jewish Sunday school.

Second, and this is perhaps the more important reason, the parents wanted to send their children to Sunday school because they wanted to make them aware of their ethnic identity, to acquaint them with Jewishness through Jewish history and customs. But why become aware of ethnic identity and of "Jewish customs"? Because parents want their Jewish identity explained to their children, often as a *defense* against hardships they might run into because they are Jews. Representative of this rather widespread sentiment was the comment: "A Jewish child, he's something different, he's never one of the boys in a Gentile group, even if he's the best guy, he's one of the outsiders, the first to get abused, and if he doesn't know why, it's going to be a shock. It's part of his training, the Sunday school, he needs it."

A number of parents of six- and seven-year-olds were particularly clear in their hopeful expectation that Sunday school would supply the children with answers about their identity. It seems to be at that age that questions first develop in the children's play groups as to what they are, in terms of religion or nationality. The children come home and ask their parents what they are, and are they Jewish, and perhaps even "Papa, why do I have to be Jewish?" Here the Sunday school is asked to come to the rescue. One father reported of his son now in Sunday school: "He can probably tell me more than I can tell him."

It is not only the Sunday school that is child-oriented. The entire community shows itself child-oriented: during the first fourteen months of existence, the largest part of its organized adult activities was for the children. B'nai B'rith nearly collapsed because its leadership was drawn off into the task of establishing the Sunday school; and after the school had been set up, the lodge immediately went to work on a Chanukah party which it hoped to make an annual event. Even among those who wished to found a congregation, a goodly portion explained they wanted it exclusively for the sake of the children: "I don't believe in praying . . . in God . . . I want it for my son and daughter. I want them to know what it's like. I have had the background . . . I remember I enjoyed it at the time."

The Jewish holidays have become perhaps the chief mechanism of teaching and reinforcing Jewish identity. All the "happy" holidays—Pesach, Purim, Succoth, and Chanukah, especially the last—are emphasized and made into children's festivals. At Chanukah time 1948, when the Park Forest Jewish community consisted of less than twenty families, the problem of Chanukah versus Christmas first presented itself to Jewish parents. A year later, the problem loomed so large in everyone's mind that people discussed it wherever they gathered. The Women's Council devoted its November meeting to "techniques of Chanukah celebration," that is, techniques of competing with Christmas.

By late November, the non-Jewish friends of the Jewish children are eagerly awaiting Christmas and Santa Claus. Naturally, the Jewish children are inclined to join in these expectations, and ask their parents for Christmas trees. In 1948 and 1949, the parents acted quickly. One mother explained: "The F.'s had a big menorah in their window, that was very fine, maybe I'll do the same next year. . . . I could put my little menorah up there, I could wire it, is that O.K., we could have different color lights—no that's too much like Christmas." Another parent said: "My child wanted a

Christmas tree and we talked her out of it. . . . I make a fuss about Chanukah to combat Christmas, I build up Chanukah and she appreciates it just as much."

Meanwhile, the adults were not nearly so lavish in providing for their own needs as Jews.

Park Forest has a number of families, either Reform or mildly Conservative, whose social life before moving to Park Forest took place within a congregation. Some of these joined a wealthy congregation in Chicago Heights—especially those whose own income and social position were more or less equal to that of the Heights community. In addition there are a number of families, probably less than ten, who have maintained enough of the traditional system of religious attitudes and ritual practices to be called Orthodox or Conservative. They favor the establishment of a congregation, preferably Orthodox or Conservative, in the village.

But for the remainder, the very large majority of the Jews, religious institutions and practices play no role. Of forty-odd families interviewed, more than half reported that they observed no customs or holidays, and had not attended synagogues or temples "for years." Ten reported attending High Holiday services only; seven attended on High Holidays, some other holidays, and a few Friday evenings during the year.

For the majority of Park Foresters, the problems of traditional observance (such as the kosher home) or of attending religious services simply do not exist. They spend Friday nights as others do in Park Forest, entertaining, or going out, or staying at home. Saturdays are reserved for work around the house, shopping, visiting, and taking care of the little things suburbanites have no time for during the week.

There are, however, two religious patterns which are still observed, not universally but by many. First, as has been indicated, there are those holidays and traditions that concern the children. Second are those aspects of death and birth that relate the Jew to his parents. Several of the men remarked matter-of-factly that they were not interested in religious observances, but added just as matter-of-factly, "except of course *Yortzeit*" (anniversary of the death of a parent). Another said: "The only thing we did—at my son's birth we had a rabbi at the circumcision, mostly for my wife's parents, they would have felt bad."

Some people celebrate the Jewish holidays by spending them with parents or in-laws, not as religious holidays but as family get-togethers. One woman explained, jokingly: "I believe Rosh Hashanah should be two days, Passover too, for practical purposes. One day we go to his family, the other to mine."

There have been some attempts to establish the beginnings of a religious institutional system in Park Forest. In January 1949, when the Jewish population did not exceed twenty-five families, the group already had a rabbi-substitute, a man with some Jewish education who roamed through the Jewish community and from his Conservative background ministered to occasional religious needs. "Someone needed Hebrew writing on a tombstone, they were told to call me, someone else wanted *Yizkor* [prayer for the dead] or *Yortzeit* services, they called me. . . ." Various groups have talked sporadically about setting up a regular congregation.* Most interesting in this demand for a congregation is the reason given by many supporters: "They'll have more respect

* In November 1950, after the completion of this study, a congregation was finally organized.

for us, to show that we have arrived, that we're not merely a bunch of individuals." The "they" refers, of course, to the non-Jewish neighbors.

Uninterested as Park Foresters may be in "the Jewish heritage," they are nevertheless very much Jews. Clearly and unmistakably, that is, they remain both matter-of-factly and by conscious design members of identifiably Jewish groups. This Jewish group may be another Jewish couple with whom they spend much of their time; it may be a regular and more or less stable group which gathers, in full or in part, almost every weekend and on special occasions. These groups make up the informal Jewish community, the "spontaneous" community that did not require professionals and organizers to be created.

For the most part, this informal community exists at night. In the daytime, when only housewives and the children inhabit Park Forest, the Jewish housewife participates in the general court social life. She interrupts her household duties to chat with a neighbor, while "visiting" over a morning cup of coffee or while watching the children in the afternoon. In most cases, there is no distinction here between the Jewish and the non-Jewish housewife; they belong together to the bridge and sewing clubs that have been established in many courts. There are a few courts in which religious or ethnic cliques of women have formed, and where "visiting" is restricted to such groups. In most courts, however, there are few ethnic distinctions in daytime social life. This applies even more to the men when they participate with other men in court life on weekends (and occasional evenings) in athletic teams and poker clubs. As one of the women observed: "The boys are real friendly. I imagine they don't think about it [ethnic distinctions] but the women have different feelings. Women have little to do; they talk about it in the afternoons."

At night, however, in the social relations among "couples," the Jewish husband and wife turn to other Jews for friendship and recreational partnership. As one person summarized it: "My real close friends, my after-dark friends, are mostly Jewish; my daytime friends are Gentile." Of thirty Jewish residents who listed the names of Park Foresters they see regularly, ten named only Jews; ten named mostly Jews, and one or two non-Jews; ten named a majority of non-Jews or only non-Jews. And many of the people who named both Jews and non-Jews pointed out, like the person quoted above, that their most intimate friends were Jewish.

There are, of course, all types of friendship circles in this informal Jewish community. One of the largest groups is made up predominantly of older, well-to-do Park Foresters, many of them previously active in big-city Jewish congregations and groups. Most of these men are employed by business or industry, or in the non-academic professions (medicine, dentistry, law, engineering). A second group consists largely of young academic intellectuals (research scientists, teachers, writers) and their wives. A third is made up of people who have only recently emerged from lower-middle-class Jewish neighborhoods, and are just exploring, with occasional distaste, the life of the middle- or upper-middle-class American Jew. And there are many others.

It is easy to explain the tendency to find friends in one's own group, even when this takes one from one's own front door, as it does in Park Forest. As the Park Foresters say, "It's easier being with Jews"—it is psychologically more accommodating, and there is less strain in achieving an informal, relaxed relationship with other Jews: "You can give vent to your feelings. If you talk to a Christian and say you don't believe in this, you are doing it as a Jew; with Jewish friends you can tell them point blank what you feel."

One man, who had been converted to Judaism in his twenties, when he was married to a Jewish girl, became disturbed, at an informal party, over a discussion of how to inculcate Judaism into the children, "and keep them away from the goyim," and felt it time to announce that he had been until a number of years ago a member of a Christian denomination. The declaration broke up the party, and upset many people. After that he felt: "From now on, they'll be on their guard with me, they've lost their liberty of expression, they don't express themselves without restriction now. At a party, if anybody says something, everybody looks to see if I've been offended and people are taken into a corner and told about me." This man has adopted the Jewish religion, is bringing up his children as Jews, and has been more active than the average person in Jewish community life. Yet he is no longer a member of the Jewish in-group, although he remains a member both of the Jewish community and his smaller Jewish group. In his presence, the group sheds the informality and intimacy of the in-group, and is "on guard."

There are many Jewish Park Foresters who reject these in-group attitudes as "chauvinistic," and when asked about their friends, are quick to reply that they do not distinguish between Jews and non-Jews in choosing friends. But these Jewish Park Foresters, too, feel that they differ from the majority of the non-Jewish Park Foresters—and not only because their friends are Jews. The focus of these feelings of difference was summarized by one person: "I have a friend who is not Jewish who told me how fortunate I was in being born Jewish. Otherwise I might be one of the sixteen to eighteen out of twenty Gentiles without a social conscience and liberal tendencies; he is cruel and apathetic. . . . Being Jewish, most of the Jews, nine out of ten, are sympathetic with other problems, have more culture and a better education. . . ."

These feelings have a basis in Park Forest reality. The Jews are distinguished by a feeling of "social consciousness," by concern over political and social problems, by a tendency toward a humanistic agnosticism, and by an interest in more "highbrow" leisure activities: foreign films, classical music, the fine arts, and in general the liberal intellectual-aesthetic leisure culture of America, and perhaps the Western world. Jews who seek other people with whom they can share these attitudes and interests tend to find other Jews.

Just as Jews form a large proportion of those interested in "culture," they form a large proportion of those interested in the self-government of Park Forest, and in other local activities. Although in November 1949 the Jews made up only 9 per cent of Park Forest's population, eleven of thirty-seven candidates in the first two village elections were Jewish. All but one member of the first Board of Education, and half of the original six-man Board of Trustees, which runs the village, are Jewish. The community newspaper was started by a group of women many of whom were Jewish; the American Veterans Committee and the local affiliate of the Democratic party were organized with the help of a number of Jewish men.

If for a moment we take a broader view and consider non-Jewish Park Forest, we discover that the Jewish community is only one of three quite similarly organized ethnic-religious groups. Both the large Catholic group (close to 25 per cent of the village population is Catholic) and the smaller Lutheran one also consist of a religious body, men's and women's social organizations, and a more or less extensive informal community. The two Christian groups, unlike the Jewish one, are organized primarily for adult activities, but also emphasize the Sunday school. Both communities developed much more quickly than the Jewish one—largely because there was much less internal disagreement as to what to do and how to proceed—and both were in 1949 already engaged in building programs. The Catholic and Lutheran groups are primarily religious bodies (although they are in part ethnic groups), and have fewer members who reject the group culture. Those who do reject it can quite easily "resign" and become part of the large amorphous body of Americans not strongly identified by religious or ethnic groups, something that is much more difficult for the Jew.

In its first year, the Jewish community was very sensitive to the problem of anti-Semitism. Just as every newly arrived tenant would try to recognize other Jews, he would also try to discover the attitudes of non-Jewish neighbors toward Jews. This led quickly to the sprouting of a grapevine which transmitted actual cases, suspicions, and imagined occurrences of anti-Semitism throughout the Jewish community, and sometimes dominated conversation among Jews. A number of people complained strongly that there was a great deal too much talk about anti-Semitism. Actually, there has probably been very little anti-Semitism in Park Forest. If anti-Semitism played any role in the formation of the community, it was the fear and expectation of anti-Semitism rather than actual experience of it.

Park Forest has changed since this study was made, and will continue to change in the future. Nevertheless, the Jewish community has already become oriented around a number of elements which are not likely to change.

Whereas their parents were not only socially "clannish" but culturally different from their non-Jewish neighbors, the adult Jews of Park Forest are "clannish" but culturally not very different. (Or, rather, their cultural distinctiveness, when it exists, is not along Jewish lines.) Their adjustment to American society and their present status can be described as one of cultural assimilation and continued social distinctiveness. It is this feeling of Jewish togetherness which provides the impetus for child-orientation, for the parents' insistence on a Sunday school, their transformation and use of the Chanukah holiday, and the unending attempt to indoctrinate the child with a sense of Jewishness.

This child-orientation is the mechanism that would seem to guarantee the existence of the ethnic group for another generation, even when the adult carriers of the group's culture are ambivalent about it, or have rejected it. So long as Judaism is the curriculum for teaching and transmitting Jewishness, the traditional behavior patterns will be studied, discussed, and taught.

A major force in the development of the Park Forest Jewish community has been the "Jewish professional," who so far has been the spearhead, "the catalytic agent," as one called himself, in the process of community formation. It was Jewish professionals who helped bring the Jews together, started the men's social organization, tried to organize a congregation, helped in forming the Sunday school, resolved the crisis that resulted, and have since supervised Jewish education in the village.

The Jewish professional is a new man on the Jewish scene. He is not a rabbi, but a leader of adults, a youth worker, a teacher, a fund-raiser, a social worker, a contact man, a community relations director, etc. The Jewish professional may not have special training in how to start a Jewish community, but he is expert at being Jewish, something other Park Forest Jews are not. Sometimes this expert Jewishness is a part of his background, and his reason for becoming a professional, sometimes it is the result of a desire to work in the Jewish community, sometimes it is only a career, and the professional's activities in these organizations are for him a means of advancing in his career. Whatever his motives, however, the Jewish professional, rather than the rabbi, would seem to have taken over the initiatory role and the largest part of the work of creating the formal Jewish community. In the informal community, his influence is much smaller.

A final factor for an understanding of the Park Forest Jewish community is the sexual division of social labor that takes place within it. The Jewish informal community is based on the Jewish woman. It is she who generally inaugurates and stimulates acquaintances and friendships, who founds the social circles and sets their pattern and content. Most of the men seem to lay less emphasis on ethnic association, and although there are some all-Jewish male groups, male activities are more likely to take place in groups which more or less ignore ethnic distinctions. In general, the women live a greater part of their life within the Jewish group, and are more concerned with it and about it than the men. In Park Forest, and presumably in communities like it, they seem to be the most influential element in determining the nature of "Jewish" activities. At a somewhat later stage these activities may be handed over to the men.

As to just how representative the events and processes that took place in this one Jewish community are, it is hard to say. Certainly, however, it would not be claiming too much to suggest that the Park Forest Jewish community offers much illustrative and prophetic material as to the next major stage in the process of Jewish adjustment to American society: the stage in which it is the relations between the second and third generations, both American-born, not the relations between a foreign-born first and a native-born second generation, that are the crucial ones.

XIV *Ernest Stock*

Washington Heights' "Fourth Reich"

At a party given by a New Jersey Jewish
community, a Princeton undergraduate mentioned that
he knew Professor Einstein. "Tell me," one of the community leaders asked the young man, "is Einstein as
conceited as the rest of the German Jews?"

The undergraduate happened to have come from
Germany himself; and he could not help wryly reflect-
ing upon how many disparaging remarks about "those
German Jews" he had been subjected to. They are "conceited," they "stick together and won't mix with the
rest of us," they are "arrogant," they are "schemers,"
they are "mercenary"—a long list of accusations sound-
ing not too much unlike the ideas about Jews generally
harbored by anti-Semites.

In part, this attitude undoubtedly stems from the
fact that the old-established Jews in Germany have a
long record for looking down their noses at Eastern
European Jews, whose kin and descendants now make
up the bulk of the American Jewish population. One

young German immigrant said flatly, "They have never forgiven us for July 1938." He was referring to the Nazi deportation of Polish Jews to the No Man's Land between Germany and Poland—a measure which some of the native-born German Jews regarded with apathy and even, it has been said, with a certain feeling of relief at its affecting "only the Polish Jews." Needless to say, this particular speaker was oversimplifying the matter; and most American Jews are, of course, happily unaware of the details of this and similar episodes.

There is, it is said, a small minority of the new immigrants who even here still persist in being contemptuous of Eastern European Jews. Some especially, who left Germany in the early days of the Hitler regime under no personal duress and with most of their property intact, expected that they would be readily accepted in "Aryan" circles here. When their hopes were disappointed, they made no real effort to find an entry into American Jewish circles, and haughtily confined themselves to their own group.

But among the post-1938 immigrants a decidedly different attitude prevails. They never deluded themselves that they came by choice, that they did not have to emigrate. It is true that many of them, too, were disappointed when they encountered social barriers between Jews and Gentiles: they had expected to find American society equalitarian in every sense, and it came as a shock to discover how much it is a series of rather tight ethnic enclaves. Although Jews in pre-Hitler Germany were organized in legally constituted religious communities (*Gemeinden*), the social relations of the German Jew were by no means restricted to his fellow Jews; German Jewish professionals frequented the homes of other German professionals, whereas, in New York, Jewish doctors and lawyers tend to visit the homes of other Jewish doctors and lawyers. But as the newcomers became more aware of the structure of American society, the initial disappointment lost significance, and they were more and more ready to seek the company of American Jews without inquiring too closely as to what side of the river Oder they came from.

There are, finally, the relatively few survivors of the death camps, and those who spent the war years in such places as Shanghai, living on the generosity of the American Joint Distribution Committee. These people identify their fate with that of Jews from Eastern Europe, and some now feel closer to the Eastern Jews than to their former countrymen.

But varying dates of arrival constitute only one differentiation in the many-stranded make-up of what is called the German Jewish group. (Incidentally, the expression "refugee" from the lips of an American has a most distasteful sound to the immigrant; nevertheless, the word is freely used by the immigrants themselves—almost all of them by now American citizens—when they refer to one another. In its English form, it has become a part of their German vocabulary.) One of the most trenchant distinctions is that between the Germans and the Austrians. The Austrians refer to the Germans as *"Yeckes"*; for the Germans the Austrians are simply *"die Wiener."* The gulf between the two groups is very wide. They have their separate clubs and congregations, and their members rarely mix socially. They don't even live in the same neighborhoods. In New York, where perhaps two-thirds of the immigrants are concentrated, the main Viennese districts are midtown Manhattan between 72nd and 96th Streets and some sections of Queens. The Germans, for their part, have moved *en masse* to the uptown section of Manhattan known as Washington Heights, settling in an area that lies, roughly, between 160th and 180th Streets and west of Broadway, and that the immigrants themselves have dubbed *"das vierte Reich."*

The Jews of Washington Heights constitute the solid core of the wave of immigration from Germany. It is difficult to say exactly how many of them live there, but the circulation department of the German-language weekly *Aufbau*, which is read in almost every German Jewish family, reports that it sells some 6,000 copies in the area. If the average family has four members, an estimate of 25,000 persons might be fairly accurate. This constitutes about 20 per cent of the 129,582 persons admitted on immigration visas from Germany and Austria between 1933 and 1944,* but it may be assumed that an additional ten or fifteen thousand arrived during those eleven years on visitors' visas and later received permission to remain permanently. (Since 1944 the influx of German Jews has been negligible.)

Even so, the size of the German Jewish group is extremely small compared to earlier waves of immigration, when hundreds of thousands of immigrants arrived in a single year. But this numerically insignificant group has nevertheless managed to cause a flurry on the American scene within a very short space of time. One striking fact that may do much to account for the success of the group is that this immigration has been almost 100 per cent middle class, an entirely new phenomenon in American social history.

America usually expects its immigrants to start on

* This figure is from *Refugees in America*, a study compiled under the auspices of the Committee for the Study of Recent Immigration, directed by Professor Maurice R. Davie of Yale University, and published by Harper in 1947.

the bottom rung of the economic and social ladder, and this is the one rule of the game that the German Jews have refused to accept. To cite one example: there were several thousand doctors in the group, and all of them were determined to continue practicing their profession. The great majority have done so, but they have had to face some real resentment on the part of their American Jewish colleagues, especially since the medical profession in New York is already, in the opinion of many of its members, overcrowded. There is also, on the part of those American Jews who remember the intense struggles of their own parents and grandparents, some feeling that the Germans are trying to have things too easy—and, what is worse, succeeding.

To be sure, the immigrants themselves have in some ways added fuel to the flames. Everyone has heard stories of German Jews boasting about their former glories and the virtues of the German way: *"Bei uns war es besser."* Perhaps the most popular anecdote in this connection is the one about the dachshund who remarks to an American dog: "In Germany I used to be a St. Bernard."

There is no doubt that a considerable number of the immigrants took a certain reduction in the living standard they were accustomed to, especially during the first period of their adjustment here. But there were also a great many others who tended to glamorize their former estate, which in reality was never so comfortable as life between Fort Washington Avenue and Broadway. In some cases these romancers manage to make their pretensions stick, but rarely with their more sophisticated fellow immigrants. Those who came from small towns and villages will be haunted by that fact to the end of their days, at least so far as their cosmopolitan cousins from Frankfort, Cologne, or Berlin are concerned. Many of the other social distinctions that prevailed among Jews in Germany have been effaced, but this one of small town against big city persists. It is not uncommon to hear children arguing among themselves about where their parents came from, and families that moved to the cities only a short time before emigrating will now informally claim their last residence. A few months ago, I was told of an elderly lady who looked at a furnished room on 180th Street and decided it was not for her because the bathtub did not quite suit her. "And do you know," said the landlord, who was telling the story, "she comes from——, and I will bet my last penny there wasn't a single bathtub in the whole village."

Whatever nostalgia for the "good old times" actually remains is not to be confused with a longing to go back. The thought of returning to Germany is never even discussed, and probably no more than a hundred of the immigrants have actually gone. For most, the break is complete, much more complete than it was for immigrants from Eastern Europe; there are no letters going back and forth, no families to support, no wistful voyages to the old home town. Now and then someone with a claim to property flies over to speed things up, but these business visits are limited to the absolute minimum required, and invariably the travelers are glad to get "back home"—which means, without any mental reservations, back to the United States.

What prompted the pioneers among the immigrants to settle up there in Washington Heights is now shrouded in the semi-legendary past of 1933 and the years immediately following. Perhaps it was the—at the moment somewhat shabby—gentility of the neighborhood, which, along with the style of the buildings, the parks nearby, and the cool breeze from the Hudson

in the evening, carried vague reminders of the bourgeois residential sections of the German cities.

By now, of course, a number of the immigrants
are established on the lower West Side, some even on
Fifth Avenue and Park Avenue. Others were attracted
to more outlying districts, especially Forest Hills and
Kew Gardens in Queens, where the German Jews seem
to mix more readily with their American neighbors,
frequenting lodge meetings and community centers in
much larger numbers than on Washington Heights.
(The Queens group is younger on the average than the
group in Washington Heights, and their very moving
away often signified an intentional break with the restricted social environment of the Heights.) But most
of the immigrants have stayed up there, south of Fort
Tryon Park and north of where Fort Washington Avenue runs into Broadway. Perhaps more would have
moved away if war and the housing shortage had not
intervened. But the chances are that the solid core of
them will stay on even when apartments have once
more become plentiful, simply because they don't like
to move once they are settled down. And somehow
those twenty or thirty blocks have by now taken on a
very homelike quality.

There is, however, little that is aggressively German about this neighborhood, in the way that York-
ville is aggressively German, with its German restaurants, German movies, travel bureaus, and *Bierstuben.*
True, the *Staatszeitung* is displayed on all the news
stands, but so are the Jewish *Day* and the *Forward.*
(They are for the "natives"; the German Jews don't
read Yiddish.) The German Jews, although in some
ways proud of their antecedents and still secretly convinced that it is a mark of distinction to have been
born in Germany rather than in some Polish village

with an unpronounceable name, have on the whole a very nice sense of tact. The shops they have taken over on Broadway and 181st Street, from candy stores to five-and-tens, are no different from any others except for the accent of the man behind the counter, and, perhaps, the fact that the windows of their bakeries contain some of the most succulent butter cookies produced in the Western Hemisphere.

These bakeries are among the most tangible manifestations of the German Jewish hold on Washington Heights; although they dutifully turn out a certain quota of sweet and fluffy American-style *challah* on Fridays, they devote their main efforts on that day to the production of the German *barches*, which has a hard crust covered with poppy seed and is not sweet in taste. Another tangible contribution of the German Jews to the Washington Heights scene is an excellent candy shop on 181st Street, the original store of the Barton chain which has since spread all over the city, setting an example of Orthodoxy by faithfully closing for Sabbath from sundown Friday to sundown Saturday. Apart from these shops, any citizen of the Heights must admit that it is a gustatory wasteland when compared to, say, certain districts of the West Bronx. The German Jewish cuisine differs but slightly from the somewhat stodgy German *Kueche*, and it has been modified only by the enthusiastic adoption of canned food by housewives who work during the day. Gefilte fish and other characteristically Jewish dishes are unknown.

Nor can the women of Washington Heights compete with the West Bronx ladies when it comes to dress. One black dress, one brown dress, and one blue dress are considered an entirely adequate wardrobe by many. This is in line with the general strain of frugality that runs through the colony: a man will boast to a friend who is wearing a new suit that he has bought no new clothes since he came over here—though this boast is now heard less and less frequently from women.

If you ask a local resident what the outstanding contribution of his group has been to Washington Heights, he may smile slyly and point to the stylish building of the Harlem Savings Bank at Broadway and 181st Street: "They built that with our money." It is possible that the bank would have moved from its old ground-floor offices diagonally across the street even without the arrival of the immigrants, but anyone willing to take the trouble can see with his own eyes that the German Jews line up by the hundreds at the tellers' windows every Friday afternoon to deposit a good part of the contents of their pay envelopes. And tight-lipped bank officials will come across with the information that a "substantial number" of the breadwinners have long ago reached the $10,000 maximum for federal insurance on savings accounts, and have started a second or third account in the name of another member of the family. Insurance salesmen, somewhat more talkative, assert that the percentage of lapses on policies taken out by the immigrants is zero.

Many families are still using the heavy German furniture they brought over in their packing crates twelve and fifteen years ago. The center of the traditional living room is a massive table with straight-backed chairs around it; along one wall stretches the so-called "buffet," a two-story cabinet used to store linen, china, and silver. In the top half, a glass showcase, knick-knacks and small antiques are exhibited. Part of another wall may then be taken up by a bookcase almost ceiling-high, with the books protected from dust and the mere browser by a locked, glass-paneled door.

With others, this type of furniture remained crated while the family settled temporarily in a small apartment. Later, as storage charges mounted, the oak, walnut, and mahogany was sold for what it would bring. Or sometimes it cluttered up the first dwelling place only to be thrown out on the move to the second, when the owner discovered that moving charges here are based on weight rather than cubic space. Today American furniture has replaced German neo-baroque in most of the living rooms; but where space permits, the vast German twin beds—each bed almost the size of an American double bed—have remained in the bedroom. They may not look very up to date, but they are too comfortable to be thrown out, and besides a bedroom is not meant to be a show-place anyway.

The Jews of Washington Heights do "stick together." It is in the very nature of such a neighborhood that it tends to keep social relations within the group. And it is in the nature of any group of new immigrants to settle in a place where the pioneers of their kind have already broken the alien ground. Then inertia and their inherent German conservatism keep most of them from seeking new vistas. The average German Jew over forty is most content in his home or with a circle of friends from his home town speaking German. Outside the home, he is likely to be happiest in a German Jewish social club, formed either for the purpose of playing *Skat* or merely for *Kaffeeklatsch*.

Professor Davie's study, mentioned above, states that in a nationwide cross section, 46.8 per cent of the recent immigrants had mainly other recent immigrants as friends, 40.3 per cent had mainly American friends, and 12.8 per cent had friends equally divided between the two. Among those living in New York, however, 61.3 per cent had only other recent immigrants as their

friends. (Those living in small towns and any but the
largest cities are more or less compelled to go outside the
immigrant group for their associations; although there are
occasional instances of immigrants in the smaller cities
being given the cold shoulder by the established Jewish
families, easy adjustment is the rule.) Probably the
count for Washington Heights alone would be higher
still. And within the section itself association is to a
high degree governed by place of residence. For instance, a twenty-year-old girl reports that when her parents lived near Yeshiva College on 185th Street and
Amsterdam Avenue, where the "natives" outweigh the
immigrants, all her friends were American Jews, but
when they moved to the corner of Fort Washington
Avenue and 170th Street, a section where 75 per cent of
the tenants in most apartment houses are immigrants,
she gradually lost track of her American friends and
began to associate with "my own kind."

Of even greater importance than place of residence
in determining the immigrant's associations is the age
at which he came to the United States. As was to be
expected, the high school generation—those who were
still young enough to start high school or at least to
complete a substantial part of it in this country—had
the least difficulty in "assimilating." Professor Davie es-
timates that 15 per cent of the immigrants were in this
"under sixteen" category. Many of them showed an unusual degree of adaptability, and the records of George
Washington High School, on 190th Street, abound
with the names of immigrant youngsters who after one
or two years in the country reached the head of their
class. In 1943, an immigrant boy set a record for scholastic achievement at this school.

These children quickly lost their German accents
and became generally indistinguishable from their

native-born classmates. The importance of this can hardly be overestimated: often the German accent makes the difference between complete integration in American life and permanent status as an "outsider." As a rule, the children speak German only at home, or they reply in English when their parents speak to them in German. Yet fundamental estrangement between the old and the younger generations, once the rule in immigrant families, seems to occur very rarely in this group. The parents encourage their offspring to imitate American customs and are proud to see them become such complete *Amerikaner*. True, they may shake their heads when Johnny (formerly Hans) remains glued to the television set all afternoon watching the Yankees, or when Joanie doesn't come home from the movies until eleven, but they are in general resigned to the fact that "children are brought up differently over here."

Middle-class Jewish homes in German cities (and what home wasn't middle-class?) had about them a certain aura of great warmth and security. That atmosphere is largely lost in America. With women working outside the home, the tight family structure is broken up and parental authority suffers, especially as the children become the authorities on American ways while the parents remain in many respects perpetual "greenhorns." The home in Germany was the mainstream of culture. The same home on Washington Heights is not yet rooted in anything that might be described as American culture. For one thing, there isn't so much reading any more—work and subway travel are too demanding. The books that do get read are not on a level with the German works that still fill the bookshelves, and immigrants who were as a matter of course well read in modern German and European literature are likely to know nothing about, say, William Faulkner or Ezra Pound or F. Scott Fitzgerald. (Hemingway was popular in Germany in translation.) This is true even of men in the intellectual professions, such as doctors and lawyers. The only exceptions are the few men who teach on the college level, and those professionals and artists who have achieved general recognition in their fields, and with it a circle of professional friends and associates outside Washington Heights.

Occasionally boys or girls from cultured homes are frustrated because they cannot find companions at school with whom to share their interests, if these go beyond movies, cars, and sports. This problem is of course not peculiar to young immigrants, but belongs to adolescent intellectuals in general. In the German Jewish group, however, it is somewhat intensified by the desire to leave the German background behind and assimilate to American life; many young people are anxious to move out of their parents' circle, and yet find the social life of the YMHA's and other American youth groups unsatisfying. Some have remained outside all organized social life; some, naturally enough, have found their way into organizations within the Zionist movement.

The decisive step towards integration is always marriage into the established group. Professor Davie's researchers found that 62.4 per cent of the male German Jewish immigrants married German Jewish immigrant girls, leaving 37.6 per cent who married outside the group—an exceptionally high proportion for a recent immigrant group. The bulk of this large minority is, of course, supplied by the high school generation; in most cases, the boys take the initiative by dating and then marrying American Jewish girls, though it sometimes also works the other way. In either case, the couple gravitates inevitably away from the German and toward the American environment; no more German is spoken, and the American parents are usually more favored by the couple.

As a rule, the German parents are at first mildly opposed to this type of "intermarriage," feeling that their child would be happier with a mate of their own background. The mothers are convinced that German Jewish girls make better *Hausfrauen*, and that German Jewish boys are more stable and more predictable. But usually everything works out all right in the end. (Intermarriage between German Jews and Gentiles, it might be mentioned, is an extreme rarity.) At some of the "mixed weddings" the gulf between the two parties is accentuated by the practice of having the bride's and groom's relatives and friends sit on separate sides of the aisle, and later the German and American Jews tend to cluster in their own little groups. At one such affair recently, the rabbi in his speech recalled the story of Ruth—which may have been somewhat farfetched.

Those young people who were too old to go to high school when they came, and started to work immediately, have found it a good deal harder to make social contacts among Americans. The most telling indication of this is the fact that very few of them marry outside the group. Most of these young men and women at one time made a determined effort to break down the barrier, did not quite succeed, and then retreated. Many of them have never entirely got rid of the German accent. It is the members of this age group, now in their late twenties and early thirties, who will prolong the collective life of the German Jewish group after those who came here as mature men and women are gone. Most of the young men served in the army, which in many cases gave them their first contact with "real Americans," but, with a few exceptions, they came back to Washington Heights, literally or figuratively. The exceptions were in the main the veterans who took advantage of the GI Bill to go to college (the majority of these had had some American high school training before they entered the army).

Some of this generation went to evening high school or college, but that experience yielded few American contacts. They have formed a plethora of clubs of their own: soccer clubs, hiking clubs, social clubs, etc. The youth group of the New World Club alone sponsors half a dozen of these. The members of these clubs have often felt uneasy about the way they have isolated themselves, and have made some efforts to widen their social horizon.

Most German Jews vote dutifully, and with pride in their citizenship, but active participation in local politics is the last thing anyone thinks of. Although there were, of course, Jewish politicians in Germany, they just don't feel at home in the American political climate. Few of them have ever set foot in the Heights Democratic or Republican clubs.

A number of the German Jewish community organizations do function within larger American Jewish organizations, which seems an ideal way to assuage the desire for general recognition and affiliation to the larger community while at the same time retaining the advantages of being "among ourselves." Examples of this type of group are the Leo Baeck Lodge of B'nai B'rith, the Daniel Frisch Lodge of B'nai Zion, and a Theodor Herzl Society which in due course became District 81 of the Zionist Organization of America, one of the most active Zionist Districts in New York. A group of World War I veterans of the German army, known as the Jewish Veterans Association, has a large membership in Washington Heights. It cultivates friendly relations with the Jewish War Veterans of America, but the fact that the members of the two organizations once fought on opposite sides remains an obvious obstacle to outright affiliation.

Somewhat of a class apart within the older group are intellectuals. As a rule they move in a small circle of other German Jewish intellectuals, including those who used to be lawyers, journalists, or teachers on the other side and are now either manual or white-collar workers. Their attitude might be summed up as follows: they have no hostility toward the American environment, no prejudice or snobbishness, but their outlook on life is different from that of their American counterparts, and thus they feel more at home among themselves. Many of these men have also sensed at one time or another that Americans don't feel completely at ease in their presence. They have been, at first encounter, the object of polite interest, but there was often hardly enough common ground to keep it up. A favorite topic of conversation among the Germans is still the incongruities and, from the European point of view, the amusing aspects of the American scene, which they discuss more freely and with more gusto among themselves. The Germans do nevertheless admire a great many traits in the "typical American"—his energy, his lack of social inhibitions, his good humor, etc.—but they feel themselves just a little too worldly-wise ever to be like that themselves.

The New World Club is probably the most remarkable of the one hundred and fifty or so organizations the German Jews have set up for themselves. The club started its career in 1924 with the descriptive but somewhat unimaginative name of German Jewish Club. In December 1934, the renamed club began what

was to become its most important activity: the publication of a monthly newsletter, *Aufbau*. Today
Aufbau, a 28- to 54-page weekly, can be found on most
news stands from the Battery to Spuyten Duyvil Creek,
and on a good many others from Johannesburg to Stock-
holm to Montevideo, and its subscription list includes
addresses not only in all forty-eight states, Canada, and
South America, but also in the Belgian Congo, Nyassa-
land, and New Zealand. The paper seems to have found
the right formula for acting as a link between German
Jews everywhere.

The contents of *Aufbau* show plainly that, however
restricted its readers' contacts with American Jews in
the flesh, they feel very much affected by what happens
in the Jewish community at large. *Aufbau* has had a
Zionist orientation from the beginning, though it might
be called a moderate one, and Jewish community activities on behalf of Israel have received full coverage in
its columns. Similar coverage has been given to non-
Zionist community activities. Among the paper's regular features are political commentaries by the editor,
Manfred George; they are well-informed, sober, and in
the best tradition of European journalism. There is also
theater, film, and art criticism on a fairly high level, a
column dealing with the doings of refugees in Hollywood, a women's page, community news, and a "News
from Israel" section. Outside contributors of the paper
have included such figures as Thomas Mann, Fritz von
Unruh, and the late Franz Werfel, and the columns of
Walter Lippman and Harold Ickes were regularly
featured for years.

The advertisements in each issue mirror the
business success of a portion of the group, in such fields
as summer resorts, furs, women's wear, furniture, books,
jewelry, insurance, shipping, investment, automobiles,

cameras, etc. On the other hand, the ads do not reveal how many former businessmen—big and small—have failed to gain a foothold in the intensely competitive business world here; Professor Davie reported that only one out of six former businessmen had a business of his own, the rest were employed. As in American society as a whole, financial success has pretty much become the determinant of status in the community. With former peddlers become factory-owners and former factory-owners putting clothes on the racks of department stores, it is hardly surprising that all but the subtlest of social distinctions have been blurred.

What of the religious life of the immigrants? At first glance, it appears to be flourishing. Every week, some twenty German Jewish congregations, most of them on Washington Heights, publish the schedule of their services in *Aufbau*. But all twenty together have fewer than 10,000 members, and a great many of those never come to shul except on the High Holidays.

Contrary to the widely held notion that the Jews of Germany were the most "assimilated," a vast section of the German Jewish middle class formerly adhered to a conservative brand of Judaism, which included strict observance of the Sabbath with regular visits to the synagogue. In the cities of Germany all Jewish life had revolved around the *Gemeinde*, and in order to be a recognized member of the community one had to take part in the religious observances. In the United States, however, religious observance, which had been part of the pattern of life in a fairly homogeneous community, has been gradually abandoned. At first, some people worked on Saturdays; those who had businesses of their own kept them open. The fight for a living in the new country, they claimed, was too exhausting; they had neither time nor energy left to practice religion. There was also the argument that in a world where one's relatives are burnt to death, there could be no God. For these and other reasons, religious observance declined, and today the German Jews of New York are perhaps less observant than their American Jewish neighbors.

In New York, the German Jewish congregations—for they are no longer "communities"—are almost all of the Conservative type; there is only one nominally Reform congregation, Habonim; its services, however, would be called Conservative by American standards. Most of those who had been Reform in Germany either dropped the whole thing or else they joined an American Reform synagogue. A few of the German synagogues are Orthodox, the most important of these being that of Rabbi Breuer, who headed the great Orthodox congregation in Frankfort. The members of this congregation—close to a thousand of them—constitute the most closely knit community within the German Jewish faction; it is said that their children only marry the children of other members. Doubtless this is an exaggeration, but it is true that this Orthodox congregation is one of the few in which the younger people actively participate in religious life; in most of the others, the rabbis complain that "the young people don't come"—a familiar enough complaint in American Jewish life as a whole.

Nevertheless, some of the congregations are expanding, remodeling old quarters, and building new ones. One rabbi, who is also the president of his congregation, negotiated the purchase of the $400,000 property in which his synagogue is situated, financing the purchase partly through a bond issue to his members—a sign, perhaps, of the sense of stability which has succeeded the first anxious efforts to "get settled."

XV

Milton Kaplan

Private Enterprise in the Bronx

Westward from Crotona Park, the Bronx drops so precipitously that a sled, unimpeded, can start at Fulton Avenue and hurtle past Bathgate, Washington, Park, and finally come to rest at the bottom of the valley on Webster Avenue. Of course no sled ever did it, in my day. There were the car tracks and the Elevated at Third Avenue; the New York Central ran through the steep canyon dug out of Park Avenue, and there were car tracks again on Webster. Besides, the ashes that the worried businessmen cast into the drifts after each snow storm made the descent impossible. Standing on the crest of the hill at Fulton Avenue, we eyed the prospect that sloped so tantalizingly towards the west, and then turned and prudently trudged on to Crotona Park to breast its safe and gentle hills.

When I was a boy, I lived in that valley, on Washington Avenue. Even in 1920 it was fast becoming a slum. The tenement houses were old and crowded. We had a coal stove in the kitchen, and I remember going down to our cubicle in the cellar and bringing up a pail of coal for the fire. We still had gaslight for illumination. Steam and electricity finally did come to our house, but not quickly enough to hold the more affluent tenants. They had moved out. The trend was ever west. From Prospect Avenue in the East Bronx, at one time quite fashionable, they moved to Fulton Avenue, then jumped to the Grand Concourse, and finally nestled against the Hudson River at Riverside Drive. That was as far west as they could go. After that there was nothing left but Long Island or Westchester.

We stayed behind. Poor families didn't move, unless they were evicted, and somehow we kept a desperate grip on our four dark rooms. The darkness didn't bother us much; we spent most of our time outdoors. The boys played baseball (outdoor baseball with a hard ball; there was no nonsense about soft-ball baseball in those days) in Crotona Park, and punchball right in the gutter outside the house. Manhole covers served as home plate and second base. First and third bases were chalked in. Our game was interrupted only occasionally by automobiles. They still weren't very numerous in our neighborhood. A great feat of prowess in those days was to punch a rubber ball two "sewers"; that is, to hit the ball two manhole covers away. The game of punchball that brought ball and fist into direct and savage contact has disappeared from the streets of New York. I wonder why. Today, the boys wield a broomstick in the gutter game of stickball, a vastly inferior sport.

For extra diversion there were the back yards, where the cats prowled night and day, the lots on the east side of Park Avenue, the freight yards on the other side of Park Avenue, and for the adventurous, the Jerome Woods, today known, I suppose, as Jerome Avenue. We made fires in the lots and roasted "mickies," potatoes that we had stolen from home. We dared each other to jump from the roofs of the stationary freight trains. Once we ventured into a freight car to explore its contents. A railroad detective was waiting for us as we emerged with packs of gaudy labels intended for U-No-Us Bruckner carbonated beverages. We scattered and ran, holding on to our orange-colored loot. I vaulted a fence and ran all the way home, terrified.

I'd like to think I led a wild and dissolute boyhood in the good old American tradition, but I'm afraid it was pretty tame. Of course, we dangled from the pedestrian bridge over the New York Central tracks, and even climbed down occasionally and flattened against the wall as the train streaked wildly by, but I can't remember anyone's ever being hurt. We had our block fights, too, 174th Street against 173rd Street, but even that degenerated into an innocuous melee with all of us surrendering our block loyalty to the private pleasure of flinging paper bags filled with sand at anyone who came into range. Once, someone threw a milk bottle, but it went wide of the mark, perhaps intentionally, and that scared us all and broke up that particular fight, and we all went home feeling exhilaratingly wicked.

We didn't have many playthings. We had roller skates—"Ball-Barions," we called them (the kids still do, I've discovered)—and we raced in the gutters despite our mothers' passionate warnings, and we hitched on the backs of wagons and cars. Someone had a bat. I don't know where he got it; I know he didn't buy it. We didn't buy baseball bats. I had a catcher's mitt, a black one that I got in exchange for two hundred (I think) United Cigar coupons that I had saved up (my father smoked). Naturally I became the catcher of our baseball team, and I broke every finger in my right hand learning how. I caught without a mask, chest protector, or shin guards. I just squatted behind the batter and caught, the United Cigar mitt between me and the lop-sided, black-taped ball we had to use and re-use. The outfield played barehanded. Sometimes the first baseman was the only other player on the field with a glove. The scores in those games used to run up into the twenties and thirties. Still, Hank Greenberg rose out of our neighborhood.

Nobody had a bicycle, although we did have home-made wagons, constructed from a box, a shaft, and four wheels wrenched from an abandoned baby carriage. Sometimes boys in a frenzy of impatience did not wait for the carriage to be abandoned. We made adequate scooters out of two shafts of wood nailed together perpendicularly and roller skates that had at last outlived their usefulness.

This isn't meant to sound pathetic. We didn't feel pathetic in the least. We accepted poverty as we did the weather. It simply was inexorable and inescapable and we lived our lives accordingly. We never dreamed of buying a bike, although sometimes we chipped in and rented one for an hour, and all of us took turns riding. (We never had to learn, it seems; we just got on and pedaled away.) We never asked our parents for money except for a nickel for an ice cream sandwich. The ice cream sandwich marked the climax of the day. The candy-store man would slip a thin wafer into a rectangular metal holder, wedge an incredibly thick lump of ice cream into it, and then top it with another wafer. In these effete times children eat ice cream cones and chocolate pops. We didn't have the pops; we did have cones, but scorned them. We all ate ice cream sandwiches—it was a community exercise. Together we went in and bought them and then sat on the curbstone and ran our tongues around the perimeter and then tentatively sank our teeth in and nibbled one corner.

Of course in slack time we didn't have ice cream. Because of the vicissitudes of the garment industry, our year was divided into a slack and a busy season. In the busy season, my father just got along; in slack, work petered out.

My mother did what she could to protect the children from the full impact of our poverty, but we felt it. It reached us in our beds in the low rumble of the nightly discussion. My mother wanted my father to earn more money. My father insisted he was doing his best. "I can't help it," he cried. "There is no work."

My mother, thinking of us, would keep on talking. Finally my father spread his arms open in a gesture we learned to recognize. "What do you want me to do?" he wailed. "Break a bank?"

Once in a frantic effort to still my mother's entreaties, he did break a bank. He left the house one morning intent on finding work. He came home that evening grim and uncommunicative. We all knew that he had failed. But when my mother drew in her breath to begin the same old tirade, he quietly spilled a heap of dimes into her hand. He didn't bother to explain how he had earned them. Long afterwards he told me he had broken open my dime bank, which in the course of years munificent relatives had managed to fill to capacity. I think I had five dollars in it. My father lived in constant terror of my mother's finding out, and from the very first wages he got after that, he refilled my bank. I was never the wiser. I had tucked it away in some drawer or other. It was my money, I suppose, but I knew I couldn't spend it.

Clothes were patched and mended, and a new suit had to be planned for months in advance. We bought tables and chairs only on the installment plan. There were things I wanted but I knew better than to ask my parents for money. I wanted books. The public library, it was true, lent books, but I wanted my own. Besides, the library didn't keep Frank Merriwell and Tom Swift. Tom Swifts were sold in the combination stationery and book store on Tremont Avenue for the impossible sum of seventy-five cents, but I could get them secondhand from the fellows on the block for twenty cents or so. They also got their copies secondhand. I never knew anyone on the block who ever bought a book firsthand.

Later, when the radio first reached into our consciousness, I longed to build my own crystal set in a cigar-box chassis, but I needed money for the parts, especially the earphones. I cast around for means of earning money. The traditional methods of mowing lawns and running errands were out. The asphalt was our lawn and the housewives were too thrifty to pay for running their errands. They ran their own, or sent their children.

Fortunately, however, our neighborhood was bare of private telephones. After a while, it is true, telephones became quite common, but at that time I don't remember anyone's having one. One went down to the corner drugstore and used the public telephone. If anyone wanted to reach one of us quickly, he had to call the same drugstore, and the druggist somewhat disgruntled (he was interrupted frequently) would dispatch one of the boys hanging around the corner to get the "party."

That's where I came in. But my scene of operations was not the drugstore—that territory had already been taken. I hung around the candy store on Bathgate Avenue and 173rd Street that sold the jumbo ice cream sandwiches. Bathgate Avenue on that block was still a pleasant tree-lined street, and the pushcarts had not yet invaded its residential privacy.

While waiting for the telephone to ring, I played boxball with the other fellows engaged in the same business. Using the lines of the sidewalk boxes as boundaries, we slapped the ball back and forth, "slicing" and "cutting" until we became miraculously adept at the game. But the shrill summons of the telephone always stopped us, even in the midst of an exciting volley.

We took turns answering the telephone. The first time I took a call, I was terribly excited. I was so nervous that I couldn't even hear what the man at the opposite end of the line was saying, and I had to make him repeat the name and address. Finally I got it and, overwhelmed with gratitude, I blurted "Thank you!" into the receiver and darted out of the store. I've forgotten the name of the "party," but to this day I remember the address. It was 1685 Bathgate Avenue and the lady I called lived on the second floor. She gave me a two-cent tip. It was the first money I had ever earned.

I got to be quite skilled at it. I would get the person wanted on the phone and resume my boxball game, keeping one eye on the booth, which I could see through the window of the store. As soon as my client emerged, I stopped playing, but I was never guilty of anything so gauche as advancing towards him or stretching out my hand. I waited with what I hope was studied nonchalance, but I must confess that as experienced as I became, I couldn't stop my heart from pounding. Usually the "party" knew the amenities and would slip me a coin or two, and the transaction would be over. Satisfying the professional curiosity of my colleagues as to the size of the tip, I would then turn back to the game.

I soon learned to gauge my clients. Men were more generous than women. Joyous news made people prodigal. A blossoming romance became a regular source of income since I would be kept busy calling the young lady to the phone. As the affair ripened, I would have to summon the girl even more often, sometimes several times a day. Naturally the size of the tip diminished in somewhat direct proportion to the frequency of the calls. But I did not complain, for I recognized the advantages of security and a regular income.

The best days for business were Saturday and Sunday. During the week the period between seven and eight-thirty in the evening was a critical one, and I managed to get there in time for the really "fat" calls. A girl bright-eyed and radiant meant a nickel tip, which was tops.

People behaved differently when they got bad news. Some passed me by blindly; others sought me out and pressed a large tip into my hand. Businessman though I was, I felt vaguely guilty at taking it; I had been instrumental in bringing the tears into their eyes. I even attempted a few times to give the tip back but they never took it. Once a girl whose engagement had been broken by phone—I overheard her responses —came out crying bitterly and ran all the way home. The next day she found me and stuffed a quarter into my unwilling fist. I stared at it incredulously and I think I told her it was too much, but I'm not sure. The fellows talked about it for weeks afterward, and it tarnished forever the luster of the nickel tip. The girl married someone else soon after and moved away.

Strange as it may seem, I didn't tell my mother about earning the money. She wouldn't have approved of my working; she would have insisted on my going into the park and playing. So I couldn't buy my earphones—there would have been too many embarrassing questions. But I found that I could use the money to buy books. I always had books around and a few more aroused no suspicion. I think I managed to fill in a set of the Bronco Boys and another set of the Motor Boys. Boys don't read books like those any more.

Part of my money, however, went into the working capital of a new business venture. In the summertime, the same candy store did a land-office business with a staff of private entrepreneurs. I became one of these.

I'm working this out backwards because I'm not sure of the details. This is how I think it went. I got a case of soda, twenty-four bottles in all, for which I paid $1.20, five cents a bottle. In addition, I paid a one-dollar deposit to assure safe return of bottles and case. I received gratis a load of ice, a bottle opener, and a fistful of straws which I stuck into my shirt pocket. The soda was put into my crude wagon, the ice tucked in between the bottles, and my younger brother and I made for Crotona Park. This was strictly a summer trade, and, for that matter, good only on Sunday. In those days people worked a full day on Saturday.

We first went to the ball park near Fulton Avenue where the semi-pro team, the Asburys—later the Everlasts—played their weekly game. It was there that one Sunday, to my horror, I saw the star pitcher of Morris High School pitching for the Asburys, a professional team! Evidently I was the only one who noticed, for he finished his amateur athletic career in a blaze of glory.

He was the first pitcher I had ever seen who could pitch a drop. After that game I changed my style and concentrated on my outcurve.

From the ball field we slowly made our way towards Indian Lake. Business at first was pretty slow because we had to charge ten cents a soda and we had to wait for the return of the bottle. A broken bottle meant a deduction of three cents from our profit. If it was a sunny day, the young men were out with their girls, rowing, strolling, or sitting on the benches around the lake. Then it was easy to get rid of our bottles; the sports thought nothing of a twenty-cent romantic gesture. We had to wait for the girls, though, because they sipped their orange pop daintily through straws. The young bucks just tossed it off.

We had to get rid of our stock within an hour or so; otherwise the ice melted and our soda turned warm and unpalatable. Often in the glare of the hot sun we looked longingly at our wares, but we held back and compromised by sucking on a chunk of our ice. After all, drinking our own soda meant not only a loss of the five cents we had paid for it, but also the five-cent profit we could get for it, a total loss of ten cents! On very hot days we could get rid of a case in less than an hour and go back for another one, but usually we had to be content with a day's profit of $1.20. The sum was so respectable that I felt justified in bringing it home to my mother. She kept the dollar and gave us twenty cents.

As I grew older I found out that the money earned was not commensurate with the time and effort. In my summer vacation from high school, I decided to get a regular job. Some genteel pride in my mother made her protest, but I soon overrode her objections. We needed the money.

I was fourteen at the time, too young for a full-time job, but I managed to get a *Bronx Home News* route, for which I paid five dollars a week. For this I got a supply of the *Bronx Home News* (now *Post Home News*) and a notebook containing the names and addresses of my customers. The area I covered stretched from Webster to Fulton, five square blocks of crowded tenements. Each customer paid twelve cents a week, and I figured I could clear a net profit of about eight dollars.

The job seemed easy enough. On every day except Sunday I got the papers early in the afternoon and was through about five o'clock. At first it was slow going, but I soon mastered the technique. I learned, for instance, that any key could open the occasionally locked door of an apartment house, and I gained entrance without having to ring the bell. I find that information useful even today. I left my wagon with the papers downstairs and took up only the required number of copies. There were no elevators and even a few extra papers got heavy after a climb of five flights of stairs. The superintendent always got a free copy because his good will was indispensable. Delivering to superintendents was a hazardous undertaking. They all lived in the darkness of the basement and kept dogs, presumably for protection against prowling marauders like me. There was one dog in particular, a Great Dane or something, who always bounded out of the depths of Third Avenue to fix me paralyzed against the basement wall. I would have to hold out the free copy of the *Bronx Home News* as identification, and with an ingratiating smile I would advance slowly, while he growled menacingly. I would slip the paper into the door and then back out carefully, still smiling and fighting the impulse to run.

Meanwhile my baseball activities continued apace. I still had my catcher's mitt, many times repaired, and I was the only catcher the team had. Accordingly, the team planned its schedule to suit mine. We played our games in the morning and I delivered in the afternoon. That summer, however, we joined the *Sunday World* Baseball Tournament and that meant that our team, the Cyclones, one day found itself with an important game that had to be played in the afternoon. After a hurried consultation, the entire team threw itself into the concerted effort of delivering papers for me. I drew up a list of customers for each member of the team, and in less than an hour all the papers were distributed and I was free to catch for the team. We lost, and as a result our team was eliminated from the tournament. Moreover, that Saturday, when I made my collections, I had to accept a reduction from virtually every customer who had not had the benefit of my personal service. Most of my teammates had just thrown the papers anywhere, and those who paid some heed to the list I had given them had not bothered to fold the papers and insert them between the knob and the doorjamb in the proper way.

Maybe it was because of that, or because we lost the game (I had thought we had a pretty good chance for the championship), or perhaps because collections weren't going so well—I was netting only about five dollars a week—anyway, for some reason or other, I lost interest in the *Bronx Home News* and carried my route just long enough until a replacement could be found.

Besides, I was going back to high school. I was scheduled to take Latin and I knew I was meant for finer things.

XVI *Samuel Tenenbaum*

Age of Learning

Brownsville, you should know, was originally settled by the overflow of people that spilled out of the tenements and slums of New York's East Side. There they had lived, with innumerable children and innumerable boarders, in railroad flats with the front and the back room sucking up a dim light and the middle rooms dark, with no warm water, no central heating, no bath, and the toilet in the yard. So the East Siders journeyed to this strange remote section of Brooklyn, reached by ferrying across the East River, followed by interminable trolley rides; and later, when a bridge was built across the river, by elevated transit lines at a cost of a nickel.

Here, they thought, they could escape the squalor, the noise, the fetid odors of pushcarts laden with foods and flies. Weren't there in Brownsville green fields, and, a little way up, real cows and real farms? And didn't children walk out to these farms with pitchers to buy the milk, fresh as it came from the cow's udders? And didn't the wife buy vegetables in season direct from the farmer?

And didn't goats and pigs wander around the fields and
streets? And didn't the bread-winner, when he came
home from work at eight or nine o'clock at night, after
milling for an hour or more in the horribly congested
trains, also taste of this new life? For what good wife—
after her husband fell into the kitchen chair and tried to
keep his eyes open for the evening meal—would not save
a glass of that milk for her husband? And didn't that
glass of milk, fresh from the cow, hold sufficient strength
and goodness in it to overcome the evils of the foul city
and the dark, dank factory?

Soon these journeying East Siders made up the
largest Jewish community in the world. At one time,
Brownsville and its environs numbered two hundred to
three hundred thousand Jews (exact figures are impossible to establish), making its Jewish population considerably larger than that of present-day Jerusalem and perhaps one-sixth that of the State of Israel.

Yet, unhappy to remark, how many noisome features
of the East Side slum quickly reappeared in the farmlands
of Brownsville! With a world of building space to choose
from, speculators erected rows on rows of tenements
and jerry-built, identical private houses, all railroad flats,
so that light and sun were here, too, rare and precious.
As on the East Side, in sweltering heat the citizens sought
relief at the candy store, with its "syruped" seltzers, ice
cream, and malted milk. Here too were the fire escapes,
loaded with bedding out "to air" and in summer also with
children and grown-ups. The kitchens, dull, luridly
lighted, were still on public view from the street. In them,
one could view the panorama of Brownsville home life:
the husband disrobed to the waist, the children coming
in and out, for food and reprimands, the tired, monoto-
nous, plodding steps of the wife, as she fussed with pots,
pans, dirty dishes, as she washed and ironed clothes. And

in Brownsville, too, as on the East Side, the immigrants found sweatshops—real sweatshops—to work in for starvation wages, while a small minority of the more ambitious scrimped together a few dollars and opened shabby little candy stores, grocery stores with empty shelves, dark, uninviting dry goods stores, delicatessen stores with rickety chairs.

The homes were dull by comparison with the street, which was the scene of neighborhood living. When a child became sick enough to be taken to a hospital—may it happen only to one's enemies—the entire block was sad. No polite ladies peeped from behind curtains. In Brownsville, the women were curious without curtains, and you may be sure that little escaped them. When a girl strayed and had an illegitimate child: woe to that girl and woe to that family!

In all of this, I assume, there is nothing unique, nothing that is not more or less true of all poor, dispossessed communities. But this is not really my story, which concerns a Brownsville in which there was such a love of learning, such a respect for ideals and idealists, as I have encountered nowhere else.

Today, children may go to school as part of a compulsory routine. In Brownsville when I knew it, school was a major occupation, not of the children alone but of the whole neighborhood. Every teacher was discussed with the minute detail a jeweler devotes to a watch; the principal of the local public school had the same authority and prestige as the most learned dean of our most respected university. School to Brownsville represented a glorious future that would rescue it from want, deprivation, and ugliness. It did not matter how poor and poverty-stricken these ex-East Siders themselves may have been—when it came to education, nothing was too good, no sacrifice was too great for them to make. Harvard, Princeton, Yale—the lowliest Brownsville family did not regard these institutions as too good for their children.

As I recall my childhood, we were all measured in educational potential. Next to an allegation of illegitimacy, nothing more damaging could be said than: "He has a stuffed head. In school, he's put back and left back." The relative scholastic progress of the children provoked intense jealousy and rivalry among neighbors. On coming home from work, the first question the good Brownsville father asked was: "What happened in school?" And the child had to bring out the test papers and the marks.

"My Milton got all A's." Milton's mother would look down her nose at Harry's mother, whose son "got all B's." Don't talk of failure—then the whole house went into mourning.

The Abramowitz family included five sons and one daughter. Mr. Abramowitz, a successful butcher, was regarded as a real millionaire: the women said he had "at least ten thousand dollars." They lived in a detached house with a porch, and at night, the women said, Mrs. Abramowitz's big pots "overflowed with meat and every luxury that a stomach could imagine . . . like a hotel. . . ." But all did not go well in this troubled world for the Abramowitzes. Five of the six children did poorly at school and the meat was as lead in the Abramowitzes' mouths; no one envied them. "What can you expect of butchers' children?" said the women. "Butchers' children remain butchers."

As tall, powerful Mr. Abramowitz hewed away at big chunks of meat, one could feel his sense of frustration and inferiority. One child, David, showed promise: he did well at school, and he went regularly to the library and took out big books. After the family had reconciled themselves, with some difficulty, to the fact that the other children would never be great scholars, it concentrated all attention on David. When David did well in school, the whole Abramowitz family—parents, brothers, and sister—felt that they had done well. When David entered Columbia, the whole Abramowitz family felt that they had become Columbia students. When David took an examination, the whole Abramowitz family sweated it out. When David became a lawyer and opened his own office, Mr. Abramowitz wanted to cover his big butcher shop window with signs advertising the fact. David had to speak at length and persuasively before he convinced his father to substitute a small, dignified announcement. Henceforth, in Mr. Abramowitz's store the important thing was not the meat, but David, "my son, the lawyer."

I remember an elderly lady, thin, anemic-looking, and very, very sad. She came regularly to our home, always with an old creased shopping bag made of black oilcloth. When she came, my mother would gather old bread, left-over food, and whatever good food she could spare. We never regarded her as a beggar or as one asking charity. In fact, we all respected her. Her son was attending medical school. She was a widow, with two other small children, and her son had no one but her to help him. I remember the time she came to make a cash loan: her son was being graduated from medical school and he now needed money to open an office. My mother gave her ten dollars, which was an enormous sum for my family in those days. It would never have occurred to my mother not to make this sacrifice for so holy a purpose.

I still remember the pride with which my family looked forward to the forthcoming social visit of the doctor himself. He was coming to repay the loan personally. We had known his mother, but we had never seen the son. My mother gave the house an unusually thorough cleaning. Every member of my family was there, even my father. When the doctor came in, he was offered the best seat. My mother took out her best dishes and served cake, which she had baked especially for the occasion. As I look back at this incident, I perceive with what humility and respect my parents regarded what they thought was an educated man. My family didn't want the ten dollars which the doctor was now returning; neither did they know how to refuse it. So finally, at the end of the visit, when the doctor held out the ten dollars, my father held back from taking it; my mother did also. Since the doctor looked foolish holding the money, my mother finally stepped forward and took it, but held it in her hand lamely until the doctor left, as if not knowing what to do with it.

If any social hierarchy existed in our community, the European Gymnasium student ranked high, next higher came the European university student, but the aristocrat of them all, the possessor of the most exalted rank, was the Russian social revolutionist.

There was Moses, with his thick glasses, frail body, and worn threadbare coat, from whose stuffed pockets protruded bundles of newspapers and magazines. Moses had been active in radical Russian circles and when I knew him he was an anarchist, a vegetarian, and a Darwinist. In our house, he always sat at the head of the table, and he was always welcome for a meal or for any courtesy he might ask. I listened fascinated as he discussed politics or read to us from the voluminous "literature" he always carried with him. By occupation a house painter, Moses was frail and sickly, and what worried and puzzled my father was how he managed to make a living; for, in fact, Moses never seemed to be in need of money. Many years later, by chance, I encountered Moses' boss, and, naturally, we began to talk about him. "What kind of a worker was Moses?" For an answer, the man laughed. "You couldn't expect work from Moses, not from Moses!" he said. And then he told me how in the middle of a job Moses would get into long political and philosophical discussions with the other workers. I asked, "Why did you keep him?" "Moses!" he exclaimed. "Fire him! How could he make a living? With Moses, one did not try to think of profit. Why, he knew more than a professor."

Occasionally—not often—we would be defrauded, as in the case of Mr. Freedman, and the big books he took from the library, and his flowery and ornate Yiddish, so that frequently we did not understand him. Mr. Freedman boarded with the parents of a friend of mine. When I visited the family and I looked into Mr. Freedman's room, I saw him, true enough, bent over a book, but fast asleep. I even saw him at times pick up a book and, although he tried to keep his eyes open, in several minutes they began to droop. I began to suspect the intellectuality of Mr. Freedman and I imparted my doubts to my mother. At first she refused to listen, but she, too, had had occasion to observe the learned Mr. Freedman bent over a book, but fast asleep. For a while she was a little cold to Mr. Freedman but this did not last long. Soon she was welcoming him to supper with her old cordiality. "A man," she told me afterwards, "who has dealings with such learned books can't be ordinary."

Even those who scoffed came to pay tribute, in their own way. Among the Brownsville settlers there arose a group who prided themselves on being hard-headed and "American." They sneered at education and their measure of a man was not how learned he was but how large his bank balance: "How big a check can he write?" Their favorite folk-tale was of the man who applied for a job, which paid a pittance, as sexton in a synagogue. He was turned down because he was an illiterate. And, continues the story, he went into business and now he is president of the synagogue.

But this same group went into the market to buy professional men as husbands for their daughters. Since doctors in Brownsville represented the apex of knowledge and wisdom, they could command a dowry of as high as twenty-five thousand dollars, pre-war value. At times, a family might subsidize the schooling of a promising student, with the understanding that when he was graduated from college he would go through with an arranged marriage. Dentists, too, had a market rating, and they commanded dowries ranging from ten to fifteen thousand dollars; teachers and accountants fetched about ten thousand; pharmacists, seven to eight thousand. Optometrists, veterinarians, engineers—all commanded a price, depending on the amount of education and the prestige of the occupation.

In other neighborhoods, the ice cream parlor, the poolroom, the dance hall was the favorite gathering-place. In Brownsville, it was the library on Glenmore and Watkins Avenues. There we got to know one another, there we argued about books and writers, there we made intellectual discoveries. We were first-generation ghetto immigrants. Our taste in literature did not come to us by family tradition; we ran across books and authors by chance, mostly by hit-and-miss. Hence, our password: "Do you know of a good book?" I "discovered" Jack London, Upton Sinclair, Oscar Wilde, Bernard Shaw, H. G. Wells; and I am indebted to a friend, my high school teacher, who introduced me to Balzac, Romain Rolland, Zola, Anatole France, Maupassant.

A book such as *Jean Christophe* was kept hidden in a special alcove, carefully guarded by a vinegary librarian. I remember how she scrutinized me to see if I came up to specifications, whether I was of the right age and maturity. Never have I seen anyone—before or since—hand out a book more unwillingly and disapprovingly, as if she herself had somehow become an unwilling accomplice in a plot to undermine public morals. If the truth be told, many of my books seemed to come from that forbidden section, so that the librarian, even when I didn't ask her for a book, developed a special disapproving eye for me. I remember by chance picking up *Dame Care*. I began reading the book in the stacks, standing up, hour after hour, how many I will never know. I was brought back to this world by flickering lights, which was the librarian's signal for closing time. I now own *Dame Care* but I have never re-read the book. My wife, who has read it lately, tells me it's so-so.

The library was something more than a place where one went for books. Here one met and made friends, those from high school, but even more important, those men and women who had little formal schooling, who worked in factories and were Socialists, anarchists, Zionists, Macfaddenites, chiropractors, atheists, food faddists, sun worshipers, Buddhists; men and women who wanted so much from life: to be great writers, to be great humanitarian leaders, to be innovators of world-shaking importance.

In the files of the library, one can find today the reminiscences of a Brownsville librarian, which he published in a professional journal about forty years ago. Excerpts follow:

". . . you are constantly beseeched for more books on sociology and for the best of the Continental literature. Your reading room is full of young men preparing themselves for civil service and college-entrance examinations. Your reference desk is overtaxed with demands for material for debate on every conceivable public question, from 'equal pay for women' to the comparative merits of the library and the gymnasium. And there are more youngsters awaiting help in looking up every single allusion in their textbooks than the assistants can serve . . . and what is better still, you have to be conservative and ever on your guard lest your reading public increase three times as fast as the library's resources. . . .

"Their reading is an odd mixture of the serious and the childish. Their race tragedy often sobers them in appearance and taste early, and as is well known they are very precocious. Sometimes a little toddler will come in whose head just reaches up to the registration desk and to the surprise of all . . . will read right off some paragraph given as a test. . . . Toward those books whose use some libraries restrict, the attitude of the adults is very liberal. No explanation completely satisfies them and their indignation rises high when they learn that libraries occasionally see fit to withhold certain volumes of Tolstoy, of Zola, or of Shaw."

I should like to tell you about Ribber, a shy, timid, sad boy. His parents were impoverished, and Ribber only managed to stay in school by selling pretzels on street corners. In school he did not do well, and in his sophomore year he was flunked out. Ribber continued selling pretzels. One day I met him in the library, and I spoke to him for the first time. I do not believe that he was more than nineteen or twenty, but he took from his pocket letters from famous universities (if I am not mistaken, one of the universities was either Harvard or Chicago) thanking him for his contributions of rare and old editions of Shakespeare and the Bible. He showed me communications with professors. In fact, he had now in his possession a rare edition of the Bible, and he was debating with himself whether to donate it to a professor in the Princeton Theological Seminary or to a professor in the Jewish Theological Seminary. He even knew what scholars would most appreciate the worth of his rare finds. He refused all payments. And how did he—this pretzel seller —find these books and how was he able to buy them? They weren't costly, he explained. "This valuable Bible," he said, talking about his latest find, "cost me eighty-five cents. I picked it up from a pushcart." It was a matter, he told me, of having the patience to seek and of being able to recognize what was valuable.

Another shrine of the neighborhood was the Labor Lyceum, the official headquarters of the Socialist party and the local trade union. Presiding over this institution was Sol Hurok, whose early entrepreneurial ability was devoted to managing the campaigns of the local Socialist party. Hurok first learned to make culture pay when, to gather funds for the party, he organized concerts with the help of top-flight artists and also with the lesser talent of loyal party members.

Early, Hurok showed that he had a unique talent for gathering dollars. Hurok would carefully coach the members of the Young People's Socialist League on the art of selling the magazines and pamphlets that both furthered the cause and helped the party's treasury. When all other Socialist party locals were conducting perfunctory campaigns, Hurok, with the same undeviating purpose with which he raised money, rallied speakers and supporters, flooded the district with leaflets, Socialist newspapers, and circulars, arranged monster mass meetings. In fact, Brownsville was among the first districts in New York State to elect a Socialist assemblyman, Abraham Shiplacoff.

During campaigns, the Labor Lyceum was the center for Socialist propaganda, but during the year the building bulged with educational activities. The courses and the lectures scorned such practical and mundane matters as salesmanship, charm, or personality. Instead,

Brownsville flocked to hear erudite discussions on such subjects as: "Moses, Jesus, Spinoza, and Marx," "The History of Human Thought as Exemplified in the Workers' Struggle Against Capitalism," "Kropotkin, Spencer, and Marx," "Dickens, Zola, Flaubert, as Interpreted from the Viewpoint of the Class Struggle," "The History of Philosophy, from Greek to Modern Times."

Either in the Labor Lyceum or in other educational forums, which dotted the neighborhood, proponents of all causes found adherents. Anarchists held meetings in which they held forth on free love, the essential goodness of man, the abolition of police and jails. Health faddists conducted campaigns against doctors, who, they maintained, were part of a giant conspiracy to keep the workers sick. Birth-control advocates here had strong support and sympathy. In fact, it was here that Margaret Sanger in 1916 established the first birth-control clinic in America. Zionists, too, in a more quiet way, were equally active.

Recently I revisited my neighborhood. I have not lived there for nearly a quarter of a century. There are still pushcarts in Brownsville; the street life is still teeming and dramatic. But the old Brownsville—the one that loved learning and knowledge—is gone. Brownsville is now "Americanized," with the movies, the radio, television, the automobile, the national chain stores (no longer independent little stores) providing focal points. Still essentially a Jewish community, the stream has not been fed by new immigrants. The shabby old tenements, more odorous now and more dilapidated, are being occupied by an influx of new minority groups, probably even more dispossessed and less advantaged than the immigrant Jews. Large numbers of Negroes have entered this community; also Italians, White Russians, Arabians, Syrians.

Brownsville residents, in the course of time getting

better jobs and becoming more prosperous, began to desert the ghetto community for more fashionable areas —Flatbush, the Bronx, Riverside Drive, the West Side of Manhattan. The exodus was especially rapid among the second generation, who, unlike their parents, did not develop close ties with neighbors, civic associations, or the local synagogue.

Not everyone left, of course. I remember one family that lived directly underneath an elevated train. The father was a pushcart peddler, but he had two daughters who were school teachers, a son who was an accountant, and three other daughters, two who worked in offices and one who worked in a factory. The girls especially wanted to move, since they felt that the shabby house harmed their marital chances. The father was adamant in insisting on remaining. "Look," the father once told me, pointing to the rumbling sound made by a passing train. "It's like music. If you look outside the window, it's always like a show." And that was his favorite recreation after tramping the streets all day—looking out the window and watching the train pass directly before him.

At times, the departure of the young from the family home had painful consequences. There were the Silvermans, whose son, a successful doctor, moved to Riverside Drive. The Silvermans one day went to visit their son. They came back disappointed. They told of a "fancy soldier," and how he telephoned, and then the "soldier" said the doctor was not at home. They went several other times, and always with the same results. After that, the Silvermans rarely spoke of their son. He would occasionally visit the family, but his visits became fewer and further apart. It would not be truthful to say that this was an isolated case. Such things happened, even to Brownsville parents.

By and large, however, successful children were ex-

ceedingly solicitous of their parents. They came back to
the old homestead for family reunions and they plied
their parents with expensive gifts. When the Cohens celebrated their fortieth wedding anniversary, a son presented
them with a tour of Palestine. Another son made a generous gift to a local hospital, and still another made a
generous donation to their parents' favorite charity. In
a family on my block, one of the sons who had become a
millionaire (a real one) lavished luxuries on his parents.
He renovated their two-family house with so many improvements and so many modern gadgets that it became
a community showplace. The parents generally protested
against such extravagance and it was clearly the children
who had the greater pleasure, perhaps nostalgic, in generously giving.

Recently I visited the library on Glenmore and
Watkins Avenues. Physically, I found the place as charming as I remembered it. The tables were polished; the
floors were waxed; the iron grillwork on the balcony
was as graceful as ever; the books were as inviting. But
there was a strange and eerie quiet. I was astonished to
learn that the library was open only twice a week, and
that even for this limited period there was little activity.
Two librarians were eager to serve me. What a change
from my youth when we waited outside in long lines for
the library to open, so that we could enter first and rush
for our favorite book!

I walked over to the Labor Lyceum. The street was
familiar, but the building itself looked strange to me. In
front of the building, huge trucks were being loaded. The
building had been converted to a factory. If you look
upward toward the roof, you can still see the name
"Labor Lyceum" clearly inscribed.

Brownsville's body is still there, but not the soul.

XVII *Isa Kapp*

By the Waters
of the Grand Concourse

A New Yorker without too strict a sense
of order and tradition can find all sorts of amiable places
to live in the reasonable confusion of Manhattan. But it
is true, and I suppose anyone with a spark of discrimination would find it disturbing, that many of these places
have no real character of their own—no particularity in
architecture, in smell, in accent. Even those groups of
streets that pretend to be neighborhoods—West End,
86th Street, Third Avenue, Riverside Drive—can show
only a few blocks that belong together. At any minute
a cross street, an elevated structure, a small walking
bridge can crash into the unity: at once there is a new
tone, new manners. One can of course find a kind of
impersonal purity in the thoroughfares, Park, Fifth Avenue, but only negatively, as in the walls of a bank, which
also exercise discipline upon money.

Unique, consistent character has to be sought in the
more parochial boroughs of the city. At the threshold of
the Bronx, just past a miniature Negro slum and the Car-

269

dinal Hayes High School, there immediately emerges a
Jewish community as dense, traditional, and possessive
as William Faulkner's Yoknapatawpha County, and
through it flows a great middle-class river, the Grand
Concourse. There is no mistaking even its inlets and trib-
utaries: the waters that seep over from the evergreened
fountained courtyard of the Roosevelt Apartments to the
modest tan brick of Morris Avenue carry an irrepressible
élan, a flood of self-indulgence and bountiful vitality,
vulgar and promiscuous, withal luxuriant and pleasurable.

The assumption has taken root in the Jewish West
Bronx that all satisfactions of palate, of vanity, and of
intellect are attainable. You can be prepared to hear that
the garage-owner's family, having shopped for ten years
at Klein's and the A&P, will one day go off for a summer
trip to Europe, buy a two-family house in a quiet residential district, sell the house at a profit and move, when
the fever strikes, to California. The dress-manufacturer's
son naturally gets his MD, specializes; the daughter becomes a psychiatric social worker. To confirm their faith
in themselves, and in America's promises, they become
conspicuous consumers of silver foxes, simultaneously
of learning, gift-shop monstrosities, liberal causes, and
Gargantuan pastries. A generous, expansive life! At the
same time, a life utterly without taste. The rugs are too
heavy, the spirit of the Jewish holiday is kept alive by fur
pieces, the frame is always more expensive than the
picture.

Still, all purchases breathe an air of not being final,
of expecting to be traded in in a few years, and this is,
in spite of waste, a hopeful sign. For, in effect, the vulgar,
predictable middle-class homogeneity is infinitely mobile,
transformable, and energetic. We will come to see that
the self-contained stable society of the Grand Concourse
makes concessions to its anarchists as well as its snobs,

and in either case, to the human need for individuation.

Take that area of gratification, Fordham Road. From the vertigo of the crossroads where thousands realize the deep satisfactions of getting a $1.98 article for $1.89 in Alexander's, and finding a creamier éclair at Sutter's, it is possible to escape, four blocks south, to a theater which was among the first in New York to devote itself to foreign-language films, Yiddish, French, recently Italian. Mongrelized by its ambivalent cultural surroundings, the little Ascot tried to be refined (was a pioneer in serving coffee in the lounge), avante-garde-ish (flung a bold challenge at the American dream that was daily unreeled under the Waterman's Ink star-spangled skies of the Loew's Paradise), and non-commercial (you could go there and constitute an audience of one). On the other hand, the RKO Fordham was the home of the heavy date, the initialed "blazer" and the DeWitt Clinton cap, red and black; while the scrawny, dilapidated University Theater played such old nostalgic pieces as *Scarface*, *Spitfire*, etc. It would not be fair to gloss over disparate elements in this borough of universities. Thus it must be revealed that there was a small inconspicuous house somewhat south of Fordham Road on which the signs announcing wining and dining were thought to be polite camouflage. I have never known anyone to exploit this inside knowledge, but the presence of such deception in the middle of the Grand Concourse lent a certain exoticism to what was in danger of becoming an oppressive neighborhood: just below was the region of medical care and funeral services.

On 174th Street, the Concourse turns eastward, and at this rather grandiose juncture looms the one-dimensional steel security of the Medical Building. The Lewis Morris, once "restricted," now contains the offices of more than forty Jewish doctors and dentists: in one building, a maternity hospital, several nose-and-throat specialists, heart men, internists, and so forth. The extravagant feeling of personal well-being is reinforced by the fact that this is no Manhattan office building, but an apartment house of two hundred Jewish families of means, in the heart of the West Bronx.

A relationship exists here between tenants and the door- and elevator-men (there are, or were, seven) that I have seen nowhere else in New York. The latter share entirely in the general house atmosphere of success and tolerance. They have a jauntiness and natural grace that seems to derive simply from ease, but then they go beyond this, to a quizzical cosmopolitanism, as though the crowding of so many urban Jewish professionals into their four elevators amused them. Every young man with glasses is hailed as professor, every adolescent female in a fur jacket presumed to be a model. The whimsy makes no apparent inroads on the complacency of the tenants, and no joke has ever been made at the expense of the elevator men, possibly because they are shrewd enough to know not only the collective but the special weaknesses of their riders, but possibly for less defensive reasons. A weak but truthful joke is told about the Negro maid in the Jewish household who answers the phone: "No, this isn't Mrs. Goldstein, this is the *shvartze*." The mark of a home where the exterior bad taste is at least neutralized, if not excused, by the interior warmth and fraternal feeling! A warm condescension is no longer wholly condescension: we call it benevolence.

One coterie in the Lewis Morris is more formal than the rest, gives in to the official nature of the house, methodically absorbs itself in its mail riding up in the elevator. But the ethos of the medical building, the real power, resides, not in such individualists, but in one of the most potent of American pressure groups, the circle of gregarious red-faced women who sit from May through October in the sunny enclosure that is reserved for them. Among the housewives who send their children to the Little Red School House, the High School of Music and Art, Columbia, even the Sorbonne, the dominant figure is that of the efficient young matron whose ambiguous expression means, I'm doing all right, the next coat is ordered, the last insured. A smug, not happy face! What is the source of the dissatisfied look that is indigenous to all Grand Concourse housefronts? Perhaps the bile of neighborly competition, perhaps precisely the involuntary community of sunny afternoons, which emphasizes the sense in the participants that they suffer a continuous displacement, that their solidity ends up in the open air. For most of them, having been romanticists in the office and *femmes fatales* in the hospital corridors, are secretaries and nurses in their living rooms. Substituted for the glamorous paradoxical moment when the secretary lets down her hair, lowers the lights, and turns on Mozart, is the futile ritual of transporting the décor of business into the home. Above the baby carriage, a tailored suit slipped over the girdle, a flash of costume jewelry on a hot sidewalk. (You have to walk at least six blocks east to see a loose cotton dress that wrinkles.) The smug look is the memory of the certificate that meant escape from the office, the spleen that works the mouth is nostalgia for the boss. Their instincts asserted and their great expectations fulfilled, efficiency becomes incongruous. Their only audience is their neighbors. Three or four young matrons can always be seen together in an impersonal, distracted intimacy. In this sort of relationship, one can live for years without an exchange of vital favors: no onions borrowed, and no babies palmed off for the day.

The young mothers are never drudges; in this class,

tradition forces grandmothers, if there is no part-time maid, to come and help out. These older women, the aggressive *balabustas*, sustain a different kind of continuous irritable gregariousness. In five minutes they find out how many rooms, how many children, troubles, what boyfriends, jobs, summer camps, how much education. As for them, they have a beautiful apartment, a talented younger daughter. If she were persistent, she could stand out among her friends in no time. Her son has a good position, his boss depends on him. They have land in Palestine, they picked out a good hill, they can retire comfortably in a few years. But the face above is stolid; no obligations on either side.

I have already implied that the side streets of the Concourse can free themselves neither from its air nor from its values. At the same time, the Concourse borrows much of its essential spirit from them. The whole character of its self-image is bound up with its absolute middle position: in geography, as a concourse leading from the heat and dust of the warehouses at its southern tip to the cool impeccable suburbs at its north; in possibility, a concourse from Bathgate Avenue uptown to Park Avenue downtown. At any rate, going east on a side street, in the oval that faces Claremont Park, conversation has a style of its own. Here, above the counterpoint of baby carriages, we made our early distinctions between world revolution and socialism in one country, between the authentic Marxists and the petty-bourgeois opposition, and formulated the vocabulary of protest. On Eastburn Avenue we ate our first *homentashen* and were told that a small glass of homemade cherry wine helps to digest a heavy meal. Here also, in an empty lot, before the sprouting of the antiseptic Lebanon Hospital, you could see between the Concourse and Sheridan Avenue the only weeds, dandelions, ivies, and wild grasses in the West

Bronx. On summer nights, portable radios, guitars, sandwiches were crowded into Claremont Park; and in the spring, a fellow picked up a girl by whistling a Beethoven quartet at her.

The Jewishness of the Grand Concourse, until recently a disorderly self-conscious phenomenon, also borrows some of its strength from the class below, the streets east, where rituals are accompanied by *esprit* and determination, and no one is vague about the forms. It is true that tradition is mainly invoked through the Jewish menu and the synagogue club, and probably with the most practical considerations in view. But the noticeable thing is the pleasure that exists in continuing Jewish habits. If the Grand Concourse draws upon 86th Street and Park Avenue for its *public* Zionism, its philanthropy, its flair for organization, it takes from those other streets on the east its *kugel*, its Friday candles, and its shrug of the shoulder. Influenced by opinion and taste from above and below, the Grand Concourse is in a sense cosmopolitanized. It has elements of classlessness, thus catholicity, and at the same time has the firmness, substantiality, and accrued culture of a definable class. It can both eat its cake and have it.

It seems to me very possible that the middle cultural position, unclear as its inclinations and its self-definitions are, provides the best breeding ground for Jews as human beings. As intellectuals, as artists, as social idealists, it gives them, certainly, a few hurdles to jump, but with characteristic generosity provides the time and money for training. To a child brought up on the Concourse, Judaism is simply part of his unconscious absorption of culture. The fact of being Jewish is accepted, but without the distinction of being Jewish. He is as innocent of martyric feeling as he is of racial peculiarity and, in most cases, of anti-Semitism. If one thinks in terms that try to impose a universal situation upon a particular person. there is, I suppose, a kind of inauthenticity in all this. Actually, though the Jewish child has not grasped the universal "real situation," he does understand his own situation, which is urban and disorganized and always subject to his own wit and inventiveness. In his case, there is to be no waiting for miracles.

He is, so far as I can see, entirely fortunate in having a free choice. Jewish manners, irony, music, intonation are in the atmosphere, and he can enjoy them either consciously or unconsciously. If he is to become a writer, let us say, it would perhaps be better for him to study the Talmud, to read Yiddish, to stay home Friday evenings, to absorb and be able to articulate a Jewish rhythm of living, as Catholic liturgies might, for example, be a very important source of a composer's invention. Since he is, for the most part, not to be a writer, but at the least to be an adult human being, the cultural vagueness in his environment cannot hurt him, cannot spoil his pleasure in discovering Judaism or the Hasidic tales a decade later. An Americanized inauthentic Jewish child, his confusion frees him. His possibilities are boundless, therefore he is more likely to bind himself in a meaningful way, to groups, to individuals, and to ideas.

The Grand Concourse is very far from the ghetto, and possibly as far from the ghetto psychology as Jews can ever get. Here there is less pressure and anxiety (apart from actual conflict) than in the Palestinian Jewish state. Jewishness is not a calling, a fate, or a challenge, but a usable fact of life. Jews set the norm of behavior, so, as Jews, they are under no social compulsions. As opposed to Palestinians, they are, as Jews, under no patriotic compulsions. Lacking perhaps the potentiality of unifying and giving form to their tradition, they gain the potentialities of diversity and disorganization. If Gentiles want to know individual Jews, this is the place where they can be known and can deny even such rational, analytical stereotypes as Sartre has constructed. The middle class here avoids Babbittry through continuous absorption of elements of discord. Undigested (but in urban life one learns to use even undigested elements), they initiate the ferment that creates a perpetual vivacity.

In the neighborhoods where Jewry has for many years been able to take its existence for granted, and to live an undefensive middle-class life, I think it is the older, European generation that has better exploited its freedom. We have seen in this generation a blurring of fanaticism, an adaptability, that is able to stand even the breaking away of its children. The latter, rigidly associating their homes with conservatism, parochialism, and repression, have been provincialized by their own revolt, sometimes going so far as to look for moderation and gentility in non-Jewish life only. They have been amazed years later to find their parents self-consciously "progressive," self-educated, wry, mannerly, and even, having got wind of modern psychology, embarrassingly over-considerate.

But what the children will never forgive their flexible parents are the stage sets of their childhood. The parent includes his home in a sweeping casual gesture of success, and then forgets about it; but to the child, the old rooms, the mirror that covers a whole wall, the painting that shows up well above the credenza, are like sore gums that he will never stop poking. The parent has resigned himself to his faith that public assertion of prosperity must come, in cities, at the expense of *Gemütlichkeit*. What Grand Concourse home knows any more this European, pre-middle-class quality? The streets are lost to them. Instead they cultivate interiors, and the principle of display drives out the principle of pleasure. How many Concourse bedrooms are suffocated by flowered wallpaper, the *Kitsch* of domestic culture; how many windows blotted out with venetian blinds, the somber instruments of urban privacy. The "living" room receives its sagging prop of barrel chairs, mahogany servers, cut crystals. In the spring, a housewife's fancy turns to chintz drapes with figures of birds and enormous roses.

Eccentric, spontaneous taste effaces itself before the dignified concept of a "set," that dreadful harmony of a single wood, a single century's notions. Between the 20's and the 40's, colors and lines may have changed, but the urge to unity remains. If through a whole apartment you notice, with slight variations, a disturbing relationship among all the lamps, you find out it was a deliberate maneuver: they are all "Japanese Modern." The mushroom-pink of the Degas sleeve "plays up" the mauve in the rug.

It becomes the extreme imaginative luxury to go from such homes into those where pieces of furniture are chosen singly, because of the limitation of money or because someone has been unreasonably lured by an odd shape or a pronounced grain of wood to substitute for the heavy completeness of the Concourse even a capricious, uninformed vulgarity. But in the very atmosphere where possessions have come to mean so much and indicate so much, they are most impersonally acquired. The prepossessing family succumbs to the ultimate degradation of calling in the interior decorator (she gets a twenty-five per cent discount on the fabrics) to match the drapes to the sofa ruffle, the kitchen oilcloth to the shelving.

Behind their massive pieces, these bourgeois are hard to confound. Ingenuousness is a quality they have lost. A kind of lumbering sophistication operates for them in sexual matters as well as in politics. Here, Marx is neither

a shock nor a mystery, nor, to be sure, very much of a
historic figure. So, too, this is perhaps the only kind of
Jewish home in which jokes about virginity and contra-
ception can be exchanged between fathers and daughters.
Such early sophistication has, of course, very little to do
with an attitude of simplicity or pleasure toward sexual
experience. It assumes, on the contrary, the existence of
insidious appetites which cannot be gratified. The joke,
in fact, lies precisely in the frustration. Out of the homes
where the vocabulary of sexual banter is breezily absorbed and flaunted, come emancipated, excitable, prud-
ish adolescents who are able to discuss "orgies of petting"
in the most academic way, and to develop prejudices that
strike midway between the stag dinner and the social
worker's brochure. If the children finally come to think
in a more natural way, the knowing parents then impose
an implicit protocol of silence. The vocabulary for sexual
enjoyment is sparse.

On the surface, the Concourse milieu would seem
to be a natural enemy of the instincts, and of taste, but
in practice it is, by the greater profusion of its minerals,
and by its density, likelier ground for creativity than the
looser, more conscientiously watered soil of Greenwich
Village. In its aesthetic clutter lies the potentiality of
strong individual opinion. Where good taste is an assumption, as often as not evasiveness is bred, and a tactful neu-
trality that is habitual and mechanical. In these homes
on the Grand Concourse, tact has to be relearned, as
does taste, thus there is no danger of relaxed alertness.

In spite of oppressive elements, the final effect of the
middle-class home is not a stifling one. We must make a
distinction between the suspicious hostility toward unfamiliar ideas and manners in the lower-middle-class
home, which is conservative, and the humorous condescension of the older generation's "You'll agree with me

ten years from now" along the Grand Concourse. The first paralyzes, the second provokes. To the first you continue to make the irritable compulsive concessions that create inward hysteria; to the second, no concessions are possible, necessary, or seriously expected. In fact, left dissatisfied and unrealized by their work, rather than debilitated, Concourse parents seek and appreciate any kind of stimulation. They are challenged, rather than overawed or puzzled, by their children. It must be remembered that en route to the Grand Concourse apartment, they stopped off at one of the side-streets to the east. Therefore, ten years from now, if their children should really be ready to agree with them, chances are that *they* will be the ones to protest.

XVIII *Morris Freedman*

The Jewish College Student:
New Model

In 1895 Morris Raphael Cohen passed his entrance examinations to the College of the City of New York, receiving a gold medal for having made the highest mark of all the candidates. He reported the event as follows in his autobiography, *A Dreamer's Journey:* "Even when I went home I could not realize that I had actually passed. My mother at that time was bedridden, and when I told her that I had passed the examination and was thus admitted to college, a flood of tears came into her eyes. . . . When one of my aunts remonstrated with my mother, 'You cannot afford to send your boy to college,' she replied, 'If need be I'll go out as a washerwoman and scrub floors so that my Morris can have a college education.'"

At the same college I recently heard the story of a bright youngster who was removed from school by rich relatives shocked to learn that he had been wasting his time studying books. With his parents' approval and his own wholehearted assent, the relatives put him to work as a salesman learning their business.

Between the extremes of the immigrant turned scholar and the native son saved by the business world from the fate of a college education, falls the history of the Jewish student in America. The avid "grind" reaching out to embrace diverse fields of learning (Cohen spoke authoritatively on law, logic, philosophy, history, literature, mathematics, and—if his contribution of a question to the radio program "Information Please" was more than a gag—baseball) has given way to the college man of as few intellectual parts as he can get away with, choosing his career with calculation and shrewdness but not heart, instinct, devotion, or a sense of sacrifice.

Morris Raphael Cohen became for the generations of the 20's and 30's a veritable folk hero. He was the Paul Bunyan of Jewish intellectuals, and tales of his gigantic mental prowess were recounted with loving exaggeration, as though anything could be true of him. The heroes of today are the practical men, the rich, the successful: Billy Rose, perhaps, or the department store magnates, or Bernard Baruch, especially in his role as financier (students at one of the branches of City College have been talking about having the name of their school changed to carry Baruch's name). Even the college intellectuals seem to be more aware of the popular successes—Arthur Miller, Norman Cousins, Clifton Fadiman, Abe Burrows: the men whose accomplishments may be directly measured by their celebrity or income—than of such "highbrows" as Lionel Trilling, Ernest Nagel, Alfred Kazin, or Sidney Hook.

Jewish students have attended almost every college and university in the country. But it may be claimed with good reason that the typical Jewish student in America during the 20's and 30's—insofar as there can be a typical

Jewish student—was the one who attended New York's free City College. For many years now, probably since the 20's, CCNY's student body has been about 80 per cent Jewish, and it has been estimated that fully one-third of America's present Jewish college graduates attended City.*

The composite image of the City College student is of an argumentative intellectual, a sometimes brilliant, loquacious, rather truculent young man, who is partial to radical politics, disrespectful of authority, and whose erudition is as catholic and unselective as it is occasionally superficial. During the "golden age" of City College, roughly the 20's and 30's, he is supposed often to have known more on any particular subject than many of his teachers. Certainly in the 30's, he was the select of the select. There probably has never been such a large student body in history that was winnowed so carefully for scholastic ability as the one at City College during that

* When the Brooklyn and Queens municipal colleges were created to supplement City, many Jewish students entered the new schools, but then these new institutions took on much of the character of City College itself. New York University, a private institution with regular tuition fees, began in late years to attract Jewish students whose parents had some money. It was felt that a degree from NYU had more value because it was paid for and did not carry the "stigma" of coming from a "Jewish" college. The irony of this is that, outside New York City, NYU and CCNY are generally confused. Some Jewish students went to one of NYU's colleges (which has a somewhat lenient scholastic standard for admission) because they couldn't get into one of the city colleges, which—since only a limited enrollment could be accepted—have had to maintain higher entrance requirements. Columbia University, too, always had a substantial number of Jewish students in its undergraduate colleges, and of late the proportion has increased greatly. In the great private universities of the East—notably Harvard, Yale, and the University of Pennsylvania —a large proportion of the Jewish students were from "the town," and perhaps were not strikingly different from the "City College type." Elsewhere outside of New York, various municipal and state colleges have had substantial numbers of Jewish students. It is hard to say how much these did or did not conform to the City College type; at any rate, they certainly weren't so numerous or so homogeneous as to create their own stereotype.

period. The depression was a perfect time for young people to go to college; there was little else to do. The minimum high school average for admission to City College kept rising, as more and more applications came in, until it hovered somewhere around 90 per cent. And in those days a high school average, like so many things, was worth more than today.

The concentration on classroom accomplishments made for the rigid, and sometimes snobbish, exclusion of other than purely academic pursuits. The Jewish student was concerned about his grades with a fierce, concentrated competitiveness. His favorite sports were chess and ping-pong, the football team was a joke, and for many years only the business students were understood to know or care about the basketball team. He was careless in dress (often out of poverty), worked at various jobs after school (for the same reason), and was quite gauche in worldly matters—City being, until recently, an all-male school at its main campus.

He was emotionally sensitive and was therefore often especially drawn to such subjects as literature and art. He was known to work his intellect for the sheer exercise of it. Philosophy classes would frequently degenerate into Donnybrook Fairs as insults, definitions, and counter-definitions were violently tossed around. Those students who hadn't committed themselves to an ideology might argue passionately on various sides of a question, trying ideas on for size. Intellectual chaos was accompanied by emotional confusion. Students were often involved in messy personal relations, at home, with their girl friends, with their teachers. A small number of Jewish students majoring in English, when they came to read Gerard Manley Hopkins' poems, were so overcome by his compelling ecstasy that they toyed, at least in talk, with the idea of Catholicism—which offered discipline, security, guidance, and, to judge from Hopkins, an emotional life of high intensity and beauty.

Of course, there were students and students. Not totally uncommon was the quiet, shy boy who was attentive in class and who plodded through his school work with a minimum of interference from irrelevant activities. And there were also the "Joe College" rah-rah boys: interested in dates, sports, fraternity life, and the like. These latter made some noise and were always coddled by the administration, who saw them as forming an island of normality in a sea of alienation. But it was a small island, with few settlers.

Writing anonymously in 1930 in the *Menorah Journal*, a prominent American writer gave this description of Jewish students at Columbia University:

"One of [the] Jewish types that has worked itself into legend is the 'student.' He is a man who is solely interested in his work, a skeptical searching man, absorbed in text or tube, not only indifferent to but incognizant of the social appurtenances of eminent academic scholarship; crusty, without the amenities, armed with a mighty scorn of the world's estimate of his work. There are Gentile scholars of such sort, of course; but the type, the 'pure intelligence,' the almost disembodied mind, is something that has been identified with the Jew. . . ."

Everyone agrees that the Jewish student has since changed; but it is almost impossible to get meaningful statistics to document the matter.

Many of the college officials I consulted made a great show of not knowing or caring whether or not their students were Jewish. This exhibition of indifference might have a point in an institution where Jews do not constitute somewhere over 75 per cent of the students. Where they do, such self-imposed ignorance, however honorably motivated, seems rather pointless. A dean of one of the city colleges wrote me that ". . . we do not ask our students whether they are Jewish, Mohammedan, or whatever else," and then sent me a highly detailed sociological examination of the student body in which just about every other question was asked. The study was made with the object of helping the administration understand its students better.

In spite of its studious avoidance of any question on Jewishness, and though some non-Jewish students are included in the statistics, this study does offer a number of interesting facts about today's Jewish students. Only a little more than half of the students covered by it have parents both of whom were foreign-born; in the 20's and 30's, the proportion was closer to 100 per cent. (I remember an instructor in history once asked our class how many had parents born in Europe. Every student raised his hand.) The family income of the majority ranges between three and five thousand dollars a year, a good deal higher, probably, than that of the families of yesterday, even taking into account the general inflation. The improved economic status of today's student may be seen dramatically in the hundreds of students' automobiles that are parked daily in the streets around City College.

There has been a major shift in the occupations of the students' fathers. In the 20's and 30's immigrant fathers were concentrated in the garment and the unskilled trades. Today, almost 20 per cent are retail merchants; about 12 per cent are salesmen; 10 per cent, professionals; 12 per cent, garment workers. If a knowledge of English is considered a sign of integration in American life, the shift to the first three occupations mentioned, in which some facility in English is required, would seem to indicate an increasing integration. Almost 90 per cent of the fathers attended school for some period; 11 per cent were graduated from professional schools; 4 per cent from college; 16 per cent from high school; and 17 per cent from elementary school (these figures are not overlapping). About 80 per cent read two or three English-language newspapers a week, magazines occasionally, and have been more than once to legitimate theaters. Many have visited various sections of the United States; a few have been abroad. Only 26.3 per cent of the families attend religious services regularly. In the 20's and 30's, the newspaper of the immigrant parents was likely to be Yiddish; there were few English magazines in the home; the parents visited only the Yiddish theater; they spoke English with some difficulty; their traveling was limited to summer visits to the Catskills or the Coney Island and Rockaway beaches.

The dean of one of the undergraduate private colleges in the East said to me: "I would say that you can almost no longer distinguish Jew from Gentile among the students. Jewish boys are not exclusively the 'greasy grinds,' as all were once thought to be, although one or two may still be; yet on the whole they still seem to be superior in their studies. They belong to all types of organizations, their interests being as widespread as those of other students. They major in every subject. Most student-newspaper editors and reporters, however, still are Jewish, just as in the old days. The Jewish boys wear the same soiled white shoes, the same mixed coats and jackets, have the same crew haircuts, and attend the same social affairs as everyone else. As a matter of fact, the social mixing at the dances is as complete as mixing in the classes.

"It's hard to say whether this leveling of differences is an altogether good thing. While it is probably a good thing that Jewish young men are showing an interest in a much wider choice of professions, most of them do not have that burning compulsion to learn that marked the boys of yesterday and perhaps inspired those around them. Today, I would say Jewish boys show little if any difference from their fellows in their attitudes toward education."

The war, which interrupted the academic careers of many students, created the interesting laboratory situation, when the veterans returned, of students who normally would have got their degrees in the 30's or 40's being placed side by side with boys fresh out of high school. The age gap between the two groups was often as much as a dozen years, and there was little contact between the youngsters and the older men. The groups constituted two nations, firmly separated.

The veterans—yesterday's students—were serious about their learning to the point, sometimes, of being stuffy. A good number had dropped out of college some years before the war, in the late 30's, and had come back with the aid of the GI bill of rights. A college education to most of them was in no sense a buffer between adolescence and the real world of maturity. Nor did they consider a college degree merely an asset in job hunting, although some were at college cold-bloodedly for this reason alone. (Some, it must be admitted, were in school purely to collect benefits.) Most of the veterans were curious and eager with a nervousness and impatience reminiscent of the students of yesterday, and instructors who had almost forgotten what it meant to have their mettle tested found themselves invigorated and stimulated.

The younger students, who for a time after the war were in the minority, contrasted sharply with the veterans. This came out in several of my classes in English literature and composition. While the veterans occupied the center of the room, the others sat themselves in the corners, turning their chairs audience-fashion to watch the show. The veterans did their work conscientiously, frequently exceeding the assignment; they brought in outside material to illustrate or challenge a point; they accepted instruction only after a serious analysis, learning slowly (after all, they had been out of school for years) but perceptibly. The youngsters, some of whom had a genuinely native skill and fluency, kept up a rather simple-minded heckling of the whole purpose of the course when they participated in class work at all. What good can composition or literature be to an accountant or businessman?—a stenographer can take care of communications. Why bother with learning anything but the jargon in a particular trade? They suspected the motives of the interested veterans, whom they accused, quite wrongly, of "bucking for grades." A somewhat similar contrast exists still between day and evening session students, those going at night being older, more mature, and generally more like previous day session students.

The typical young student of today is considerably less "disturbed" than his brother of yesterday. The students of the 20's approached maturity in the "jazz age," with all of its manifold confusions; those of the 30's were the children of the depression and potential "cannon fodder," as we were told over and over again. In 1939, a professor at City College had his students set down their feelings about the world and make a prophecy about their future. *Life* magazine was present ten years later when the sealed envelopes were opened. "Brought up in hard times," *Life* wrote, "their prophecies were anything but bright. Three talked about suicide." The 1939 statements were self-consciously pessimistic, gloomy, overflowing with *Weltschmerz*. While these students may have constituted a special group on the campus, being all in one professor's class, their sentiments were not untypical.

They were anxious (using the term in its clinical sense) about various things. Many were uncertain about their careers. One of the students planned to be a chemist. "In ten years," reported *Life*, "he has been a civil service employee, a New York City policeman, a salesman, a metallurgical engineer, and an engineering officer in the Navy. Now he has decided on the career of a dentist and is in dental school at New York University." Another wanted to be a poet; today he is still a public accountant. Still another collected BA, BBA, MA, MBA, LLB, and JSD degrees, and now teaches business administration at a Southern university. Yesterday's students were anxious about security (in the late 30's a $25-a-week job represented the end of the rainbow: a princely income for a bachelor, an adequate one for marriage); about politics; about religion (denying it often with the zeal more appropriate to a believer); about their Jewishness (I recall one impassioned and rather ugly boy, carried away with his argument, demanding that Orthodox Jews be forced to cut off their beards, for such an "exhibition," he felt, harmed all Jews in America).

Today's student is rid of at least one important fear; he is politically freer than the student of the 30's. Anyone who has not lived through it, and in some way been scarred by it, cannot fully appreciate the intellectual terror (inquisitorial in its refinement and thoroughness) that the Communists exercised on the campus.

Always small in number, they were the most dedicated and fearless of missionaries. In the basement alcoves at City College—that dingy substitute for a student union—the party adherents held regular sway with booklets on tables, placards announcing rallies, speeches going on to nobody in particular. In this atmosphere, it took unusual courage or unusual apathy to remain outside the church, especially since joining up was supposed to be a practical demonstration of idealism and humanism. If you didn't join, you might be branded loudly and venomously as a fascist, a trotskyite (the party line was to use lower-case letters for epithets), and, worst of all, as an ivory-tower aesthete or wishy-washy liberal. There were no conservatives in those days.

In the face of the Communist assault, there were only three ways open to students, none, as it turned out, satisfactory. You could join the movement, actively or passively (the bulk of the students adhered passively: it was easiest on the personality); resist the movement (in which case you became a pariah, spoken of with contempt and disgust); or just stay outside the political arena altogether, which meant excluding a major realm of interest, acquaintance with which was necessary to a full education and a mature growth.

The Communists imposed their own Nuremberg laws on the intellectuals of the time, one of the most important of which was that Jews should never be distinguished in any way from other Americans. (The widespread disinclination to ask questions about Jewishness, when such questions may be completely free of ill will and may even be crucial in contributing to progress and understanding, is to some degree, one supposes, strengthened and encouraged by this prohibition.) For Jews, this meant they could pour out their sympathy for the downtrodden Chinese, Spaniards, Indians, and other victims of imperialism. Hitler, of course, depending on the moment, could be attacked, but not too specifically, on the basis of anti-Semitism—his anti-Semitism was depicted purely as a device of capitalism to divide the people, to offer them a scapegoat for their resentments, and so on.

At the same time, and to the Communist mentality not at all paradoxically, anti-Semitism in America (always tied tightly together with anti-Negroism) was played up for all it was worth. By joining the Communists, or agreeing with them, Jewish students could thereby simultaneously lose some feeling of their Jewishness (most Jewish Communist leaders of the time changed their names) and maintain a bitterness toward a world that insisted on mistreating Jews.

Bitterness was probably the dominant quality in the personality pattern of very many of the students of the 30's—a powerful, soul-corrosive, deeply imbedded bitterness, in its lighter moments manifesting itself in cynicism, in its heavier moments in a suicidal despair. The question of Communism was often the specific irritant. Close friendships split because of doctrinal disputes; teachers (and, in the outside world, historians and poets and musicians) were generally judged—and then sentimentally lauded or viciously dismissed—entirely in relation to their "political maturity." How could one grow up with a healthy independence of mind in such an atmosphere? It is significant, I think, that no worthy novels have yet come out of this so very rich and varied world, if one thinks of the novel as representing an integrated, developed understanding of a milieu and the people in it.

In large part, of course, it was the depression that was responsible for the radicalism. The children of the immigrants were in their teens and twenties when the dream of America suddenly fizzled. Disillusionment and cynicism and a turn to radicalism were only the immediate reactions. More deeply, the depression instilled a lasting sense of insecurity, a diminution of confident self-reliance, a disbelief that by hard work and intelligence and ambition one could achieve what one wanted. The American world showed itself then in another dimension, and, since adaptability is perhaps fundamental in our nature, the Jewish student went forth to meet the world on its terms.

The bluebird for many Jewish students became a "depression-proof" job: in a government agency, with "tenure" written into the law; in the "expanding" professions like accountancy; anywhere, that is, where the vicissitudes of individual initiative might be minimized. Creative abilities, whether in the arts or in business, were inhibited. Young writers turned to government posts, or to routine teaching, or to lucrative but unsatisfying hack writing; artists and creative musicians did much the same. For Jewish students the depression was probably more meaningful, more permanently shocking, than the war was to be.

In the 20's, students concentrated on a full education because so many jobs might be had on graduation; in the 30's they did the same because there were so *few* jobs to be had (students were then so "impractical" as to register for Greek). In the 40's, there were jobs, but chiefly for "experts," and so pinpoint specialization became the fashion.

Of course, the meaning of a college education has changed for the world at large. More students are attending college these days than in the 20's and 30's. Since a college degree, regardless of what has gone into it, has become a *sine qua non* in the most unlikely places (department store salesmen and office boys in advertising agencies, for example, often need baccalaureates), too many youngsters who are simply without the motivation for an education (and often without the intellectual equipment) crowd the classrooms of even the best schools for merely vocational reasons.

The changing attitudes in America toward Jews have also probably accounted for vocational shifts among Jewish students. The 20's saw an immense output of Jewish physicians from American medical schools; the quota system, strictly applied at the end of the 20's, began to channel Jewish students into allied fields like dentistry or into foreign medical schools or out of medicine altogether; today a slow swing back to medicine seems to be taking place as the *numerus clausus* becomes less and less respectable. Relaxation of barriers against hiring Jewish college instructors has sent many Jewish young men into graduate work. The Columbia University graduate English department has never before had so many Jewish students preparing for doctorates.

Changes in feeling among Jewish families themselves certainly must have contributed to changes in vocational plans. I remember hearing the derisive comment that only goyim became engineers (probably true at that, since the profession did exclude Jews at one time). And what was an accountant after all but a fancy bookkeeper? Today, both engineering and accountancy are considered quite respectable fields among Jews. At City College, more and more students plan to go into their fathers' businesses, which represent no longer drab poverty but a comfortable career. (Currently, one hears that the sons of the rich, graduated from colleges like Dartmouth and Princeton, are in many cases turning away from their parents, in the direction of the theater, ballet, the "little magazines"—often out of personal aimlessness rather than artistic or intellectual dedication.)

The major wish for their son of most Jewish immigrant parents was, at one time, that he *not* follow in his father's footsteps, that he *not* become a garment worker or carpenter or tailor. The Jewish student was thus forced to look for an American surrogate-father among his teachers, one who could impart the formula of how to fall into place, neatly, gracefully, in the American scene. The utter naivety in this situation of most of the teachers, usually Gentile, with no inkling of the peculiar needs of their Jewish students, helped produce a brooding antagonism between student and teacher.

Deliberately, the parents cut the student son off from themselves—for his greater glory, of course, and possibly for their own. But while the son was cast out in this area, he was at the same time made fast with multitudinous silver cords of another kind, his private life carefully scrutinized, carefully circumscribed. He was so firmly staked to the home that few ever broke away to go to out-of-town colleges, even when funds were available. After the war, when the government made it possible for veterans to go to college anywhere, it was startling to discover how many New York Jewish boys preferred to go to the city colleges so that they could live with their parents.

The parents participated with intense feeling in their children's successes and failures in school; there was no greater joy than the publication in the Sunday *Forward's* rotogravure section of a photograph of the son in academic cap, titled "A College Graduate at 18," or "A Doctor at 23." (Some overanxious parents took to sending in pictures with exaggerated details of accomplishment, so that the *Forward's* editors were eventually constrained to require documentary proof of achievements and awards before running photographs.)

Today's student appears less smothered by his family life. He is also calmer about his Jewishness. In the 20's and 30's, Jewishness for students was not only a handicap but a vestige of the old country to be discarded. Their indifference to Jewishness was also encouraged by some of the Old World ideologies of their parents, many of whom had been Bundists or of some other persuasion of socialism and had cast off Orthodox ritual. While attendance at City College dropped at Yom Kippur (partly because many instructors, Jewish and non-Jewish, let it be known they wouldn't meet their classes), the drop did not indicate the relative proportion of Jews at the college. Name-changing was common shortly before graduation. Only a handful of students belonged to the religious or Jewish nationalist societies, and these boys were considered eccentrics by the others who flocked to the political and literary, language and science organizations. When these non-committed students married and had children they gave them typical Hollywood or "American" names: Dennis, Linda, Kenneth. . . .

Today, probably fewer Levines are becoming Lanes; fewer Cohens, Kanes. Just as once there were students who made a point of not celebrating even the most important Holy Days, there are now students who make as much point of not attending classes on even the minor holidays. The feeling seems to be that non-attendance is at least a gesture of affirmation of one's Jewishness, whatever that Jewishness may consist of. (In most cases, religion has nothing to do with it.) One of the sources of names for the most current crop of babies is again the Old Testament. Hillel, the national Jewish student organization, has expanded tremendously in the last several years, at some campuses boasting membership around a thousand. Many students, it is true, belong to Hillel and attend Hillel affairs only for the social possibilities, but participation on even such grounds would have been frowned upon in the 20's and 30's.

Perhaps the most essential difference is that yesterday's Jewish students were the children of proletarians—of workers who were either Orthodox or self-consciously secular; today's Jewish students are the children of middle-class parents—shopkeepers, businessmen, professionals, who are neither passionately Orthodox nor devoted to any this-worldly ideology. The children of the last generation inevitably had intellectual problems in the natural course of their development—problems relating to religion, to their attitude to Jewish culture (Yiddish, *shul*, and *cheder*), to political outlook. The children of today's parents, on the other hand, are brought to consciousness of Jewish and general problems less by an inevitable conflict between generations than by events in the larger world. The Jewishness of the students of the 30's, insofar as it existed, was something internal and personal; the Jewishness of today's students appears to be public and impersonal, expressed in Hillel and in an attitude toward Zionism, just as the crucial Jewish events in their lives have shifted from the intimate stage of the home to the public stage of the world.

Obviously, today's Jewish student feels more secure in America—and in part this, too, relates to his middle-class status. But the drive to security seems to have brought with it a further feeling that there is never enough security.

There is, for example, the case of the Jewish basketball players who were quite willing to accept money from gamblers to throw games—for a future "security," for a "nest egg"—at a time when there are fewer problems about gaining economic security in America than ever before. Even more ambiguous was the reaction of the students at City College to the overwhelming disclosures. Many students defended the players: they were young, their heads were unsettled by their unprecedented success (the winning of the two national tournaments in 1950), they were tempted. Some students reacted with deep emotion, violently demanding extreme penalties for the accused. A good number of these were much concerned about what would happen to their chances for jobs as a result of the new blow to the college's reputation; rather plainly they were motivated by fear.

While the student reaction was not uniform, an indefinable, deep-seated, emotional shock was unquestionably felt by everyone. The basketball team had represented the emergence of City College, long the archetypical image of the underdog (at least in the minds of the students), as the equal, even the superior, of Ivy League schools and Midwestern universities. It hadn't been enough all these years to know that CCNY was the intellectual peer of other schools in the country (a feeling rather excessively, even aggressively, held); it had to be equal on "American" terms: athletically. (Proposals to adopt the University of Chicago's intramural athletic program were always rejected.) Perhaps if the team had not *lost* games—the gamblers would have been satisfied if it had won, so long as it kept within a given point margin—there might have been no substantial group which would not have wanted to protect the players.

Does this prove that the students are simply dominated by a spirit of "materialism," as many outsiders (alumni as well as instructors) believe? I don't think it is materialism in any simple sense that guides them, or that influenced the members of the team. After all, none of the basketball players went out on spending sprees—they put their money away for the future, and all of it was returned to the authorities. Again the security question. The basketball team, many students felt, had undone its own good work in public relations that had succeeded decades of Communist publicity and a generally bad press. The process of adjustment to America had been disturbed.

Yet if we take any long view, this is surely only a temporary setback—if, indeed, it is one at all—in the integration of these students into the American scene, an integration which serves to make the older type of Jewish student a dying species. The Jewish student no longer feels he is on the fringe of society or altogether an outcast; his brains are no longer his only asset. The depression seems to belong to a different age, and prosperity, together with Selective Service, has pretty much eliminated the problem of getting a job.

Today the Jewish student must often consider with his non-Jewish brother, in the traditional American manner, whether he should reject dad's offer of a job in the bank, in an accountancy office, in an advertising agency, in the factory, in the retail store. The Jewish student is today tempted by the American financial reward for diligence, ambition, intelligence, independence. "What boots it with uncessant care to tend the homely slighted Shepherds trade," when the same application in the business world can bring adequate returns with a lesser expense of spirit, with a lesser dedication? And Milton's answer that "fame is the spur" (either in this world or the other) doesn't count for much with a new generation that seeks its contentment in the traditionally pragmatic American fulfillment of personal and family security. Of course, there may be something other than the traditional American pragmatism at work. It may well be that there has been a shift since the 20's and 30's in the ideals of the American younger generation and in the climate of the campus generally—and that the Jewish student is but barometrically registering the change. More than one observer has noted the preoccupation of recent graduating classes with security—the "safe berth," and the steady income—contrasted with the more vaulting ambitions of their elder brothers; and a general slackening of "idealism" and of vital interest in the intellectual life and movements for social betterment.

Of course, not all Jewish college students have abandoned the intellectual pursuits traditional to the halls of ivy. But those who remain are not driven by their own and parental and social compulsions to be "geniuses" and get their names in the papers. There are fewer dedicated Jewish students today; they are becoming much like other middle-class young Americans. One hardly knows whether to be saddened or heartened by this. Perhaps, to some degree, both.

XIX *Ruth Glazer*

West Bronx: Food, Shelter, Clothing

When the Woodlawn Road-Jerome Avenue express rushes out of the tunnel at 161st Street in the Bronx, the subway rider catches a glimpse of rows of six-story apartment houses flanking the elevated tracks on both sides and extending far back into the hinterland. Viewing the crossword puzzle of yellow squares made by the lighted windows block after block, the outlander cannot resist musing profoundly to himself, "Ah, those poor people living out their pallid lives in regimented cells, one above the other." Luckily for him the Bronxite wedged next to him cannot read his thoughts; otherwise he would transfix him with that characteristic glare of the embattled straphanger. Pallid? Ha!

Why, there's more life, vigor, and excitement in one single Bronx apartment house at six o'clock in the evening than in a thousand elm-lined Main Streets on a Fourth of July. Visualize six little girls, none over three and a half feet high, dragging their roller skates up over the marble staircase; two or three fourth-floor mothers trying to summon recalcitrant sons to dinner; the building superintendent, flanked by irate ground-floor tenants, descending on a group of boys playing "association."

To be sure, the returning fathers, crushed by forty minutes in the subway, are extraordinarily noiseless at this hour.

The West Bronx is located in time midway between the Lower East Side (or the East Bronx) and West Side Manhattan. It is a community whose residents seem occupied full time in discovering the wonderful things produced by the world that can be had for even the moderate amount of money at their disposal. In so doing, they have created a style of living all their own.

Take any of the main arteries that mark the topography of the West Bronx—170th Street, Burnside Avenue, University Avenue, the Upper Concourse, Fordham Road. What streets anywhere can match them for sheer number in food stores, ice-cream parlors, delicatessens, restaurants, specialty shops for women and children, haberdasheries, and that special institution of the area, the "hardware" store, which maintains only the most distant kinship with establishments elsewhere engaged in selling nuts, bolts, gardening tools, and other such items. These "hardware" stores are crammed with every conceivable ingenious brightly colored gadget for the kitchen—painted bread boxes, the newest thing in shelving, 22-carat warranted gold-plated china tea sets, chromium Chanukah candelabra, ruby glass luncheon-sets, toasters, broilers, mixers, and a whole window of bottles, sterilizers, infant china and silverware, and complicated devices for warming baby food. For the West Bronx is nothing if not a *crèche.*

Indeed, the earmark of any display in the West Bronx store is the profusion. Park Avenue can have its Gristedes with six carefully polished apples bedded down in tissue paper and exposed to public view on a white lace doily. In the West Bronx there are veritable mountains of apples in all varieties, prices, and stages of edibility. From the dim, dark, cool interior of the fruit store, they proceed in carefully segregated groups, from the most expensive to the least, until finally whole bushels of green ones spill out of the flimsy enclosing boundaries of the store onto the street.

As for the bakeries, who would hazard even a guess on the number of barrels of whipped cream which are beaten up in the early morning hours behind the glass and tile façades of the West Bronx bake shops, and which later in the day make their appearance atop and inside every shape and manner of cake—including the humble coffee ring?

Where else in this world can there be found anything to compare with the Victory Layer Cake—not to be confused with the cake of the same name, say, in the chain bakeries of Manhattan? There it is a triumph in deception, with its chemically achieved batter, a composite of protein substitute for egg, karo for sugar, some dried-out milk curds, a bit of flour, and various chemical elements—sodium propionate, monosodium glutamate, etc.—topped off with that culinary super-fraud of mass-production hygienic kitchens, "marshmallow icing."

Victory Layer Cake, as defined in the West Bronx, is quite another matter. Its inspiration is clearly one derived from some heathen and sybaritic god of another time. But essentially it is a simple construction with an all too transparent purpose: to pile the largest quantity of whipped cream into the smallest cubic area. This feat is accomplished with ingenious simplicity, by spreading, between seven or eight of the thinnest slices of chocolate cake ever carved by a Bronx baker, quarter-inch layers of whipped cream, not marshmallow, not a gelatinous substitute with mere protein content, but simple, thick, rich, heavy whipped cream. It is to be noted that this triumphal concoction is purchased by the pound.

But for all the glory and glamor of his whipped-cream cakes, the true art of the Bronx baker, the real and individual cornerstone of his reputation, is his bread and rolls. Although it is true that it has not been attempted outside the area, is it so hard, after all, to whip up some cream and put it between a few layers of cake? But where else do they bake a rye bread with caraway seeds that is not a sour, heavy lump requiring paper-thin slicing to be edible or, at the other extreme, that sweetish, pasty loaf so uncomfortably reminiscent of white bread? The true rye is soft and crusty when fresh, and grows more flavorful as it ages. Any Bronxite would smile at the raptures of our more fluffy-headed lady food columnists in the metropolitan dailies when they first taste rye bread. "It's an exciting, delicious taste-treat," they chirrup, "especially when spread with fresh sweet butter." As any gourmet north of the Harlem River could have told them, it's not only a "taste-treat," but also the staff of life.

The course of the week in the Bronx could almost be plotted according to the bread that the housewife buys. Except for the occasional loaf of packaged bread, brought in conscientiously for its breakfast-toast-making properties, the daily staple is rye bread, with an occasional loaf of whole wheat or pumpernickel for variety. Corn bread has, somehow, never been able to achieve a regular position and is generally sold in half-pound or

pound chunks carved out of a huge oval five- or ten-
pound loaf. It is always bought with a kind of dare-
devil, on-the-spur-of-the-moment air. As if yielding to
some hidden and finally irrepressible impulse, the
housewife will call out, "All right, and give me a piece
of corn bread, too; but not too big." Although the Sabbath may not be observed in other respects, for Friday
night and Saturday one buys *challeh*. (In some areas,
where all sense of proportion has been lost, *challeh* is
available every day in the week.) On Sunday, rolls
achieve a sudden prominence with the Sunday morning
trip downstairs for the Sunday paper "*and* a dozen
rolls." These range in variety from the classic bagel
and its variant, the egg bagel, through the *pletzel*, Bial-
ystoker and otherwise, the seeded water-rolls, the soft
sweet-rolls, until finally at the end of the spectrum it is
hard to distinguish the crumbly yellow crescents from
cake. Recently, finding no other way to satiate the appetite of his customers for *pletzels*, the baker has added
yet another variety of bread to his shelves—"Something
New—17c—Try It—Onion Bread." All this is displayed
with a sense-numbing profusion in bins and racks behind plate glass—an element of décor that, in addition
to its decorative properties, has proved itself to be one
of the few devices capable of thwarting the thumb-and-
forefinger test for freshness.

The same cornucopia effusion marks the groceries
and the dairy stores with their windows crammed full
of row upon row of cheeses and tubs of butter, and the
appetizing stores which lure passers-by with whiffs
from their open barrels of pickles and peppers, sauerkraut and sour tomatoes. The delicatessens, however,
hide demurely behind window displays of dummy beer
cans. But for those who have eyes to see there are steaming frankfurters and knishes on the grill and untold de-

lights behind the clouded glass and shredded colored cellophane.

Only one institution remains austerely aloof from this kind of display. This is the kosher butcher store. Even the chicken market indulges in a kind of raw profusion, exhibiting trenches of vari-colored chickens for the selection of the housewives. But the butcher store is quite a different matter.

Whereas on other days the patronizing of the various food stores is a matter requiring only an ordinary degree of acumen, tact, and watchfulness, a certain air of solemnity settles over the West Bronx on Thursday. Thursday is devoted to shopping for the weekend, since Friday is given over to cooking and cleaning so that Saturday can be the day of rest ordained on Mount Sinai. Even emancipated young housewives have been caught up in the tyranny of this custom. This is the day when the housewife descends to do battle with the butcher in earnest. Small purchases during the week of "a few veal cutlets" or "a piece liver" can be regarded as minor skirmishes. The one point that must be firmly grasped is that one does not buy meat from a butcher, one negotiates. One lives in a state of armed truce.

The young bride, for example, goes through a long period of training before she dares ask for so much as a single lamb chop. This rigorous course includes elements both scientific and psychological. To know the cuts of meat derived from the cow, the calf, and the lamb is, of course, primary. (For to what end all this fencing if one simply gives away one's hand by asking for two pounds of meat for pot roast?) Even more important are the little professional tricks suspected of every butcher by every well-versed housewife. This information is generally delivered *sotto voce* as the butcher disappears to get the cut of meat requested;

viz., "If he asks you what you want it for, tell him you want to broil it. It's *his* business that you want to use it for chopped meat?" or "Make sure when you ask for *mittel* chuck, that he doesn't give you single chuck."

This masked antagonism, this deep-lying mutual suspicion between the kosher butcher and his customer, is symbolized by the customarily empty showcase. The only function of this elaborate testimonial to refrigeration seems to be to set a restraining barrier, a neutral zone, between the two contending parties. Every piece of *flanken*, every shoulder steak must be custom-cut, and each piece of meat is held up for inspection with the furtive glances, the special avowals which only a butcher knows how to utter. Occasionally a timid young woman will attempt to influence his mysterious choice as he disappears into the refrigerator. "A small piece of calf's liver," she'll say, "I hope it'll be good. It's for the baby." To dissipate the illusion that the prospective cut is not already predestined, the butcher will respond, "Whaddya mean 'good'? Would I give you a piece of liver that isn't good?" Is there a reply?

Unlike other stores, too, there is a leisurely, almost club-like atmosphere here as the women gather of a Thursday morning. Then the butcher holds court, announcing his opinions on the world, commenting on departing customers. There are no small private conversations between neighbors. No. There is an easy general public discussion and everyone is included. "Well, Mr. Pizetsner" (not "Sam," as she might say to the grocery-store man), will begin an older and more favored customer, "and how are your sons these days?" "All right, thank God; the new business in Flatbush is doing fine." "So, how do you like living in Brooklyn, Mr. Pizetsner?" "Well, it's not so bad. We have our own house. . . ." "It must be a terrible trip for you every day.

How come you don't move the store to Brooklyn?" "Listen," says the butcher, as he prepares to quarter a chicken, "everyone says the same thing. My wife wants me to give up the business. (*chop*) The boys have a good spot for me there. (*chop*) But you know what I say . . . ? (*The cleaver is suspended.*) I tell 'em, I couldn't give up my business here. Where would I ever find such customers? They're not customers. They're dolls!" (*chop, chop*) Really, could you buy in the A&P?

In view of the breathtaking variety of food which confronts his eyes and nose as he walks down any one of the main streets, the incautious observer might well conclude that Lucullan feasts are concocted each evening in Bronx kitchens and that Bronx housewives are culinary paragons. Nothing, alas, could be further from the truth. Quantity, perhaps, or wholesomeness, yes (or maybe). But variety—never. For the older generation there were certain extenuating circumstances. Burdened with the care of many children in cramped quarters, the mother of the family cooked dishes which required a minimum of preparation and watchfulness. Conservative calculation would reveal that in the first thirty years of her married life a good mother of the old school demolished 1,560 chickens and served up 6,240 portions of pot roast. As might be deduced from these figures, the older generation was not particularly aquiver over the culinary art; their approach was not adventurous but strictly utilitarian.

I remember once overhearing the following conversation in a neighbor's kitchen:

"Mmm, Mrs. Siegel. It smells wonderful. Tell me, what are you cooking for dinner?"

"Who can tell?" she replied. "All I know is that I've put up a pot of water and an onion and some meat. If all goes well and the family comes home early we'll have some soup and some soup meat. And if the water cooks out and the meat burns a little, we'll have pot roast."

Offsetting this casualness toward everyday cookery, this generation brought a certain prayerful solemnity to the preparation of certain festive dishes, where failure cannot be turned into a last-minute success. There is, for example, the delicate business of *untershlogen a borsht* (beating eggs into a borsht). The first step requires the cook to make her peace with the world and renounce all anger against her fellow mortals. Having done this, she may proceed to break two eggs into half a cup of warm borsht and pour it ever so slowly, beating it with a *steady hand*, into the soup. But if her spirit remains troubled the borsht will infallibly be streaky, and no scientific explanations to the effect that the borsht was too hot or the eggs too cold will ever convince the cook who *knows*.

Sometimes American-born daughters, learning in the institutional ads of that hallowed myth about recipes handed down from generation to generation, attempt to introduce this charming practice in their own families. There has been, however, one difficulty. The ladies from the old country have developed a kind of shorthand for recipes, something akin to the reply of the teacher who, when asked how to spell "immediate," answered "With two m's." So the girl who has painfully managed to extract and translate what she thought was the recipe for cookies, suddenly notices that she has no specification for flour. "Don't you use any flour?" she will ask. "Why, of course," replies her mother, aghast at such ignorance. "Well, how much?" she will pursue. "Who can tell in advance? Whatever the batter requires. . . ." This sort of exchange is discouraging. No wonder, despite their pride in their ad-

vanced and experimental outlook in the arts of living,
the daughters of the new generation have unwittingly
slipped back into the old inherited routine. Few, con-
sequently, escape the chagrined surprise of hearing
their own sons complain, in that classic formula, "Aw,
ma. Chicken soup again."

The truth is there are only two kinds of occasions
that utilize the full resources of the food stores. One is
the ceremonial dinner, which proceeds gravely through
ten courses, both hot and cold, in high disregard for
the eating capacities of the guests. The second, and
more common, is "having a few friends in for the evening," which inevitably concludes with a midnight
snack known as a "spread." Once having decided between the delicatessen store and the appetizing store,
the rest is according to ritual. The evening guests are
customarily presumed to have gone without food for
three days and their prospects for the future are also
not considered very hopeful. With this in mind (assuming the nod to have gone to the appetizing store) a not
ungenerous sample of every type of "home-made
salad," and of every variety of smoked, pickled,
creamed, or otherwise bedeviled carp, whitefish, sturgeon, herring, butterfish, and salmon, and half a dozen
kinds of cheeses are extracted from the trays and barrels of the appetizing store. Every suggestion of the
naive husband (along to help carry the packages)
that surely a limit has been reached, is silenced with
the slogan, "Better too much than too little."

How explain the vitality and longevity of the delicatessen and appetizing stores in Jewish neighborhoods, considering that they are, so to speak, dietetically
out of bounds, except for "occasions"? For unchanged
is the tradition from mother's time—to admit to one's
neighbor that one is having delicatessen for an evening

supper, unless there is a clear and present emergency, is to admit that one is an incompetent, shiftless wife and mother who cares nothing for the health of her husband and is cheerfully ready to poison her off-spring. Happily for the younger element and husbands, there are two types of occasions on which the holder of the purse strings may relax the first principle of any Bronx housewife—namely, No Delicatessen. The first, already mentioned, is situations of extreme emergency, to wit, a gas main has broken and the house is deprived of light and fuel; or the family has just moved and the barrel with the dishes seems to be inexplicably miss-ing; there has been a fire and the kitchen has been de-stroyed; or mother has been downtown shopping at Klein's. At other times a coalition of all other mem-bers of the household can temporarily so overpower her that she will look the other way when the provisions are brought onto the premises. But, on ordinary days, to initiate such a thing herself is to commit two other sins, in addition to those noted before. She is guilty of extravagance, because everybody knows what prices in appetizing stores are, and, worst of all, she is not Giving Her Family a Hot Meal!

For let a girl be never so flighty, let her breakfast daily on Pepsi-Cola and salami oblivious to the tears and prayers of her mother, once she is mistress of her own household she is immediately an authority on nu-trition and the intricate relations of vitamins and calo-ries and proteins to health. And it is this last that, when all is said and done, shapes the patterns of the meals and menus typical of the West Bronx. Good, healthy, nourishing food! "Can a boiled egg be bad for you?" "Who ever heard of chicken hurting anyone?" With such sweet reasonableness tradition conquers another generation.

Perhaps it is because in her youth the present-day housewife slept most of her nights on a folding cot put up in a hallway or a dining room or in the kitchen. Whatever the reason, today both sides of Jerome Avenue are lined with stores specializing in bedding: special extra-thick mattresses, extra-curly coiled springs, super-warm and light quilts made of 100 per cent imported white European goose down. Macy's, which is capable of packing a quilt with simple lamb's wool, is somehow not good enough. But it doesn't stop here. A girlhood spent sitting on hard kitchen chairs, or worse, on stiff-backed, gloomy dining-room chairs, bears fruit in the Bronx living room filled with the softest of down-cushioned chairs and sofas upholstered in the brightest of "cherry red" or "chartreuse."

Now the down cushion, as everyone knows, is like the most delicate of soufflés—every jar, every touch, the merest fingerprint is clearly visible on the dimpled surface. Although it is true that she spent her youth badgering her mother to "throw out that damn dining room set, and get a living room so that we'll have some place to sit, for-god's-sakes," the pleasure of looking at the unruffled surface transcends the grosser—and more masculine—enjoyment of sitting on it. Protests from the man of the house—"But, my God, what did we buy it for, if not to sit in?"—are met with that look of contempt which the aesthete bestows on a philistine.

The delight with the soft and sumptuous does not end with pillows and coverlets. Everywhere straight lines are abhorred. Lamps are preferred in the form of baroque vases, their shades adorned with poufs and swaths of ruffling; the drapery is of a weight and quantity calculated to set a luxurious barrier between the beholder and the University Avenue view. Wherever there is an upholstered surface, it is tufted; wherever a wooden one, it is carved into sinuous outlines and adorned with gilded leather.

But a couch, after all, is at best a couch, a chair is a chair, and a drum table, however gilded its adornments, still only a drum table. The hallmark of individuality, the sign of a discriminating owner aware of the finer things in life, is the handpainted oil painting. On the whole, they are of two types—the landscape and the portrait. The almost overwhelming preference for the landscape, or, more properly, the "scene," probably indicates that people like to get their money's worth. The scene is generally made up of four compositional elements arranged traditionally as follows: a rather gloomy green forest in the left foreground, a road winding diagonally across the picture, and a brighter area (a field of waving wheat or flowers) extending backwards from the middle distance on the right hand side. The whole is enlivened (here's where the value comes in) with a *figure* walking down the road. These classical elements, however, are changeable and interchangeable. The road, for example, may become a winding brook (in which case the figure is replaced by a swan), or the field may become a lake, or the forest and field may change places. But the formula remains, light balanced by dark, or sunshine by gloom, to put it moralistically.

There are two comments which are appropriate upon seeing such a picture for the first time:

(1) The practical—"I'm telling you, the frame alone is worth it."

(2) The aesthetic—"A picture like that, you won't get tired of looking at so fast."

I know of an exile in Tennessee who was unable to find anything in all of Nashville, or its environs, to match the splendor she remembered, and finally resorted to importing her furniture from the Bronx. You have only to step into her living room to feel yourself transported 500 miles back to the Grand Concourse. Even the draperies fall in little puddles on the floor in the prevailing manner indicating (1) opulence—"Let it be a little longer"—(2) superlative housewifery—"Her floors are so clean you could eat off them."

Bronx style extends to clothing, too, for undeniably there *is* a Bronx style, the result of an appreciation for, even a reveling in rich fabrics, in sumptuous textures, in elaborate folds, in dense colors, and in complex designs. This emerges in the extravagant hats, the weighty fall of a dress, the dark and brilliant nail polish, and the sculptured, appliquéd, and platformed shoes.

Even men can taste a little of this sheer exuberance of costume, now that it has been semi-legalized as "California style." They can have silky gabardines (just a bit more silky than Brooks Brothers would approve), smooth, rich flannel shirts, of an altogether different nature from the scratchy, plaid, woodsman's type, and brilliant, broadly knotted ties. And so—a suit is not a suit, but an experience, just as a fur coat is the achievement of a decade of yearning. It would be a shame if people didn't notice.

For Sunday afternoons the men have developed a special style suitable for airing the baby, milling about on the Concourse, visiting relatives in the neighborhood, and not inappropriate for local parties or poker sessions. This costume, often the cause of hidden, or sometimes energetically expressed, distress on the part of the wife, enables the Bronx husband to indulge his liking for informality (no tie), color (!), and comfort (sport shirt). With the aid and abetment of local haberdashers, the men have gained their first victory in a decade over the delicate sensibilities of Bronx taste which draws a sharp distinction between what is proper for everyday and what is required for occasions. The women, however, will not be deterred from their knowledge that Sunday is the day to be straitened by corsets, pinched by shoes, hobbled by skirts, and burdened by furs.

The role of the Concourse in Bronx life, like its geographical location, is central. Its once aristocratic buildings have become shabby and it no longer has its former prestige. But as the longest and broadest avenue in the Bronx it is still a name to conjure with. Do you desire a pastoral afternoon? At one end of the Concourse there is a small but intricate park, complete with bandstand and Sunday afternoon concerts. Or perhaps your taste fancies a walk on civilized pavements. There is the middle section where one may see and be seen. And at its far end is the big shopping center that is almost the lodestar of Bronx life. Here the best furniture and clothing stores display their brightest wares so that the young may gaze and be educated and the old may sigh and envy.

But the architecture of the Bronx is basically characterized by the long sober lines of six-story apartment houses, built some twenty to thirty years ago, running in a northerly and southerly direction, intersecting the main avenues. The majority of these edifices are built in a plain, unpretentious style vaguely suggesting Italian Renaissance fortresses. In harmony with their solid construction are the gloomy but magnificent hallways that even the marauding hands of three or four generations of children have not been able to disfigure. There are black-and-white tiled floors, laid out in formal patterns to resemble marble; there are gilded, pilastered walls, heavy mirrors, tables and chairs of an indefinite but regal historical period, and rococo flambeaux on the walls, unfortunately requiring the prosaic aid of electricity. The arrangement and interior architecture of the apartments also suggest palace chambers. The entrance to a meanly proportioned living room, for example, will be guarded by two elaborate French doors; the walls imitate wood paneling; the floors are parqueted; once again, there are flambeaux on the walls. Most buildings front directly on the street, but many, built on a larger scale, have center courts frequently ornamented by a pirouetting nymph or a cupid cut in stone.

The "new" houses of the Bronx (some are more than fifteen years old) are all built in a uniform "moddern" style, with white or cream brick façade, casemented windows, and chromium-decorated doorways. Their interiors are likewise constructed smoothly, with a minimum of doorways, mouldings, and decoration. Despite their great number, these houses always seem exceptional, and, somehow, frivolous, appearing at random among the "regular" apartment houses, and practically never in solid blocks.

The sobriety and regularity of the life of the West Bronx is suggested more by the even and dull architecture of the side streets than by the color and movement of the shopping avenues. This regularity is enforced by the schedule of the head of the family: when he must get up to go to work, when he returns—this sets the boundaries of the day. Few of the housewives can afford to break the pattern with club meetings and charitable activities; most are completely absorbed by the creatures of their own creation—home, children, their style of living. Only the children, and particularly the adolescents among them, are free. Probably the children are little different outwardly from other city children.

The girls play with their dolls, or mimic their mothers, or rather awkwardly play in street games. Once out of the confines of their apartments, the boys rush around the streets in packs, dressed uniformly during most of the year in plaid shirts and corduroy trousers. At play, both groups are rather anonymous. But the adolescents are another story.

When the weather is warm and pleasant, numerous islands of greenery, groupings of stone benches, and even little parks seem to appear in almost every area of the West Bronx. During the day the benches are occupied principally by mothers with baby carriages, old men talking with their friends, and old ladies sunning themselves. In the early evening these areas lose their calm. The benches are still occupied by the old, but perched on the iron railings or standing about in knots in out-of-the-way corners are groups of teen-age boys and girls. Gradually the darkness begins to seethe with their laughter and talk. Those still unattached wander casually but tensely up and down the paths hoping to be invited into a "crowd." The girls here are young, carefully made up, carefully dressed, very wise, and terribly shy and afraid, for all their outward brazenness. The boys are very bold in their new power. It is up to them to set the tone of the group, to tease the girls, to make wisecracks about the passers-by, while the girls "just die laughing." The "crowd" is free-floating in space and time. What relation can it have to a stifling apartment, to dowdy mothers, to school, to relatives? It is disembodied excitement; night after night the girls and boys are drawn by it to the same spot.

The college students soon find themselves too old for this teen-age "crowd," or too busy, or too superior. For many it meant a period of loneliness, especially if they went to City College or Hunter College, which were restricted, respectively, to men and women. (Although, as an aftermath of the war, these schools have become coeducational in actuality if not specifically.) But in the West Bronx, at least, students have one rendezvous which has as much fascination as any park railing or street corner. This is the reference room of the Fordham Branch of the public library. Here, every evening and on Saturdays during the school year, every seat is taken with earnestly studying figures. As everyone knows, of course, a borrowed sheet of paper can lead to a conversation, a conversation to a date, a date to a romance, and a romance, well. . . .

But the adolescents and the college students represent temporary aberrations in Bronx life.

Some do manage to leave—a few intellectuals, those who marry non-Jews, or take jobs in strange cities. But those who remain are slowly drawn back into the vortex of family existence and the pattern of Bronx living.

It doesn't take long for the teen-agers to discover that the generalized excitement of the crowd is not enough, and they begin either to pair up within the crowd or to find themselves boy friends or girl friends outside it. Their progression here is as simple as a pick-up in the Fordham library. Before she knows it, the young girl, who required not much more than a new suit every spring and a "good dress" for Rosh Hashonah and Yom Kippur, absolutely *needs* a "cocktail" dress, platform shoes, a fur jacket, if possible, and whatever other trappings she can afford or her mother is willing to buy for her. From here it is only a step to the suddenly awakening consciousness of interior decoration. When there emerges the chain of thoughts beginning, "When *I* get married. . . ." the circle has been closed.

So the present generation is only the continuator and the embellisher of the Bronx style. It does not revolt against the given. It does not seek for new modes of expression in its domestic arrangements. The younger generation (aside from the intellectuals, who, even so, are more infected by this milieu than they think) has not yet exhausted the present pattern. (The translation of sheared beaver into Guatemalan cotton or slipper satin into Javanese batik, or the use of leather Mexican drums for coffee tables, as against leather-topped mahogany, is a change in form, not substance.) To judge from its present unabated vigor among the newest generation, it would seem that some time must elapse before the hyperbolic extravagances of the imagination as applied to everyday living will begin to pall.

Elsewhere in this country the mechanics of living comprises only the framework within which other events are supposed to occur—like making money or belonging to a golf club, or playing bridge, or doing all the other things that handsome American families are shown doing in automobile ads. But in the West Bronx . . . there it *is* life.

XX *Irving Howe*

Spruceton Jewry Adjusts Itself

For some time I had heard fragmentary reports from several friends whose childhood was spent in Spruceton. Strange reports. . . . A Jewish community, some years ago on the verge of disintegration, now thriving, self-confident, "modernized." Yet a community not quite at peace with itself. Certainly, Spruceton's Jewish old-timers, the parents of my friends, were far from happy over the boasted "modernization." What clash of values, perhaps a local version of large problems, was taking place in this isolated Jewish community?

I took the train to Spruceton. The idea of such a trip was itself an adventure; a New Yorker going "to the country" . . . and not for a vacation!

Spruceton is a sprawling New England city of 28,-ooo people. Its long Main Street is dreary and ugly, but in its residential sections one does find that relaxed graciousness one likes to think characteristic of New England.

Spruceton has not taken any special pains to attract industry and rather prides itself on retaining something of the quality and aroma of pre-industrial New England. While Spruceton's few industries—a tannery, a railroad installation, a large printing plant, and several granite quarries—are becoming increasingly important to its economic life, they are still peripheral in the Spruceton society. The labor movement, for all its impressive membership of some two thousand in the AFL and several hundred in the CIO, exerts no major influence in the city.

The starkly visible extremes of status that cleave most American industrial cities are not evident in Spruceton. It has few mansions; the "aristocracy" of "Mortgage Hill" is small and without inordinate social power. Nor are there any slum areas: Spruceton has few unskilled workers and no Negro sub-proletariat. Most of its residents are "middle-class," in status and outlook.

This economic homogeneity is matched by an almost equally considerable racial homogeneity. Small Greek and Italian pockets, some French Canadians, and about sixty Jewish families comprise its "foreign" element. All the others are "native stock"—Protestant, Anglo-Saxon, solid, conservative.

Politically, Spruceton is of course Republican, and that without any of the scandalous concessions to the two-party system found in the southern parts of New England. One of the Spruceton Jews to whom I spoke told me that he was a Democrat but that he registered Republican. "In this town, if you don't register Republican, you might as well close shop." Probably that statement is an exaggeration. A number of Spruceton Jews had been sympathetic to the Democratic party, especially when it was headed by Roosevelt, but they did not take any pains to publicize this opinion.

Spruceton is overwhelmingly Protestant, though I did hear and overhear expressions of concern about the rapid multiplication of "mackerel-snappers," as Catholics are called. The local paper, edited by a conservative eccentric, has often sniped at the Catholics and, more recently, at the Jews, for their failure to assimilate themselves to the ways of Spruceton life—that is, to accept the mores of the majority group.

The New England equalitarian tradition, so industriously advertised by our nationalist historians, is here largely a memory of the past. What one encounters in both conversations and the local press is a rigid, heavy, almost eccentric conservatism. To be sure, this attitude is decent and polite—a demagogue like G. L. K. Smith would not find favor in Spruceton. But it soon becomes painfully evident that this is a New England with a withered and crotchety social imagination, a New England in which Sam Adams, Emerson, or Thoreau would not feel at home. Perhaps it is only the naivety of the New Yorker standing in involuntary awe of the great places of early American history, but I felt a certain disappointment at the invariably provincial and almost bigoted attitude of the many Spruceton people with whom I spoke. I found only one sign of intellectual ferment: a small chapter of the American Veterans Committee.

For all its gracious atmosphere, its aura of good living, and its lack of overt conflicts, Spruceton is full of subterranean tensions.

There are about 160 Jews in Spruceton, of whom the overwhelming majority are middle-class. (In this respect they are Spruceton's most representative group!) A few are rich—but most of the storekeepers and businessmen are just comfortably well off. There is a handful of Jewish workers but they exert no independent influence; Spruceton's temple is a congregation of solid businessmen. As I drove down Main Street one afternoon, my cab driver, after observing that my nose pointed in the right direction (upward), remarked on the number of stores owned by Jews. He thought that "bad for the town."

In its own estimate, Spruceton's Jewish community is thriving as never before. Its members live in peace, undisturbed by any open enmities, and those given to reflection feel protected by the "New England tradition." They are prosperous and live in "nice homes." (I shall not here describe "nice homes.") And they are proud of their handsome temple, a religious and social center.

In recent years the Jewish community has come together under the leadership of an intelligent "modern" rabbi, who, I was proudly informed, is "a respected figure in the city." More Jews attend his services, more contribute to relief funds than ever before. Formerly a disintegrating remnant of Orthodoxy, Spruceton's Jewish community is now a lively center of Reform or "liberal" Judaism. True, a few old-timers grumble: they don't like the rabbi's modern ways, they look down upon the Americanized businessmen who have taken over leadership. But these old-timers are numerically insignificant; in a few years their voices will be stilled by death.

The Jewish community, at first blush, shows every sign of growth and vitality; it is even becoming an accepted part of Spruceton's social life. For most of Spruceton's Jews, this is the whole story; and from their point of view I could well end here. But let us probe a little deeper.

I paid my first visit to the Old Man. His son, a friend of mine in New York, had told me that the Old Man knew more about Spruceton than anyone else.

When I first arrived at his dirty and littered junk shop, the Old Man hesitated to talk; he could not understand why anyone should find Spruceton interesting. He was more concerned with politics: Taft, "a dried-out herring"; Dewey, *a leideger kop*— "an empty head"; Churchill, *an imperialistisher banditt;* Attlee, *a sozialistisher shlemiel.* After I smiled my assent to these characterizations, he relaxed and began to reminisce. When I told him I brought greetings from his son, rapport was soon established. "A smart boy, my son, a little too much against Stalin, but a smart boy."

The Old Man was small, gentle, quite shy. His face was not crinkled, but was blocked into a series of flat surfaces separated by sharp ridges. It is the kind of face one finds in pictures of 18th-century Jews.

The Old Man came to Spruceton in 1899, when the town had perhaps six or seven Jews living in self-imposed isolation. As more Jewish immigrants drifted in, most of them went "into business" as rag pickers and junk peddlers. They were neither integrated members of Spruceton's community nor a distinct group on its margin; they crept around in its interstices. Most, the Old Man smilingly recalled, were as poor as when "*di mame hat unz gehat*"—"when our mothers had us."

During those early years between the turn of the century and the First World War, the Old Man would hitch up his wagon and, together with the other peddlers, ride to Millberg, a large city nearby, for the High Holidays. As soon as there were enough Jews in Spruceton, they began holding their own services. But "*yiden zeinen doch yiden*"—Jews being Jews—conflicts broke out within Spruceton's Jewish community. "Altogether we had maybe twenty men. So when we split into two *minyans* [congregations], each one used to fight for the tenth man." What was the reason for the split? That amused the Old Man: as if there had to be a reason! "Well"—he continued in his odd combination of Yiddish accent and Harvard broad "a"—"some of us were junk peddlers and others worked in a rag-sorting place; that's why there was a split. When they closed down the rag-sorting place, we had peace again."

For the High Holidays, they would hire a prayer leader and would play host to Jews from surrounding villages. Services were held on the ground floor of the house of the ritual slaughterer (*shochet*). Once, the Old Man remembered, "a whole gang of Litvaks, noisy and hungry," descended on his house two days before Rosh Hashonah: they were so isolated they didn't know the date of the holiday. "So we fed them. *A yid iz a yid.*"

During the years before the First World War, the Jews usually lived on Spruceton's outskirts so that they might have space to store their junk. A few more adventurous souls became door-to-door drygoods peddlers and even opened up stores. Since they were viewed primarily as a curiosity, they met with little overt anti-Semitism. The Old Man did recall one incident when his junk wagon was chased by boys shouting "Christ-killer!" "So I got down, waved my horsewhip at them, and they ran away." Only those Jews forced to by their business arrangements mingled with the townspeople; the rest kept to themselves in the south end.

Shortly before the First World War a Jew, Jake Cohen, ran for mayor. He was of course defeated, but there was less of an anti-Semitic reaction than the more fearful Jews had expected and some of them, as the Old Man put it, felt they might now "come out of their holes and look up at the sun." Jake was apparently something of a character: a captain in the National Guard, always "one of the boys," and later a producer and actor in silent Western films. "An interesting life for a Jew," the Old Man said.

In the early 20's the placid life of Spruceton's Jews was disturbed by the first overt and, thus far, the most severe outbreak of anti-Semitism in the place. Locally, they were digging into business life and provoking resentment among Gentile competitors; nationally, the Ku Klux Klan was spreading race hatred, of which some even reached Spruceton. A branch of the KKK ("hoodlehoods," the Old Man called them) was formed in the town and for a while it began to stir up anti-Catholic and anti-Jewish prejudice. The Jews became fearful, but the whole thing blew over in the halcyon prosperity of the middle 20's.

When the depression came, Spruceton was not so badly hit as most other New England towns. A nearby textile center became a ghost town, but Spruceton still had the state capital. However, New England's economic paralysis gradually spread there too, and many Jewish storekeepers had to go into bankruptcy and move away. Business failures, sharpening clashes between the old-timers and their modernized children, and internal religious disintegration all converged to make the depression the lowest point of Spruceton Jewry's history.

It is somewhat surprising that the radical political tendencies of that era did not particularly influence Spruceton's Jews. As a matter of fact, a branch of the Communist party, composed of Scandinavian granite workers, was formed in West Spruceton, but it had slight impact on the Jewish community. The older generation viewed all politics with skepticism; the younger ones, who might have been more receptive to radical ideas, had largely left Spruceton.

Thus far the Old Man had a thorough grasp of his story, but now he was clearly at a loss to explain what had happened to the second generation of Spruceton's Jews, those born and reared there. To maintain chronological sequence, I will here interpolate what I learned from other sources.

Though reared in their parents' Orthodoxy, many of these second-generation Jews rejected it when they reached maturity in the late 20's or early 30's. Those who had professional or intellectual ambitions were forced to leave Spruceton entirely, since it offered few opportunities for Jews in these fields. Some of their contemporaries who did remain in Spruceton married Gentiles. The rate of intermarriage for Spruceton's Jews is nineteen per cent and remains one of the community's irksome problems.

But even those members of the second generation who rejected religion still retained—if only because of their own uneasy status—a certain community with their parents. For instance, between the Old Man's remarks on Spruceton's Jews and those of his intellectual son there was a fairly close similarity of critical perception: both viewed history from the *outside*. It is remarkable that even those old-timers' sons who married Gentiles and were therefore driven from the fold still identify Jewishness with the ways of their parents; and to the degree that they identify themselves with both their parents and Jewishness, they concur in the old-timers' criticisms of "newcomers" and of the temple's Reform innovations. That, in some instances, their own children are being raised in non-Jewish faiths does not seem to affect this attitude.

It is not difficult to see why the Old Man, as he

hesitantly and painfully talked about this second generation, should have found it perplexing. For all his
worldliness and basic skepticism, he could not stretch
his imagination enough to understand sympathetically
either those who had drifted into cosmopolitan intellectuality or those who had intermarried. But when he
rather hurriedly shifted the conversation to the next
major stage in Spruceton Jewry's history, he was again
secure and keen in his judgment.

In the middle and late 30's a new group of Jews,
soon to become the dominant one, came to Spruceton.
They were businessmen from various New England
towns who set up stores and businesses in Spruceton.
Most were successful and became what the Old Man
laughingly called *"alrightniks."* (Throughout his nar-
rative there was an undercurrent of amused skepticism
towards events, his own account of them, and my reception of his account. What did it mean, and what did
it matter? And suppose one knew, what could be done
about it? Perhaps this was to be expected from a man
nearing his seventies, but perhaps—I will not be so bold
as to say—it was an attitude that might be described as
characteristically "Jewish.")

This group of *alrightniks* soon became the pillar
of the town's Jewish community. Why? How explain
the fact that the group that knew least about and cared
least for Judaism became the most active and sustaining
section of the Jewish community? I posed these questions to the Old Man. Again his face creased with the
irritation which inability to formulate his impressions
into leading ideas seemed to cause him. He could not
answer me, as he frankly admitted.

Above all else, the Old Man was a thoroughly
honest human being. When I pressed him about the
old-timers with whom he most readily identified him-

self (were they really so wonderful?), he admitted
that for many of them religion was a mere routine, a
rigid and meaningless formality. Though they now complained about the "liberal" rabbi's innovations, their
own religious services were falling apart and were quite
unable to attract younger elements.

Why then, since he was himself of such lively temperament and not really Orthodox, did the Old Man
still consider himself closer to the old-timers than to
anyone else?

This seemed to be a crucial point; he thought very
carefully before answering. His answer was not well
formulated, but I think it came to something like this:
The old-timers, mostly East European immigrants, continued to live within the emotional and intellectual
shadow of the Pale; in that sense, for good or bad, they
remained Jews, no matter what their politics, social
status, or religious attitudes in America. Even, said the
Old Man, when they became "*gevirim*" (rich men)
they continued in "*yidishe vegen*" (Jewish ways). But
what did that mean exactly? Well, if they were money
grubbers they were not the same kind as the members
of the local Chamber of Commerce; if they were philistines they were not the same kind as the local Rotarians.
But *how* were they different—"They didn't mix themselves up in American things." More than that I could
not elicit from the Old Man, but what he seemed
to be trying to suggest was that the old-timer Jews
were not absorbed by Spruceton. They lived at one remove from it and were therefore able to retain, in no
matter how attenuated a form, an attitude of critical
distance towards American industrial society.

At this point the Old Man went out of his way to
intimate that he himself, for all his attachment to the
old ritual, was a non-believer. (He reads the *New Re-*

public.) His attachment to the old was to some extent a habit, but even more it was an unformulated esthetic appreciation.

Once he began to talk about the current conflict among Spruceton's Jews, the Old Man felt more sure of himself.

When the present rabbi—a cultured, intelligent man—came to Spruceton over a year ago, he began to institute certain innovations. One of them, perhaps most bitterly resented by the old-timers, was the installation of an organ in the temple. When the Old Man first heard about this, he passed it off with a joke: would the temple feature "hootchie-kootchie" dancers next? A crony of his, when asked about the organ, scornfully murmured, *"Eh . . . es skripit"* ("It screaks"). Others of the older generation, however, were neither so humorous nor so polite.

The conflict came to a head during the recent holidays when the rabbi read parts of the service in English and omitted other parts. This occasioned the Old Man's biting remark: "This is the first time I have ever seen a herring that has only a head and a tail." When I asked him if the shofar was blown on Yom Kippur, he replied that it was but it sounded like a Boy Scout bugle.

A handful of the old-timers embarked on a rather pathetic hegira: since they no longer could tolerate such heterodoxy, they abandoned the temple and went to Boston and other towns where they could pray in Orthodox synagogues for the High Holidays. But the Old Man remained in Spruceton. Why? "Where will I run?" I think he meant to suggest that the gesture of protest was basically futile. One couldn't run away from the situation. In a larger city, Orthodox and Reform could split; here they had to coexist. In practice that meant giving way to Reform. He personally preferred the old ways (prayers in English are "dry like crackers") but he seemed to grasp that the old ways were doomed.

It would be pointless to report on other conversations I subsequently had with Spruceton's Jews, most of which merely substantiated what the Old Man had told me. But I do want to relate an interview with one of the *alrightniks,* for in the contrast between him and the Old Man is dramatized the social conflict inside Spruceton's Jewish community.

Mr. X received me in his expensively furnished house, a "nice home." He wore a dressing gown and tried to suggest an air of comfortable worldliness; he looked somewhat like Jean Hersholt.

Mr. X had been in Spruceton for about a dozen years, and was now a very well-established businessman. He began by deprecating the importance of the religious differences within Spruceton's Jewish community; but nonetheless, like almost every other Spruceton Jew to whom I spoke, he seemed unable to leave the subject.

He told me about the old shul in Spruceton. "It was dirty, it stank; when you went in, there were old men in their stockings and with long beards. Then they had that gargle music. . . . Well, you know, it wasn't the kind of place you'd want to bring your wife and kids to. Then some of us got together and pushed through the temple. Sometimes we did things first and asked permission afterwards, but we got things done." I ventured to remark that this was in the tradition of American business, but my feeble sarcasm did not seem to disturb him.

Mr. X felt that the Old Man was "something of a trouble-maker, a little un-American. Now we have the finest type of Jew."

"What is the finest type of Jew?"

"Well, you know, the kind that's clean, doesn't push himself or make noise; the kind that's respected and doesn't fool around with the Reds. Now we're part of the Community Chest, the goyim respect us. We're part of the town. Everyone respects the rabbi."

Then came the clincher, "I'll tell you something else. Before, when the old ones ran the show, there was a lot of intermarriage by the young people. Now there isn't. Now we are learning about being Jews, we send our children to Sunday school and we know what is going on when we hear the prayers in English."

My last question was: "Is there anti-Semitism in Spruceton?"

"No, it's not that sort of town."

The same evening I talked to Mr. X, I also met a number of Jewish women who were discussing a Zionist dinner that had been held at the town's leading hotel, at which I was staying. At this dinner there had been an unexpectedly large number of guests, some of whom had got merry and so far forgotten themselves as to sing Zionist songs. Others of the Jewish ladies felt that was "bad behavior—it makes a bad impression on the Gentiles." As one of them put it, "We have to show we're good Jews, not bad Jews." I asked her, as I had asked Mr. X, what she meant by "good Jews." She murmured, "You know. . . ."

The next morning, while sitting in the lobby of the hotel, I could not help but overhear its owner loudly discussing the Zionist dinner: "Jews . . . grabbers . . . noisy, crazy songs . . . what can you expect from them?"

I spoke to a number of other Mr. X's. Some were cruder, some more subtle, but they were all cut from the same pattern.

There is no denying that Mr. X and his fellow *al-rightniks* are fundamentally decent enough as individuals. They are, or can be, individually kind; some are rather more imaginative; and a few even have a smattering of culture, though a very thin one. Yet their basic socio-economic situation propels them as a group to a system of beliefs and attitudes that is highly unattractive and that has helped bring about their disagreements with the old-timers.

Mr. X and his fellows have had one severe shock in the past two decades: Hitler. From this shock they learned that, no matter how they may wish to, they cannot assimilate themselves (they really mean obliterate themselves). Yet they have become successful businessmen; their daily life brings them into repeated contact with Gentile businessmen whose values they eagerly seek to adopt. They wish, almost more than anything else, not to be identified with "bad" Jews—those who are "dirty," wear beards, make "gargle music," or are always "knocking things."

Experience has further taught them, as one Jewish businessman ruefully told me, that they can't integrate themselves into the town's middle-class Gentile social life. "We tried now and then to join the animal-cracker lodges but somehow most of us never got in. There was no law against admitting Jews, you understand, but still . . ." This Jewish businessman said this without any irony; to him it was a matter of deep regret.

Mr. X and his friends faced a tremendous problem, and here we can readily sympathize with them. They had to make a social and cultural niche for themselves. The old ways were out. They were not rebels or intellectuals who could generalize from their own condition. And now they had learned that even if they wished to, they couldn't become goyim. In a sense, they were more of a "lost generation" than anyone else in the world. The temple was their answer, their hope, and their solution.

The "Americanization" and "modernization" of Spruceton's Jewish community cannot be understood exclusively in terms of conflicting religious doctrines. No doubt many of Spruceton's Jews sincerely think of it that way; no doubt many of the old-timers deeply feel that the new ways are an abomination while some Jewish businessmen feel as deeply that they make religion more meaningful. But if there were only a religious dispute—Orthodox versus Reform or Conservative versus Liberal—the problem would be comparatively minor. The developments in Spruceton are a portent of trends to come—*social* trends.

The old-timers' group was disintegrating of itself. Despite such an exception as the Old Man, their most conscious member, they were for the most part people, as Kafka puts it, "who are Jews in an especially pure form because they live only in the religion, but live in it without effort, understanding, or distress." Nothing could be more absurd than for one so completely irreligious as the present writer to sentimentalize these old-timers. Their day is over and their most intelligent member, the Old Man, knows it.

Their sons likewise could not perpetuate Spruceton's Jewish community. The sons left Spruceton entirely or they intermarried, or, while formally retaining the faith, in actuality abandoned all interest in it.

That left only the third group: the *alrightniks*. They won the Jewish community by default. Thereupon they faced the problem: how reinvigorate this Jewish community so that its members could find identity and prestige while simultaneously ridding themselves of the old stigma?

I think they have solved their problem with admirable skill. The present rabbi is indeed a respected figure in Spruceton, an excellent spokesman at community affairs. A whole new social life is offered by the temple; hence, the decline in intermarriage. In the temple the Jewish businessmen can find a status and security available nowhere else. And the neatly decorous, bilingual services—an incongruous mixture of the traditional and the imposed modern—are not calculated to disturb anyone.

Second only to the temple as a focus of Spruceton's Jewish life is Zionism. The old-timers, never joiners, belonged perhaps to a fraternal organization that assured them proper burial. But the *alrightniks* find in Zionism a not too irksome means of expressing politically their new awareness of their status as Jews. This awareness is seen primarily as a financial obligation more than faithfully assumed (they are proud of fulfilling "quotas"); it is also a means of vicarious participation in international affairs and still another occasion for social life, in this instance sanctified by the mild personal commitment and thin cultural veneer of present-day American Zionism. I visited Spruceton before the recent Palestine crisis, but I am quite certain that it aroused strong feelings among its Jews. Yet it would be a wild exaggeration to suggest that Zionism impinges directly on, or in any significant way breaks the quiescent *kleinbuergerlich* pattern of their lives. No pioneer hearts beat here.

The present Jewish community of Spruceton is a perfect expression of the needs of the *nouveau riche* Jewish businessmen. It permits them to be Jews with "peace of mind"; it permits them to achieve the spiritual identity provided by religious affiliation without paying the price in differentiation of behavior and custom that Judaism once demanded of its followers. Their turn to the temple does not mean that Judaism is making them over in its image; it means that they are making Judaism over in theirs.

That is why the representative attitude of Spruceton's *alrightniks* is so middle-class: unquestioning, complacent acceptance of American society; slight interest in cultural or intellectual problems; complete absence of that deep, troubled, perhaps even agonized feeling that can result from religiosity; and, above all, a complete lack of self-doubt and self-criticism.

In the values of this group "respectability" and decorum play an oppressively dominant role. They have taken as their goal one of the least attractive traits of the American middle class: its genteel inhibition and fear of public emotional expression, its rejection of spontaneity. Hence, their uneasy feeling when they see Zionists sing at a hotel, their suspicion that such things should either not be done at all or should be confined to the intimacy of the temple.

The rabbi, an intelligent man, is aware of this state of affairs. He seems to work on the principle that once he has snared the Jewish Babbitts he should then be able to create new attitudes in them. I think he is wrong. All of Spruceton life, all of the deeply entrenched and powerfully motivated values of the business world in which most of his congregation lives and works—values that most of them unquestioningly accept—are arrayed against him. If he were to try to imbue the *alrightniks* with those critical habits of mind and ethical biases that to one extent or another are part of the old Jewish *Weltanschauung*, he would meet only with stubborn resistance.

The *alrightniks* have won. They are the bulk of Spruceton's Jewish community; they control the temple and have molded it in their own image. Their turn to Judaism is fundamentally a means of organized adaptation towards American middle-class businessman values. But what social or ethical promise can one find in it?

A Note on the Type

This book was set on the Linotype in Janson, a recutting made direct from the type cast from matrices made by Anton Janson some time between 1660 and 1687. Janson's original matrices were, at last report, in the possession of the Stempel foundry, Frankfurt am Main.

Of Janson's origin nothing is known. He may have been a relative of Justus Janson, a printer of Danish birth who practiced in Leipzig from 1614 to 1635. Some time between 1657 and 1668 Anton Janson, a punch-cutter and type-founder, bought from the Leipzig printer Johann Erich Hahn the type-foundry which had formerly been a part of the printing house of M. Friedrich Lankisch. Janson's types were first shown in a specimen sheet issued at Leipzig about 1675. Janson's successor, and perhaps his son-in-law, Johann Karl Edling, issued a specimen sheet of Janson types in 1689. His heirs sold the Janson matrices in Holland to Wolffgang Dietrich Erhardt, of Leipzig.

Composed, printed, and bound by H. WOLFF, N. Y. *Designed by* HARRY FORD.